WALK WITH ME

Charlottetown

THEN AND NOW

By **D. Scott MacDonald**

The Acorn Press
Charlottetown
2024

The author welcomes comments at:

D. Scott MacDonald
18 Swallow Drive
Stratford PE C1B 4N2
(902) 393-4999

ACORNPRESS

P.O. Box 22024
Charlottetown, Prince Edward Island

C1A 9J2

acornpresscanada.com

Edited by Laurie Brinklow
Designed by Rudi Tusek

Printed in Canada

Library and Archives Canada Cataloguing in Publication

Title: Walk with me : Charlottetown then and now / by D. Scott MacDonald.
Other titles: Charlottetown | Charlottetown then and now
Names: MacDonald, D. Scott, 1947- author, photographer.
Description: 2nd edition. | New edition of: MacDonald, D. Scott, 1947-. Charlottetown.

Identifiers: Canadiana (print) 20240352718 | Canadiana (ebook) 20240352726 | ISBN 9781773661612 (softcover) | ISBN 9781773661629 (EPUB)

Subjects: LCSH: Buildings—Prince Edward Island—Charlottetown—History. | LCSH: Buildings—Prince Edward Island—Charlottetown—History—Pictorial works. | LCSH: Streets—Prince Edward Island—Charlottetown—History. | LCSH: Streets—Prince Edward Island—Charlottetown—History—Pictorial works. | LCSH: Charlottetown (P.E.I.)—Buildings, structures, etc.—History. | LCSH: Charlottetown (P.E.I.)—Buildings, structures, etc.—History—Pictorial works. | LCSH: Charlottetown (P.E.I.)—History. | LCSH: Charlottetown (P.E.I.)—Pictorial works.

Classification: LCC FC2646.4 .M33 2024 | DDC 971.7/500222—dc23

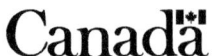

The publisher acknowledges the support of the Government of Canada through the Canada Book Fund of the Department of Canadian Heritage for our publishing activities. We also acknowledge the support of the Canada Council for the Arts for our publishing program.

WALK WITH ME
Charlottetown
THEN AND NOW

It has been almost ten years since I created the book *Charlottetown, Then & Now*. A lot has changed in the City of Charlottetown. Buildings have come and gone, with many new apartments, and roundabouts. With the help of: The Public Archives and Records Office (PARO); City of Charlottetown Archives-curator Natalie Munn; and Earle's Picture Restorations and with his consent, I have attempted to create another view of the city from days gone by. In this book I encourage you to take a walking tour of a few of our main street to view what was there then (from this book) and what it is like now. We walk on Queen, Grafton, Richmond, Prince, Great George and Water Streets. These six streets are where business was conducted for the most part. Please enjoy this walk along the historic streets of this wonderful city.

Your attention is brought to the size of trees in a couple of the before and after, however you will see much more in a lot of the photos.

When referring to specific buildings on corners, I have added "northwest or southeast" to note the exact location. ◾

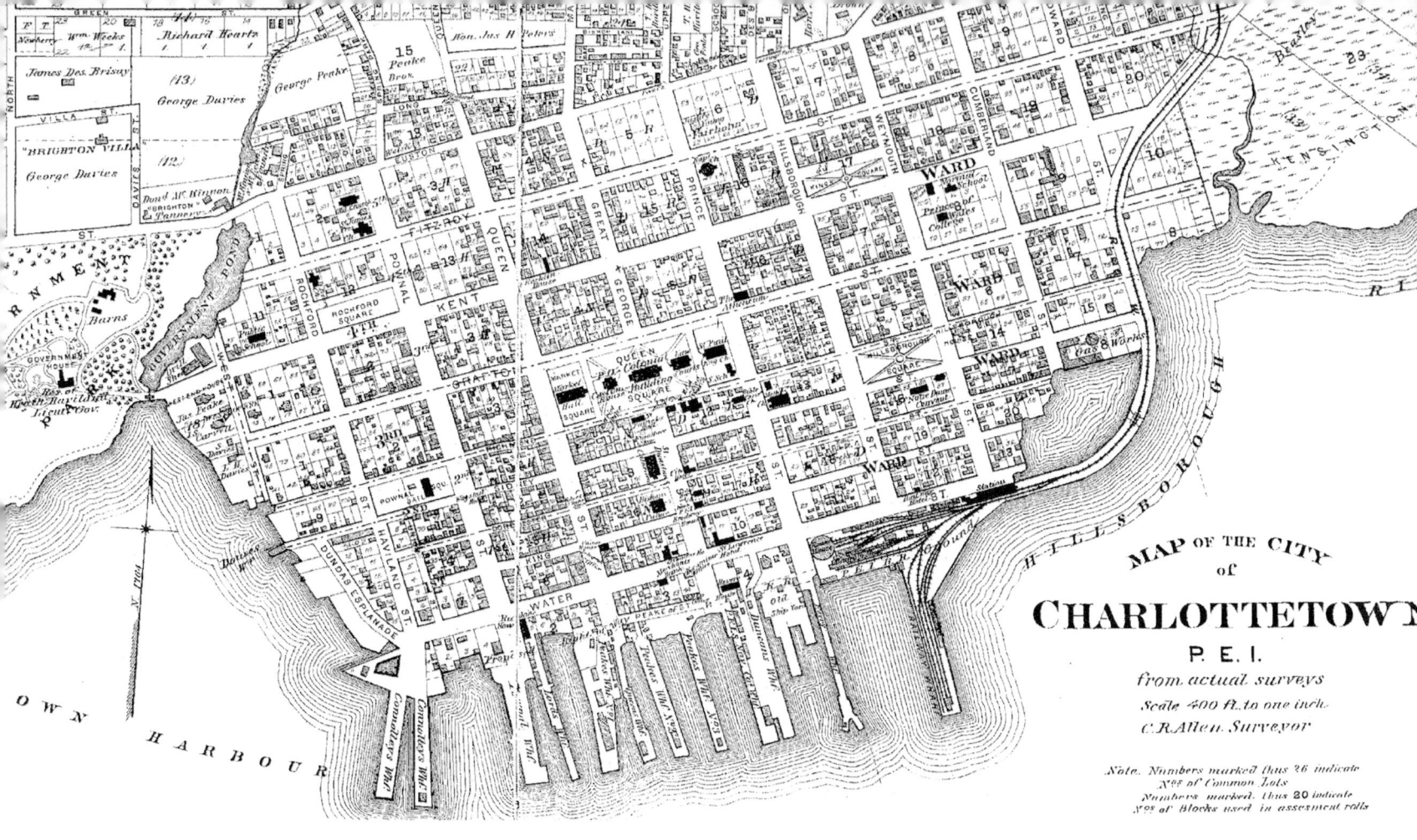

This map of Charlottetown from the 1880 Atlas may be used as an early reference to pictures in this book.

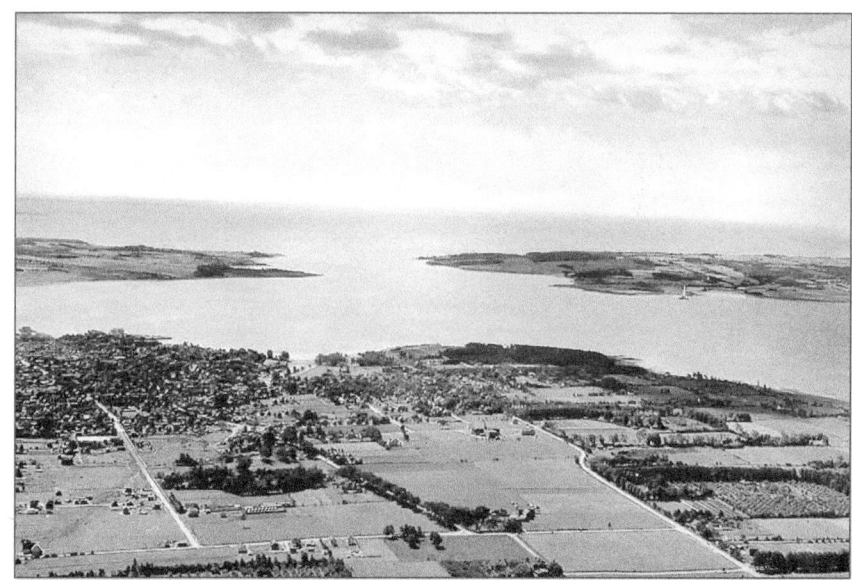

An aerial photo from 1928 shows the extensive water front wharfs. The upper part of the picture highlights open undeveloped land from Pond Street toward North River Road. The four main streets leading north from the water are, left to right are: Pownal, Queen, Great George and Prince Street.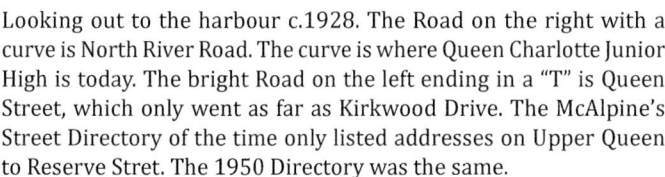

Looking out to the harbour c.1928. The Road on the right with a curve is North River Road. The curve is where Queen Charlotte Junior High is today. The bright Road on the left ending in a "T" is Queen Street, which only went as far as Kirkwood Drive. The McAlpine's Street Directory of the time only listed addresses on Upper Queen to Reserve Stret. The 1950 Directory was the same.

Across the harbour to the right you can see the Rocky Point ferry wharf. On the left, Stratford was mostly undeveloped land.

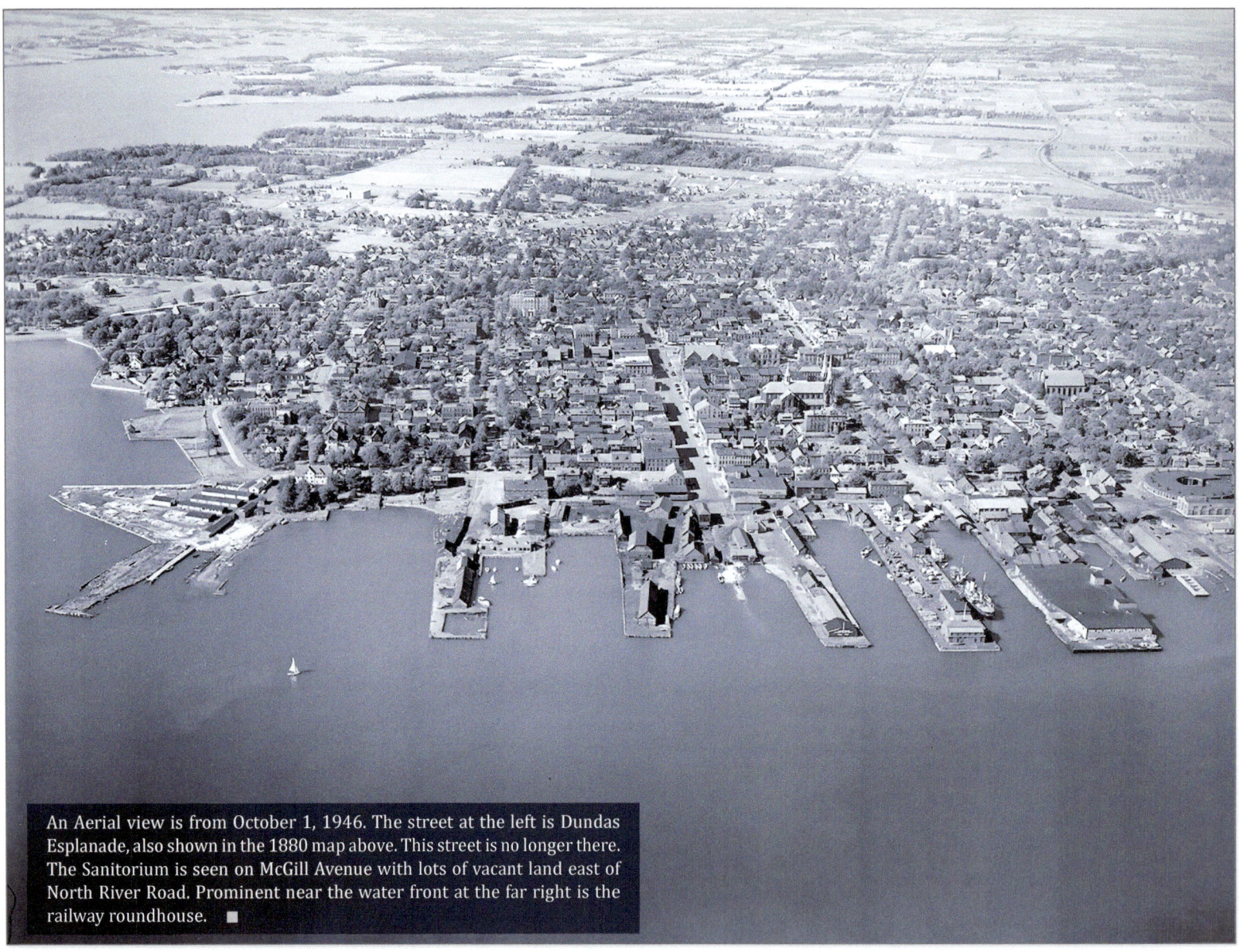

An Aerial view is from October 1, 1946. The street at the left is Dundas Esplanade, also shown in the 1880 map above. This street is no longer there. The Sanitorium is seen on McGill Avenue with lots of vacant land east of North River Road. Prominent near the water front at the far right is the railway roundhouse. ■

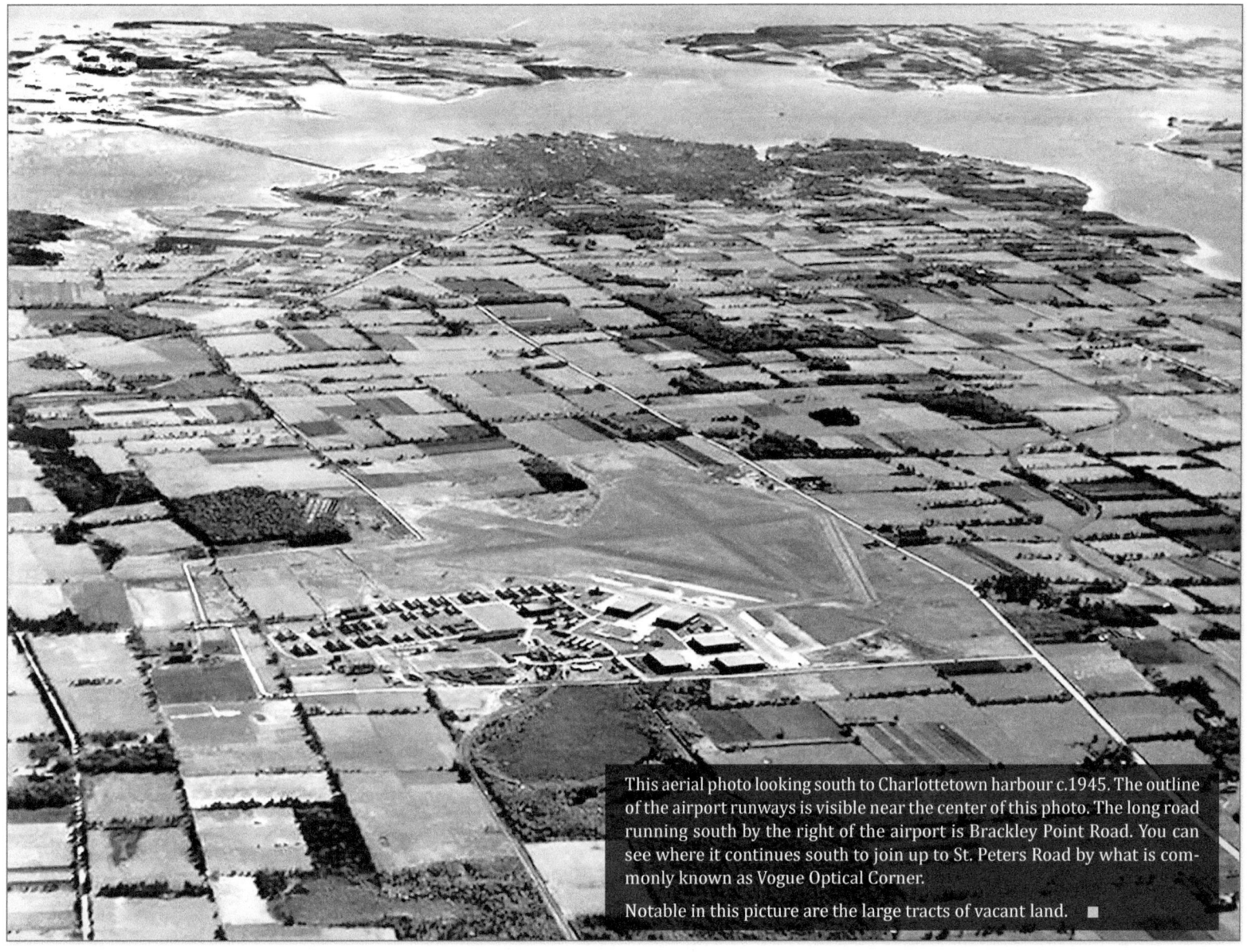

This aerial photo looking south to Charlottetown harbour c.1945. The outline of the airport runways is visible near the center of this photo. The long road running south by the right of the airport is Brackley Point Road. You can see where it continues south to join up to St. Peters Road by what is commonly known as Vogue Optical Corner.

Notable in this picture are the large tracts of vacant land. ■

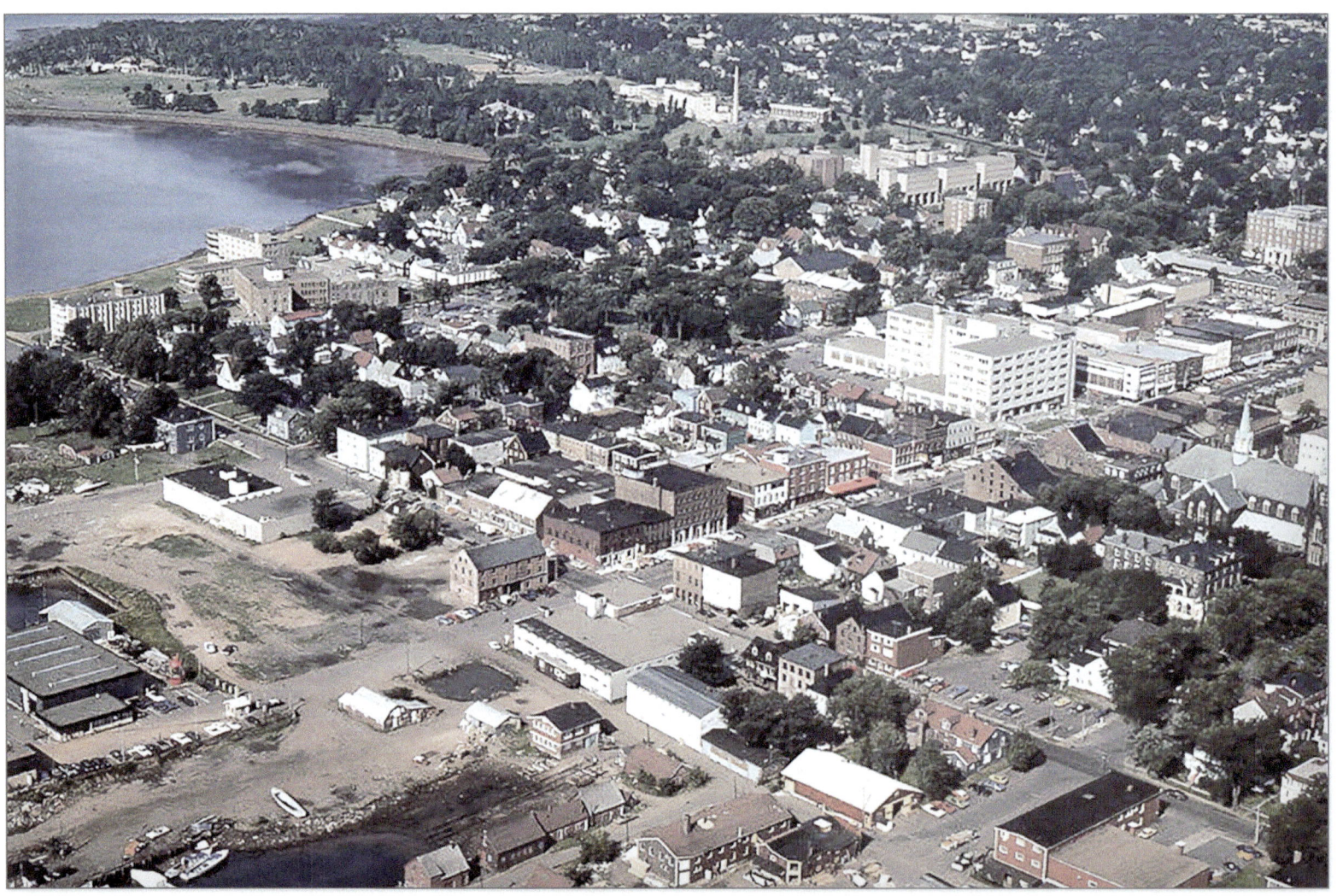

Looking northwest c.1977. The predominant light building with all the windows is the Dominion Building on Queen Street between Richmond and Sydney. Following Queen Street down to the lower left of this picture, you will note the Delta Hotel is not yet built (opened February 1984). The Merchant Man Restaurant today was then Carvel's Wholesalers final days. The Prince Edward Island Hospital can be seen on Brighton Road top center, with the Charlottetown Hospital just south of the water's edge. Straight below that, the white building with the two white stacks on the flat roof is Atlantic Wholesalers, now the location of the Law Courts. on Water Street. You can see where the train track (although removed) moved along Lower Water Street ending at the back of Atlantic Wholesalers. Moving along this track line, to the east the CN train car is at the back of DeBlois Brothers Wholesalers. The red building with the red roof is MacDonald - Rowe Woodworking. Heading up Great George Street, the parking lot is where the Queen Hotel was on Water Street following the fire on January 13, 1965. Moving up the right side of this picture you will note the Basilica and the Rodd Charlottetown Hotel. Take a good close look and you will see many interesting changes from forty-five years ago.

Queen Street

Queen Street from the harbor north past City Hall to Euston was the merchants row over the years. There the wholesalers and retailers established their trade and thrived long before the arrival of the shopping centers. Street numbers in Charlottetown are assigned from the water north, and from the water eastward. Low numbers were assigned at the water as a finite point, as there was no way of knowing how long a street would eventually be.

Freight, in the early days arrived by boat, and later by train. Lower Queen Street originally held large piles of lumber or coal, with coal being the main source of heat in the early days.

At one time the car dealers, gas stations, blacksmiths even farm machinery dealers were all south of Euston Street.

Almost seventy-five years ago, in 1950, listed in the Classified Business Directory (todays Yellow Pages) there were:

So few apartments, 30, that they were listed.

- 10 Bakeries
- 32 Blacksmiths on the Island
- 35 Canners
- 17 Coal dealers
- 4 Funeral Homes in town each with their own ambulance service
- 5 Poultry hatcheries in the city
- 16 Hotels in the city
- 14 Radio sales and service on the Island
- 15 Cab companies in the city

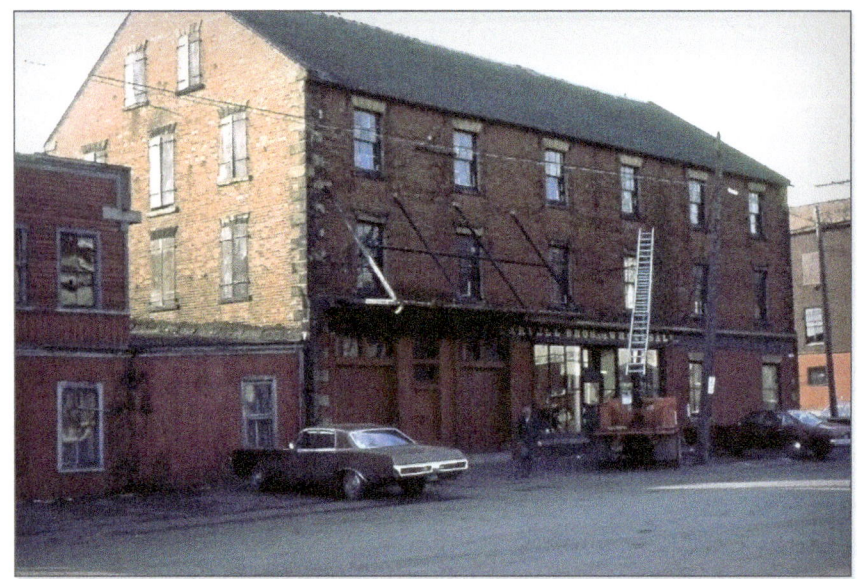

James Peake built a brick building at the southwest corner of Queen and Water in 1857. The Bank of Prince Edward Island, the first bank on the Island, occupied part of this building from 1858 to 1868. Carvell Brothers Wholesale - Fruit and Produce was there from 1862 to 1976. ▪

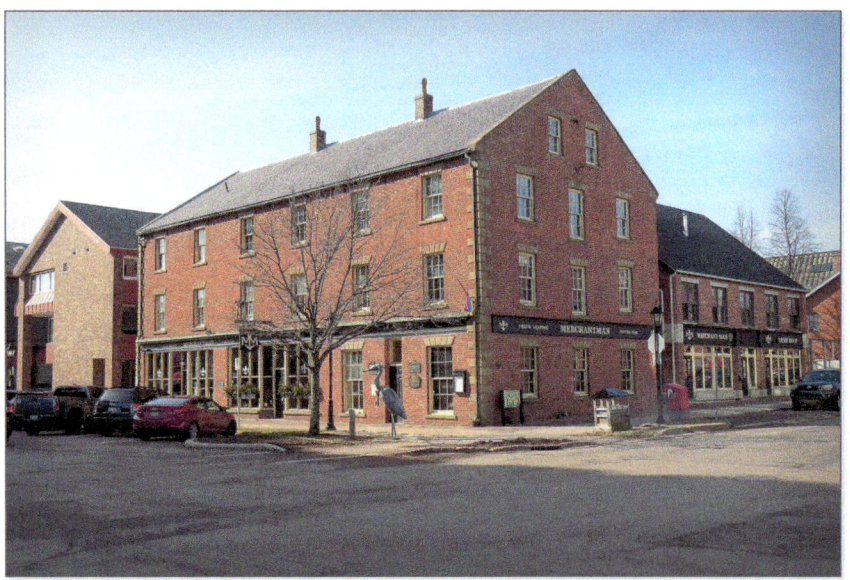

The Charlottetown Area Development Corporation acquired the building and restored it. This included adding the two chimneys which were previously cut off at roof level and restoring the slate roof. There is an historical marker on the face of the building: "Peake-Carvell Building 1857" ▪

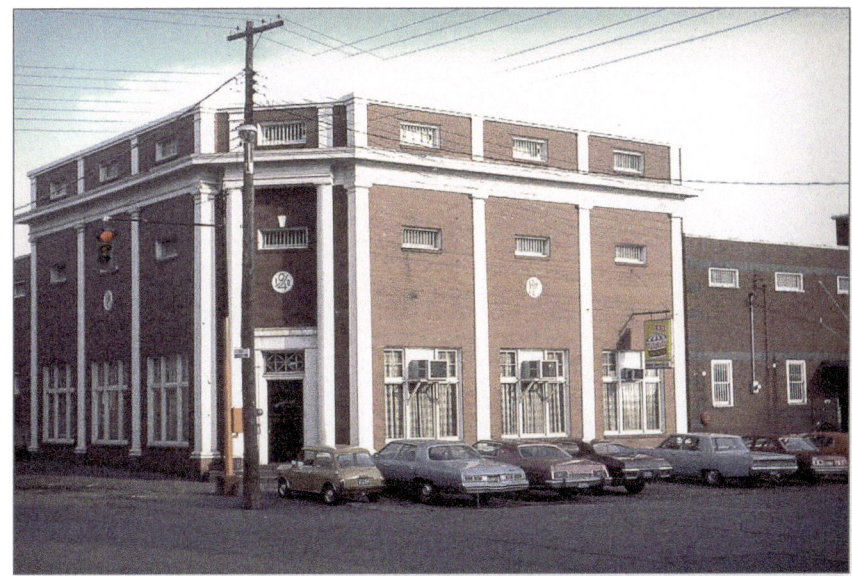

Looking north up Queen Street, in April 1977. The end of the brick building is the Carvell/Merchantman, being the only building left standing following the demolition for the Harbourside apartments and related development. ◾

DeBlois Brothers Wholesalers built this office and warehouse in 1940 (note the date over the door) on the southeast corner of Queen and Water. DeBlois was formerly at 57 Water Street, opening on June 4, 1915. From 1919 to 1940 they were located at 45-47 Queen Street. In this picture from November 1976 you will note there were traffic lights at the intersection of Water and Queen Streets.

This picture was taken in November 1976 before the building was demolished. ◾

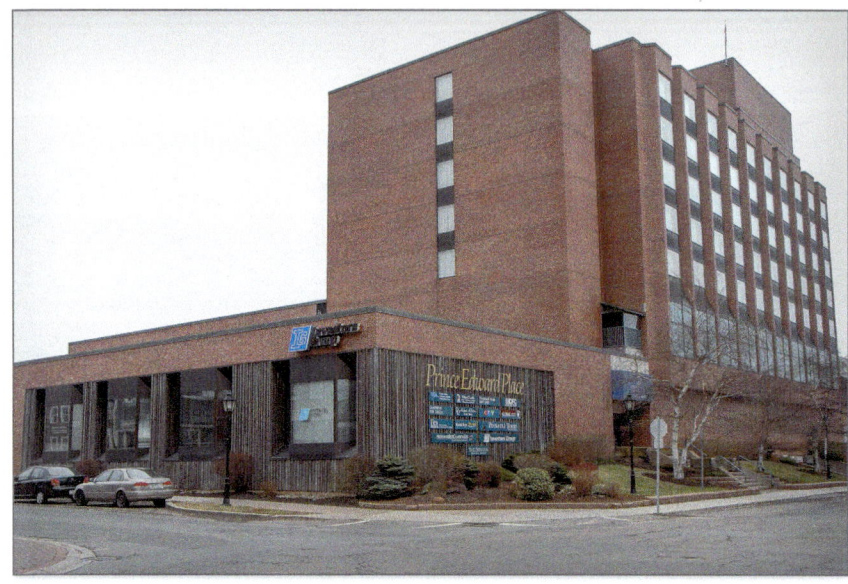

The former DeBlois Brothers site was replaced by the present Delta Hotels by Marriott Prince Edward. This hotel opened Valentine's Day 1984. as the Prince Edward Convention Centre, later called the Prince Edward CP Hotel. ▪

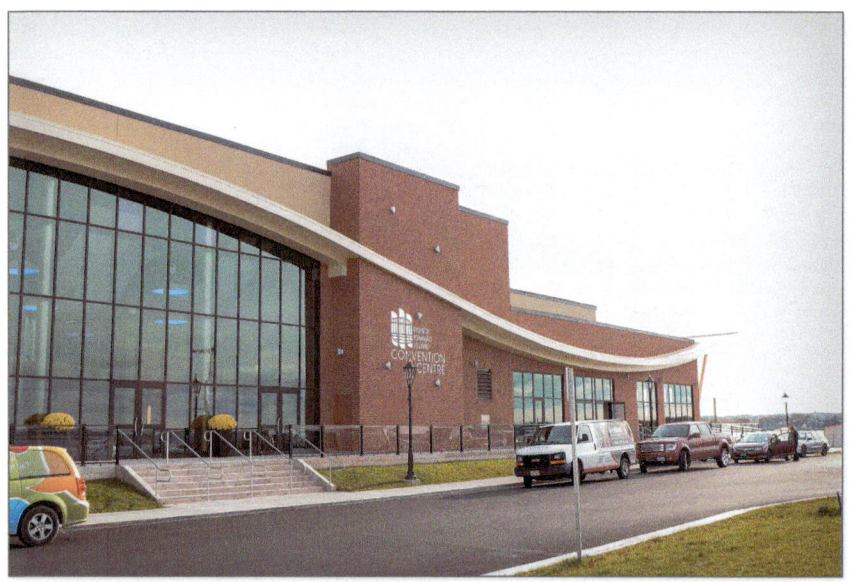

A large addition to the Delta was added in 2013 extending south toward the water to include a convention centre. ▪

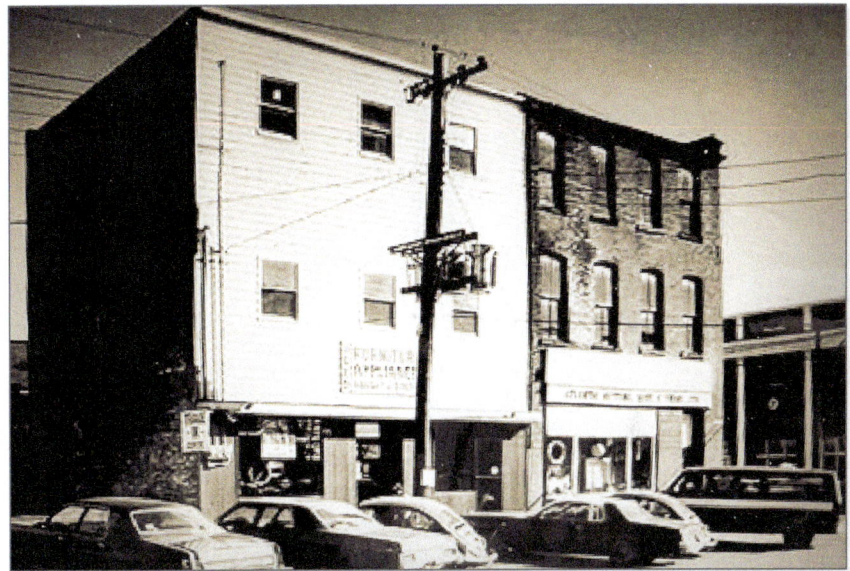

The northeast corner of Queen and Water. You can see DeBlois Brothers on the right across Water Street. In 1959, 32 Water Street was A. Kennedy & Co. ▪

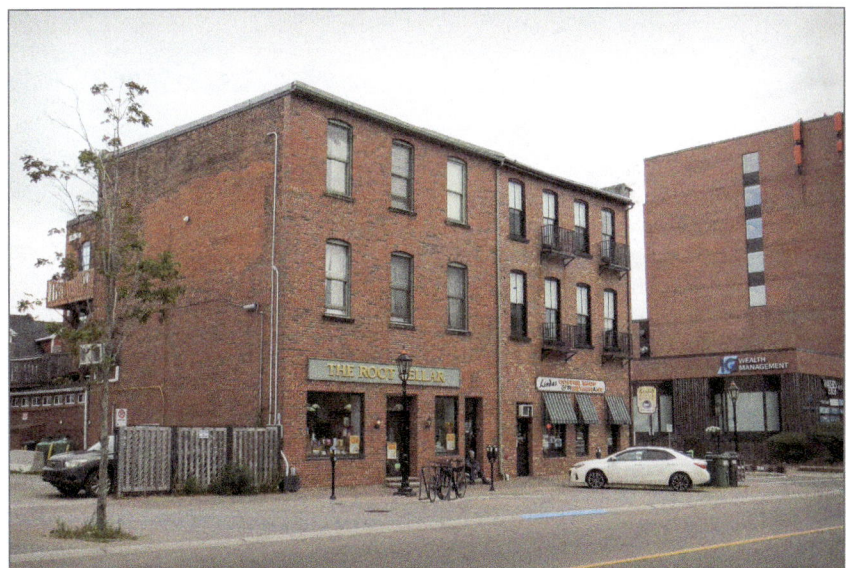

The current picture, September 2022, shows The Root Cellar and Linda's Coffee Shop. Windows were updated and all match. Some of the windows over Linda's Coffee Shop have a small European style balcony. The Delta Hotel is on right edge of this photo. ▪

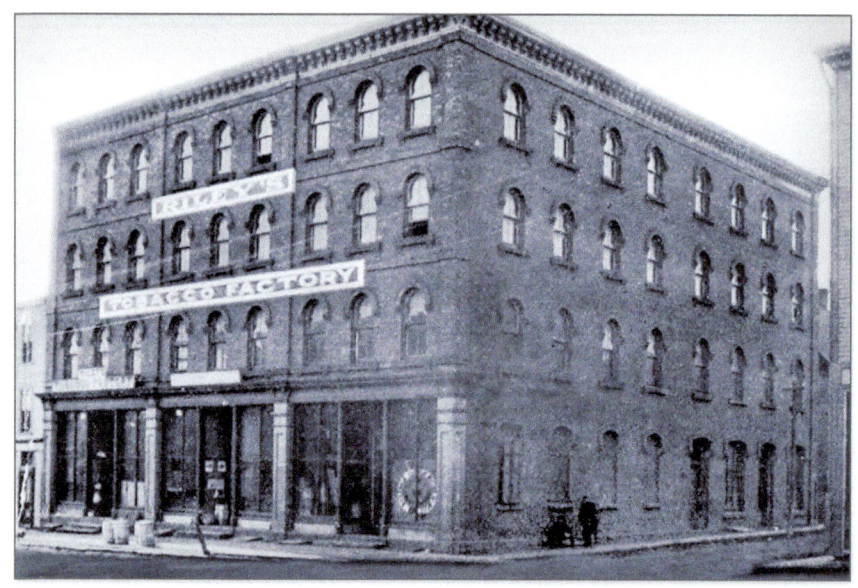

45 - 49 Queen Street: This building on the southwest corner Queen and King Streets was built in 1872 for brothers-in-law Lemuel Owen and William Welsh. Following a fire which gutted the interior in 1902, T. B. and Daniel J. Riley's Tobacco Factory, having rented a portion of the building, purchased the structure and rebuilt. The business was sold to the Island Tobacco Company in April 1954. R. E. Mutch and Company grocers, operated out of part of this building at 45-47 Queen Street. Subsequent owners were Kays Brothers Wholesalers in 1962 until 2009. The brothers Riley previously were in premises on Water Street operating there in 1885. This photo from the H. B. Stirling collection PARO. ◾

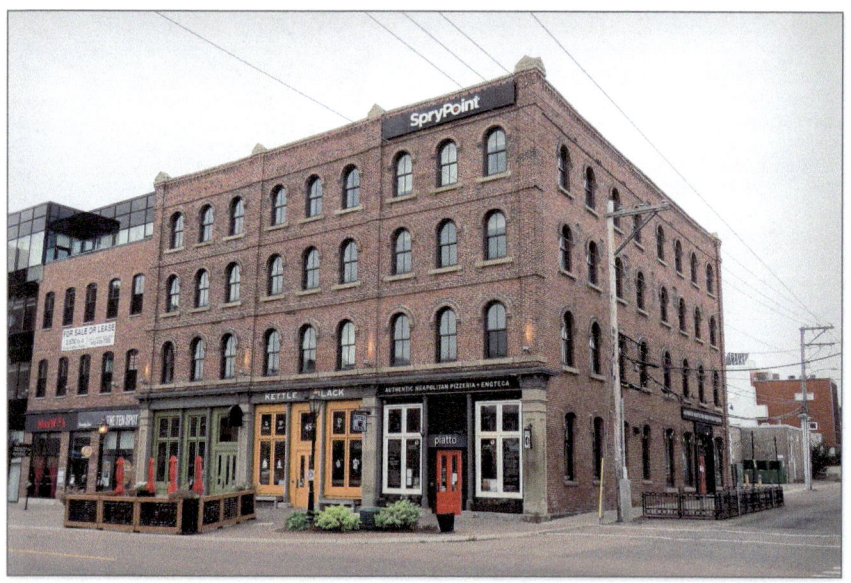

The Charlottetown Area Development Corporation (CADC) bought the building for $750,000 and following a $6.5 million renovation, this corner building is now divided and occupied by Electronic Arts, Kettle Black and Piatto Pizza. ◾

71 - 73 Queen on the northwest corner of Queen and Dorchester was built in 1866. Norton Bros (R. B. & E. H. Norton) operated here as a hardware store. It was sold on August 02, 1886 to be operated as the City Hardware Store by Norton and Fennell (R. B. Norton and Robert Fennell). Cr: City of Charlottetown Archives Gary Carroll Collection.

An article in the *Examiner* dated June 13, 1888 stated "Messrs. Norton & Fennell intend putting down a stone sidewalk in front of their store on Queen Street next week. The example thus set is worthy of imitation." Note: Sidewalks were wooden at the time.

Mr. Fennell together with an employee of the Norton firm created a new hardware store called Fennell and Chandler on July 7, 1893 to operate out of the Cameron Block at 152 Richmond Street. Fennell and Chandler later moved to new premises just north of the Bank of Commerce at 155 Queen Street. This building was subsequently a grocery store, until its present tenant, the Canton Cafe moved here. ■

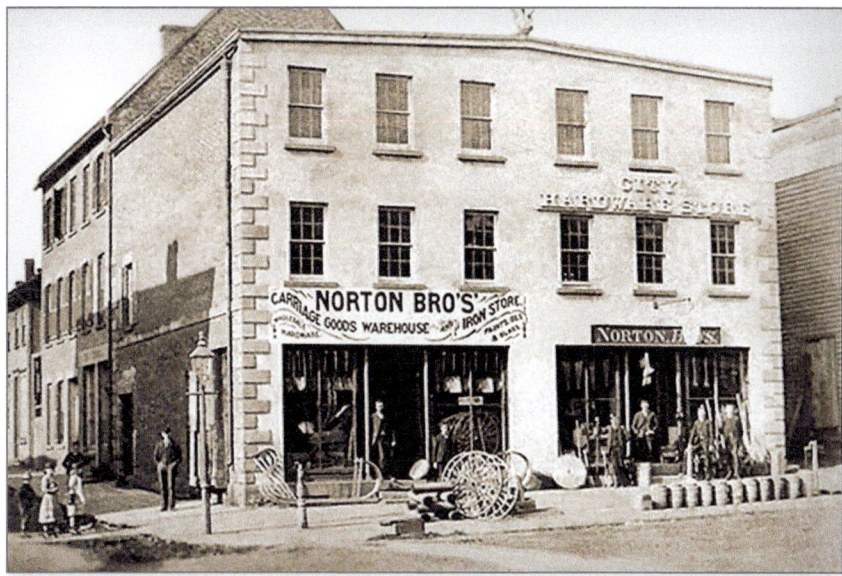

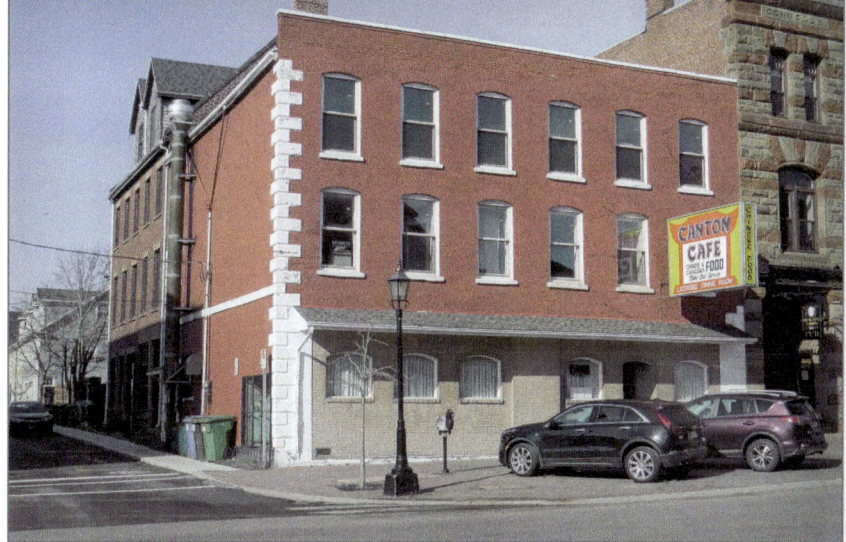

This building is most recently recognized as the Canton Cafe. The Canton Cafe opened for business on September 25, 1936 at 176 Queen Street by Sam Ling. They advertised full course dinners for 30 - 35 cents. 176 Queen Street is where Shoppers Drug Mart is today. ■

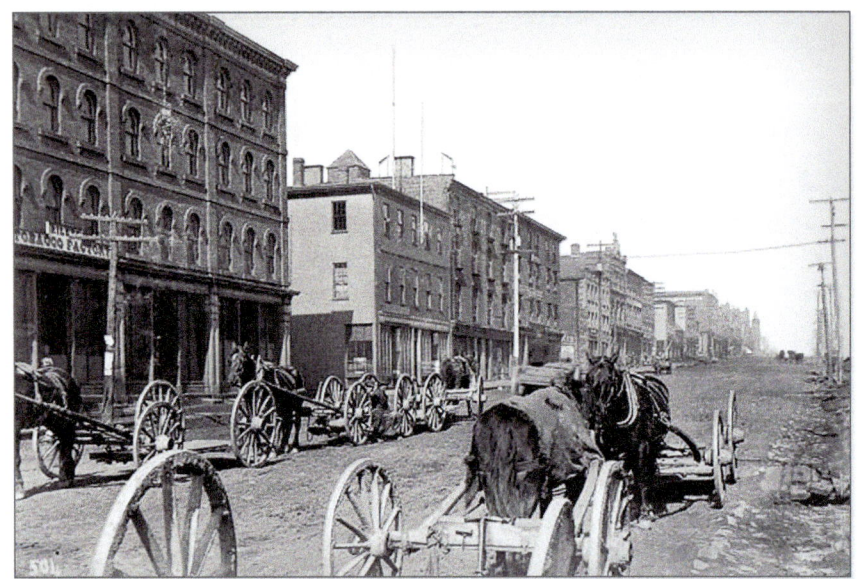

Looking north from Riley's Tobacco Factory up to City Hall. The next building highlighted by the sun, is on the corner of King Street. Up further Dorchester Street, and again highlighted by the sun is Sydney Street. The tall building, a few doors up is on the corner of Richmond. This picture was taken in c.1890. The pointed tower at the top of the street is City Hall having recently been completed in 1888.

The low slung freight wagons were designed to carry supplies from the wharf to the merchants. (PARO) collection. ▪

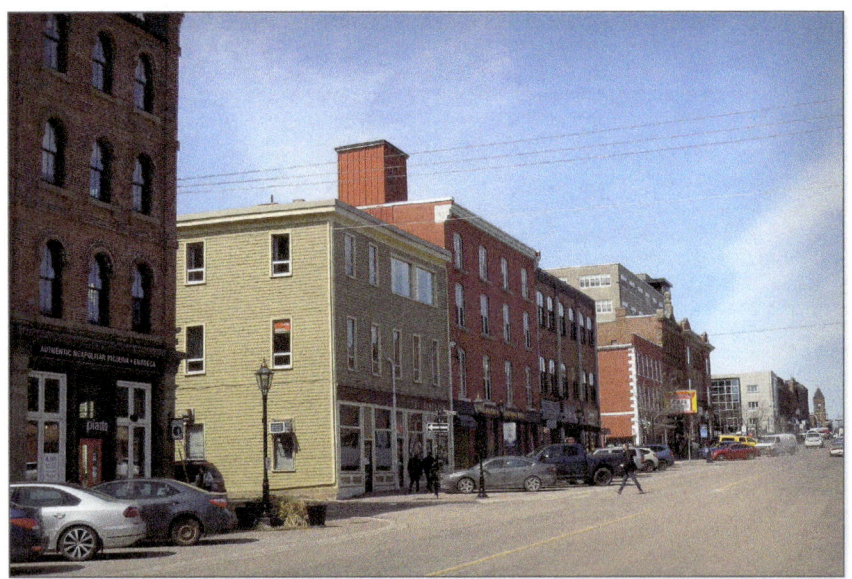

The picture from 2022. For the first few blocks, the buildings do not appear to have changed, although the road is in better repair. ▪

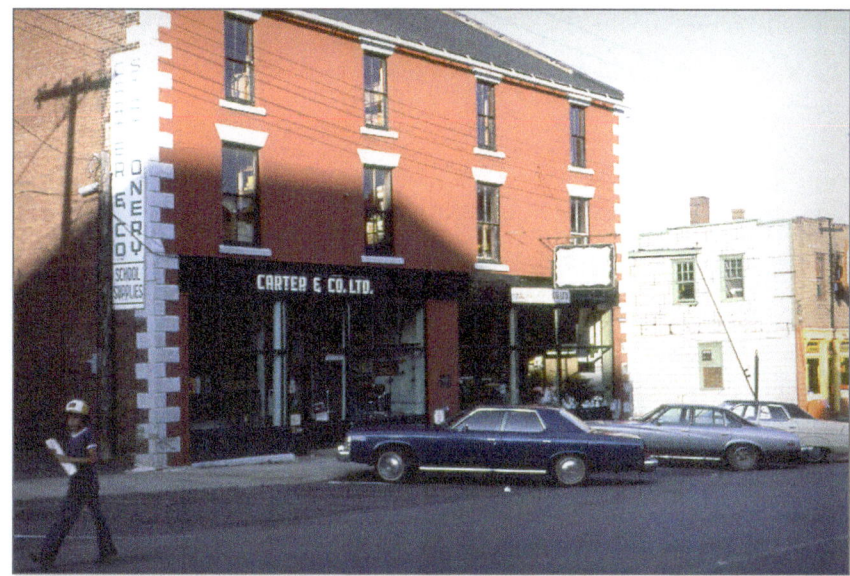

74 Queen Street, August 1979. Home of Carter & Company Stationery - School Supplies. On the right in this building was the Halifax Seed Company. Across Dorchester Street at 70 Queen: Pizza Delight, the first franchise on P.E.I. was operated by Jerry and Ishbel Connors in November 1969. This building was formerly Dillon and Spillett - Flour and Feed. They used to have baby chick in the window. ▪

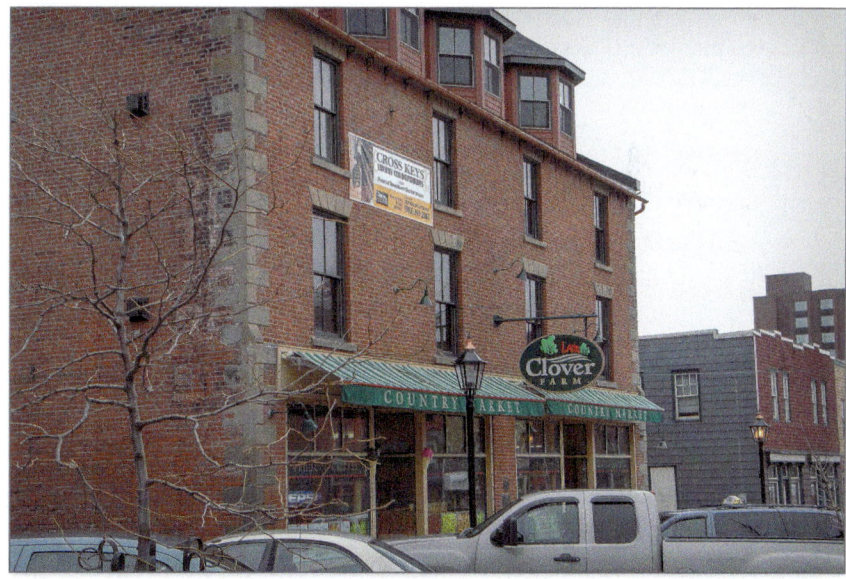

In May 2010 the site of the former Carter & Co was then Clover Farm Country Market which closed in December 2010. The sign on the third floor reads: Cross Keys Condominiums. This building has a plaque on it which reads "Duncan Mason & Co. 1855" referring to the original owner. Another plaque reads: "It was the site of the Cross Keys Tavern. The first public building in Charlottetown in which many early functions were held, and where the Legislative Assembly of Prince Edward Island first met on July 7, 1773."

This refers to the former building on the site. ▪

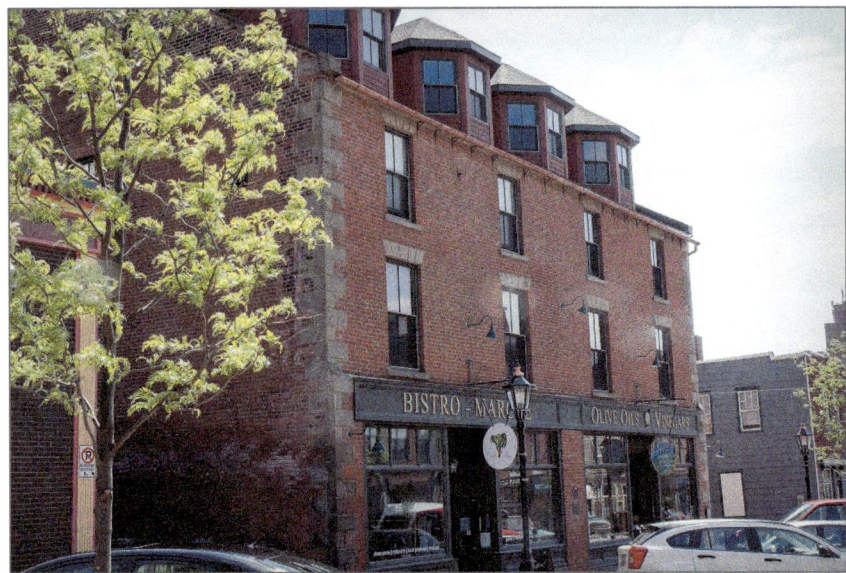

In 2013 Terre Rouge Bistro Marche was located there, with 72 Queen being Olive Oils & Vinegars. Presently 74 Queen is called Terre Rouge on the marquee. ▪

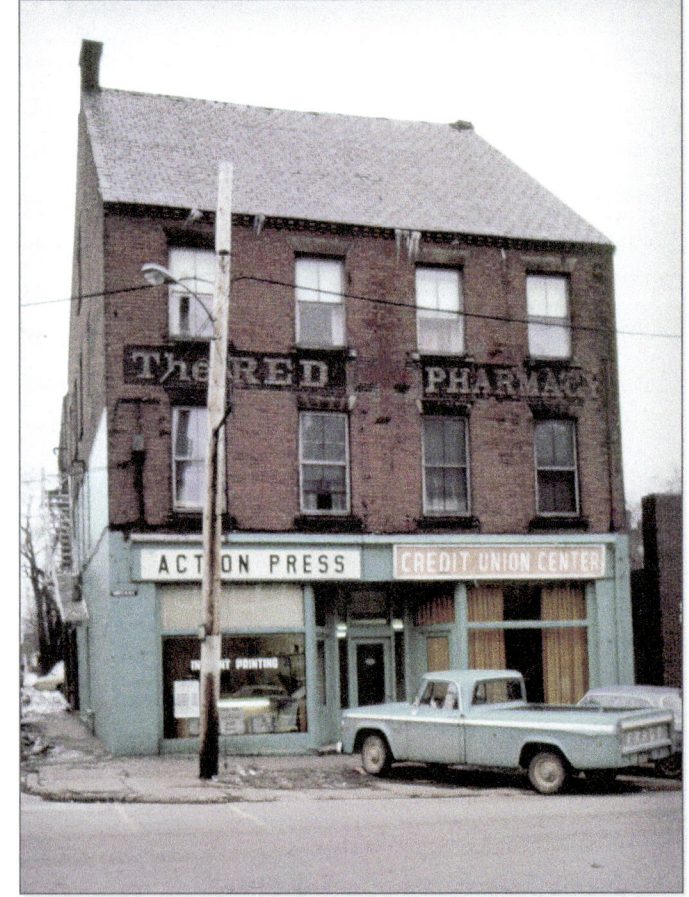

Taken in 1968, showing Action Press on the left and Credit Union Central on the right. Between the second and third floor is the sign still there from the Red Cross Pharmacy which closed in 1911. The Capital Credit Union operated out of this building from 1962 - 1968, before merging with other local credit unions to form Metro Credit Union, subsequently Provincial Credit Union. This building on the southeast corner of Queen and Sydney is now home to Sims Steakhouse and Oyster Bar.

Cr: City of Charlottetown Archives: N Munn. ▪

Looking southeast on Queen from Richmond c.1900 (PARO). The first street is Sydney. Note the wooden sidewalks, and the multiple cross bars on the poles carrying individual lines. The facade of these buildings is little changed in over 100 years. Prowse Brothers in 1920 - 60's occupied most of this first block as well fronting on Richmond Street. Barbara Anne Beauty Salon was on this block in the 1990's. Canadian Tire was located at 96 Queen Street. As their business expanded, they went from Kent Street (1939-47), 181 Great George Street (1947-52), 96 Queen (1952-60), 96-98 Queen Street (1960-66), Royalty Mall (1966-85), 685 University Avenue (1985-2014) and 20 Babineau Avenue (2014-present), having just completed a further expansion at their present location.

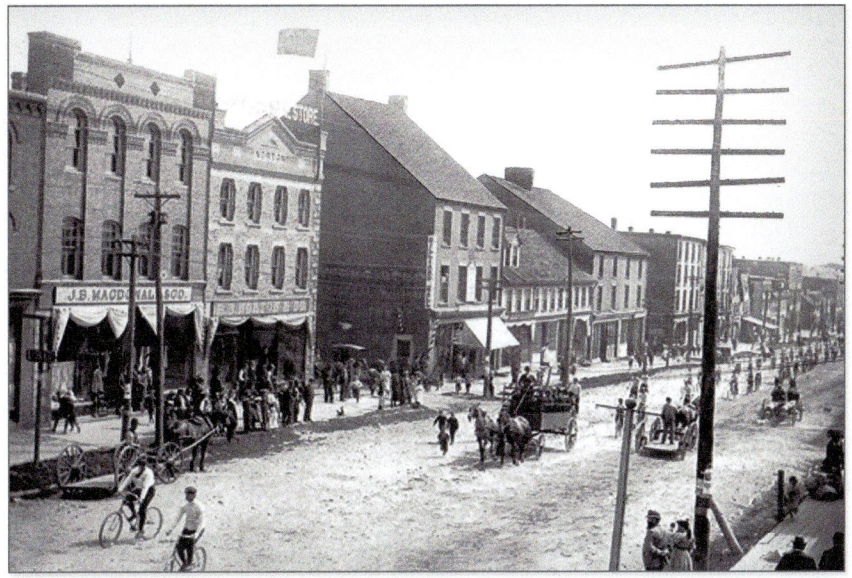

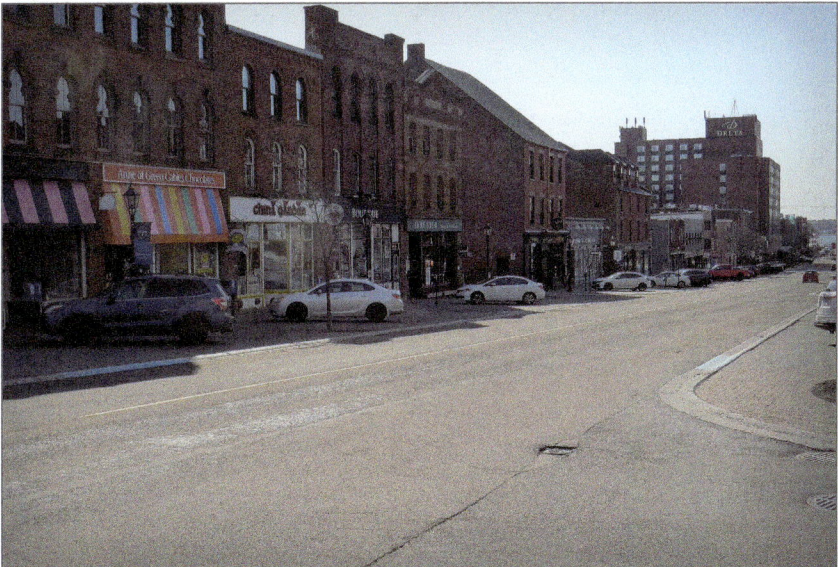

The only building that shows a change in structure is the Prince Edward Island Liquor building at 80 Queen Street.

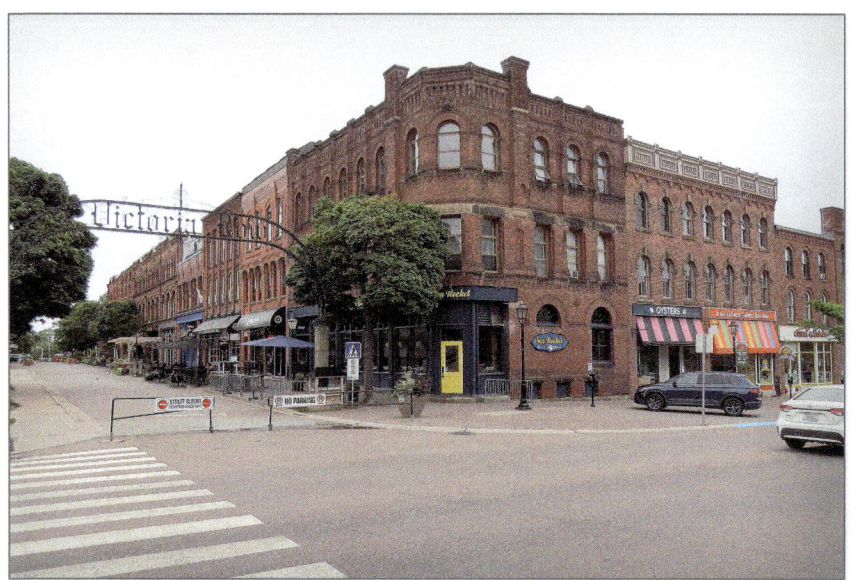

The southeast corner of Queen and Richmond was most recently Anne of Green Gables Chocolates. The building was renovated in mid 2022 and is now Sea Rocket Oyster Lounge, with Anne of Green Gables Chocolates having moved just south on Queen Street.　▪

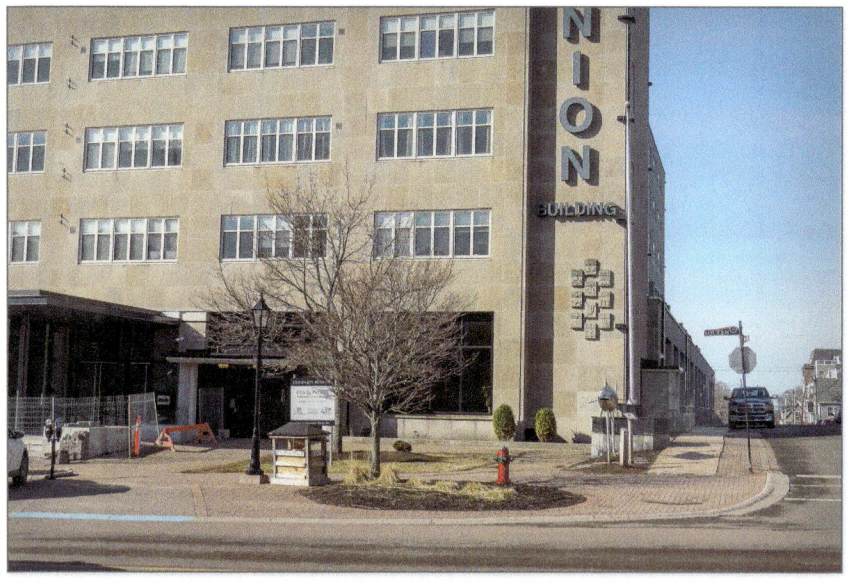

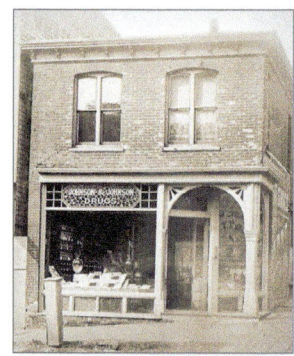

Johnson & Johnson Drugs (A. S. & R. M. Johnson) had two corner stores in Charlottetown. One on the northeast corner of Prince and Kent, and this one from c.1894 (PARO), on the southwest corner of Queen and Richmond. This building was one of many removed to erect the new Dominion Building in 1954. In 1898 the brothers operated a store on Grafton Street or Sunnyside, between Queen and Great George Street.　▪

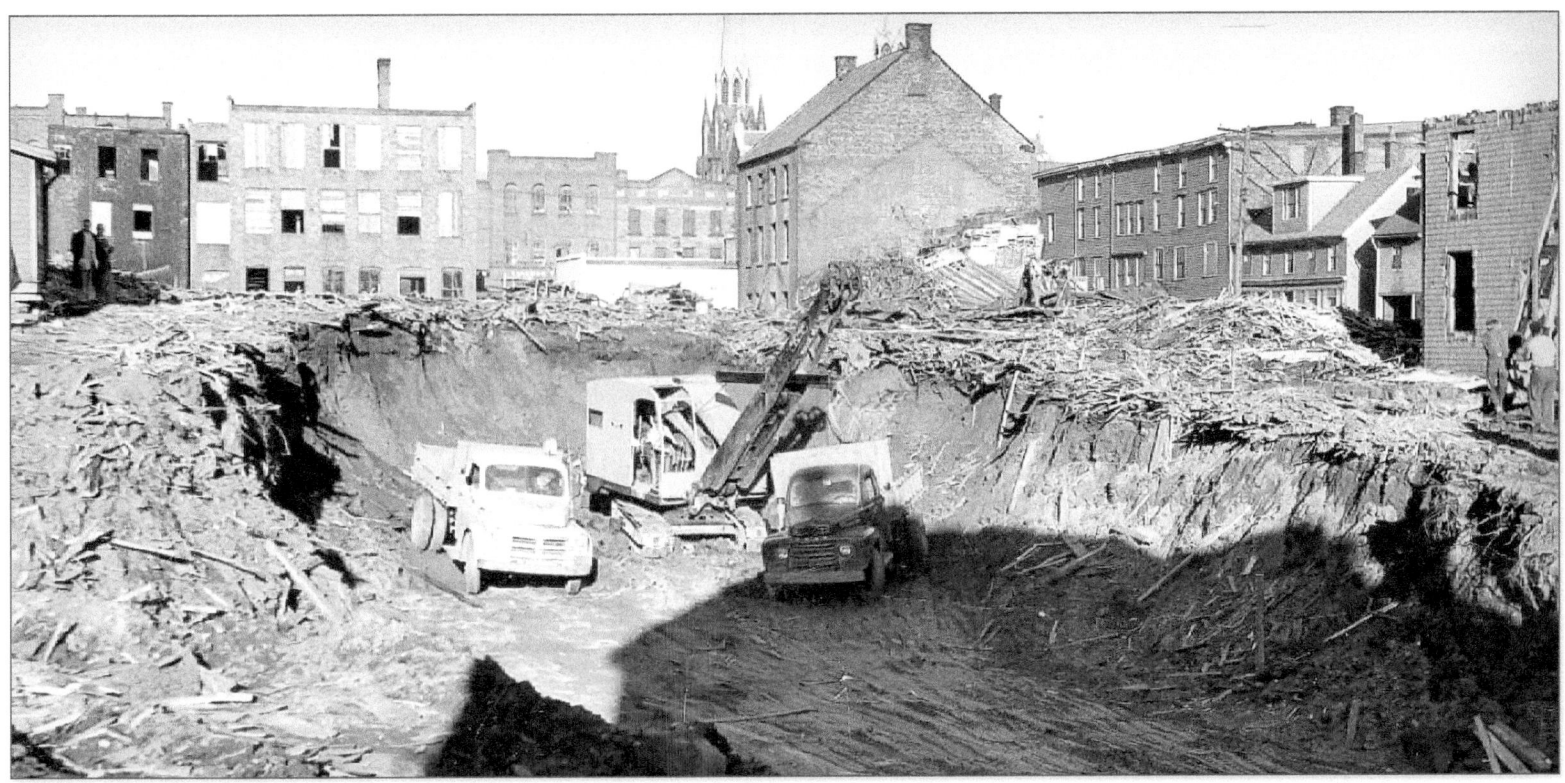

This view is the Dominion Building under construction in 1954, looking east from Pownal toward Queen. The back of the buildings on Queen are shown with most windows out. This block on Queen Street had: a service station (low, white flat roof building in center of the picture) on the northwest corner of Queen and Sydney. Next to it going north was Greendol ladies dry goods, W. H. Schwartz & Sons, wholesale grocers, and on the corner of Richmond, was Johnson & Johnson Druggist. The building, far right, is also under demolition. The three-story building with chimney front and back was slated to be demolished for this project. The other buildings to the left of this are on the south side of Sydney Street and were not part of this project. Cr: City of Charlottetown Archives.

The new federal building was originally called Confederation Building in 1956 after a naming contest. In February 1958, a new naming contest was initiated, with 61 names suggested. Only four made the short list, being: Kent Building, Jacques Cartier Building, Federal Building and Dominion Building, with the latter being declared the eventual winner. Among the other names suggested were: Metropole Building, Charlo-Kingdom Build-ing, Queen Elizabeth Building, Territorial Building, New Abegweit Building, Dominion Hall and Canada House. The reason for the change was that it was thought Confederation Building might be confusing to tourists looking for the Confederation chamber in Province House.

Recently this building was converted to condos and offices, with the first floor becoming the new Charlottetown Public Library. The library having moved from the northeast corner of Queen and Richmond, part of the Confederation Centre complex.

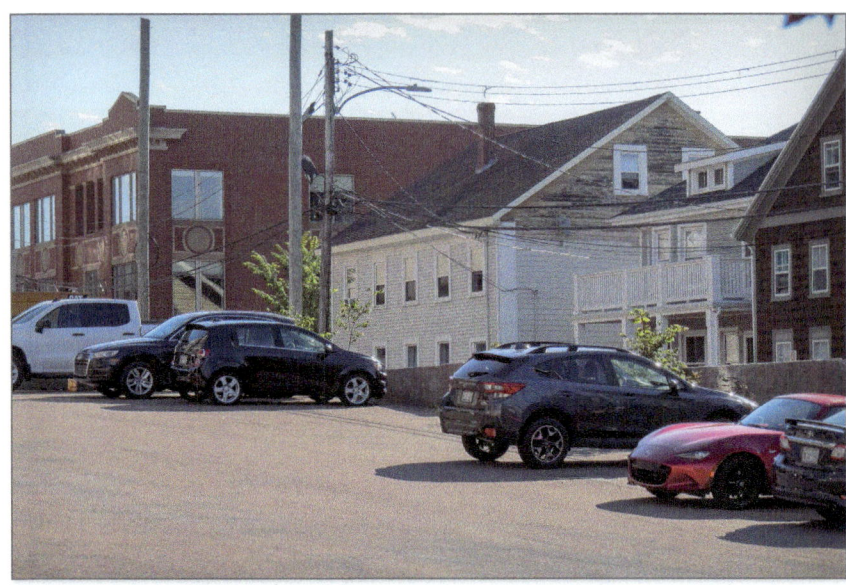

From 2022, this picture from Pownal Street looking southeast to Sydney, shows two of the houses still there from the previous picture of 1954. ▪

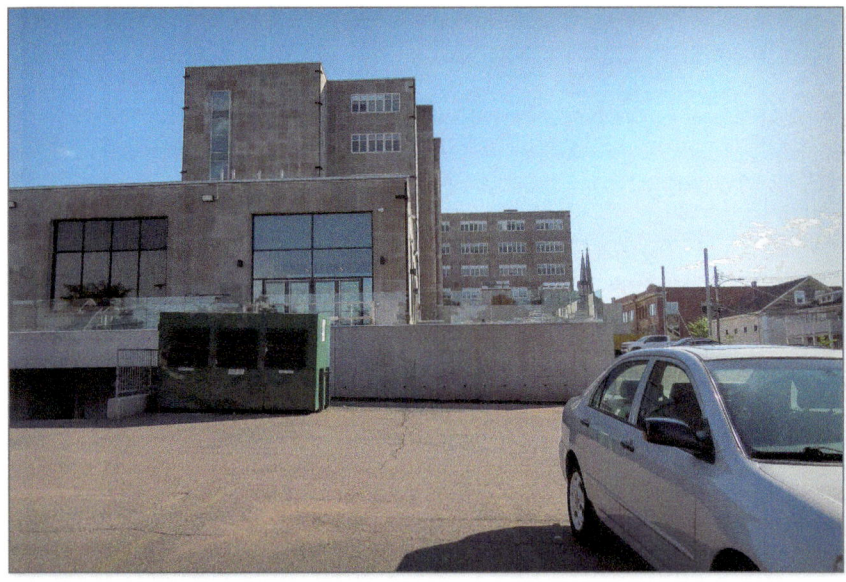

Showing the back of the Dominion Building from Pownal does not have the impact the picture of 1954 does. ▪

The northwest corner of Richmond and Queen c.1894 looking north up Queen Street. London House was on the northwest corner of Queen and Richmond (present day the Guild).

The Beer Bros building, with the new brick and stone face put on in 1888. This is the location at 113 Queen Street where F. W. Woolworth first established a presence in the city. The next building on the right with Goff Bros over the door is where Moore & McLeods opened for business. Two doors up was the location of the Metropolitan Stores.

Note the wide wooden sidewalks.

This corner of Queen and Richmond contained a building in 1868 that was moved to Water Street and placed beside the bonded warehouse (see Water Street section).

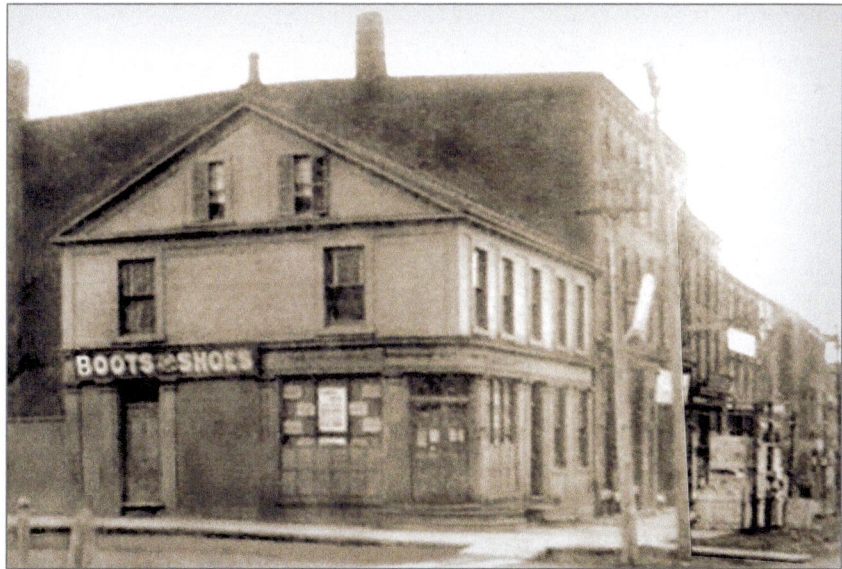

The northwest corner of Richmond and Queen c.1900. This corner was bought by the Royal Bank of Canada in 1911 and remodeled in 1912.

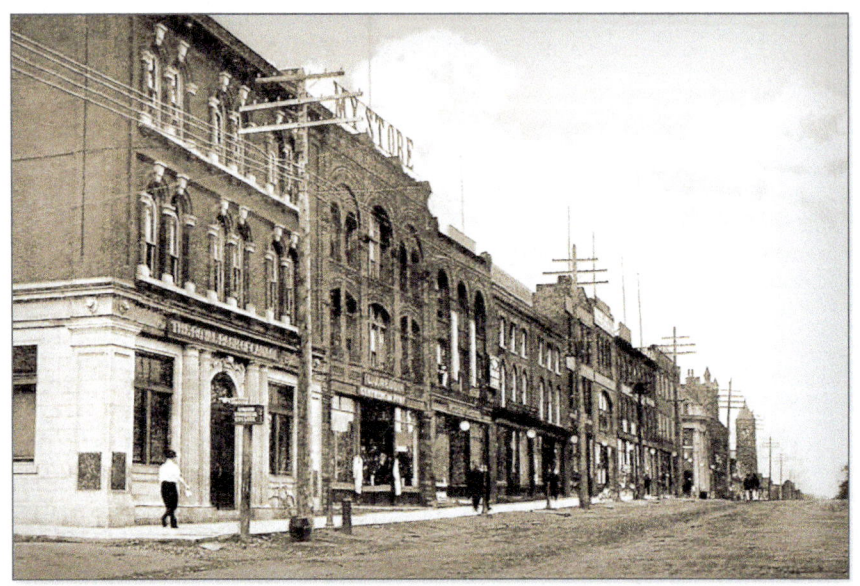

The northwest corner of Richmond and Queen c.1915. In this picture, next to the Royal Bank is My Store which was previously Beer Bros. In 1913 it was the original location of F. W. Woolworth, before moving up the street. Many will remember the Co-op store which had a back entrance on Richmond as the store wrapped around the Royal Bank. ■

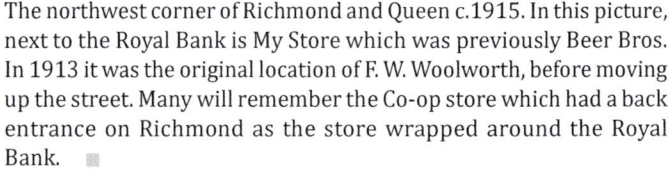

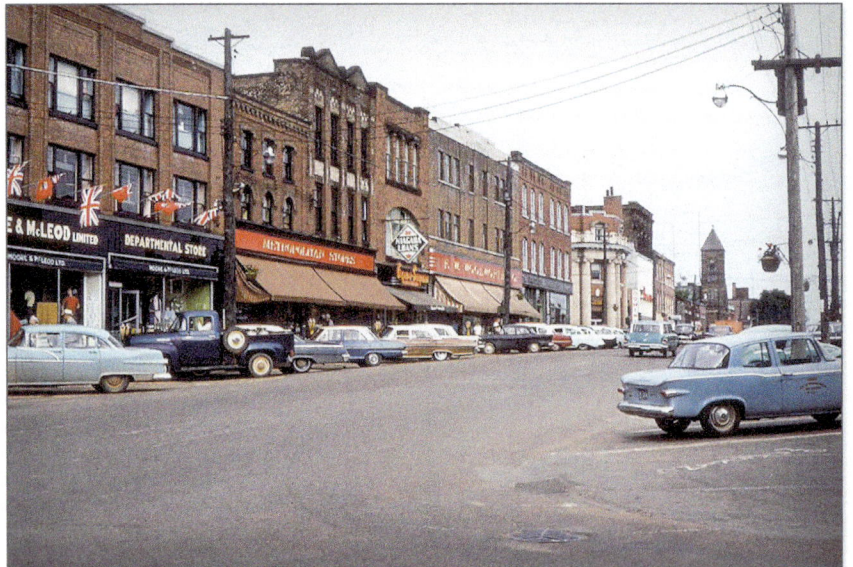

In this picture, from 1962, we see Moore & McLeod's Departmental Store, Metropolitan Stores (opened May 22, 1929), Agnew Surpass (originally opened 123 Grafton on March 17, 1932) and F. W. Woolworth (opened first at 117 Queen on June 8, 1917), with Rogers Hardware on the southwest corner of Queen and Grafton. ■

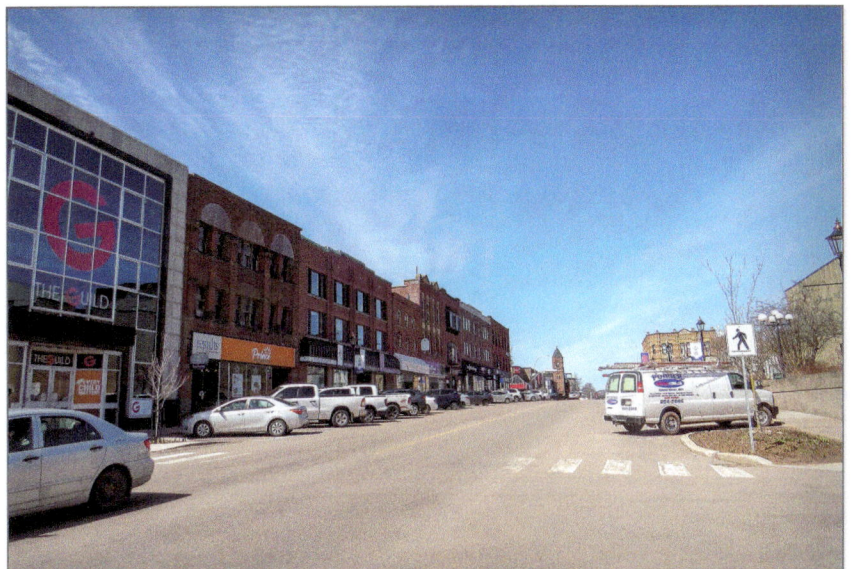

Looking north in 2022, showing the former Royal Bank converted to The Guild Theatre. The other buildings retained their original structure, with new occupants. ▪

Looking southwest from Grafton along Queen Street. The first business was Medical Hall with Dodd and Rogers next. This building at 137 Queen Street, was built in 1867 by Thomas Dodd and Benjamin Rogers. In 1871 Dodd's brother Dr. Simon Dodd opened a pharmacy called the Medical Hall. In April 1904, Benjamin Rogers took over the hardware business from Dodd and Rogers renaming it Rogers Hardware. He eventually occupied the whole building. ▪

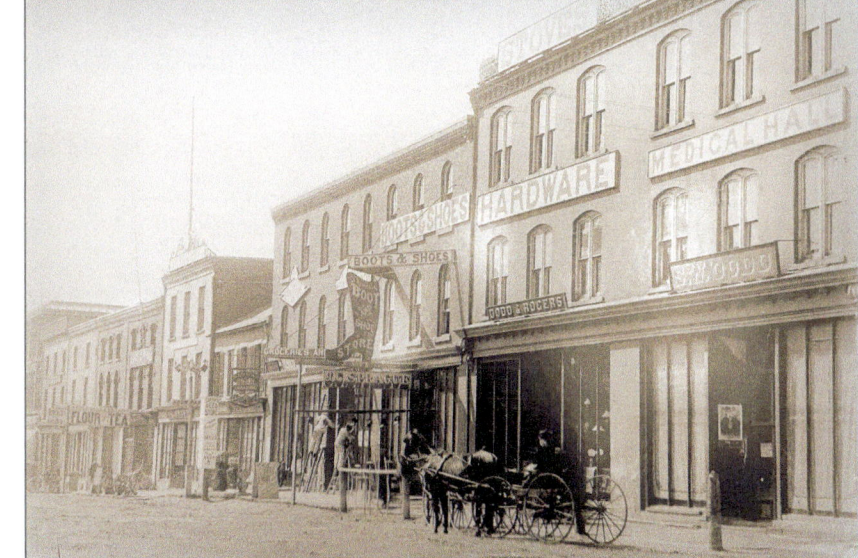

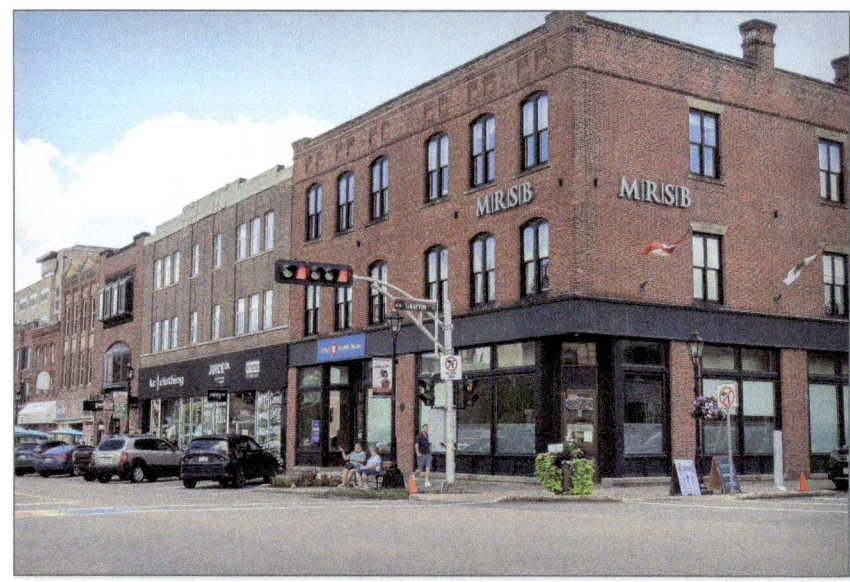

Down this block today it is: MRSB, Kinetic Fitness, Juice Co, K C Clothing, Casa Mia, Island Realty, the Charlottetown Mosque, Rising Tide Electric Bicycles, Queen Square Centre and The Guild theatre. ▪

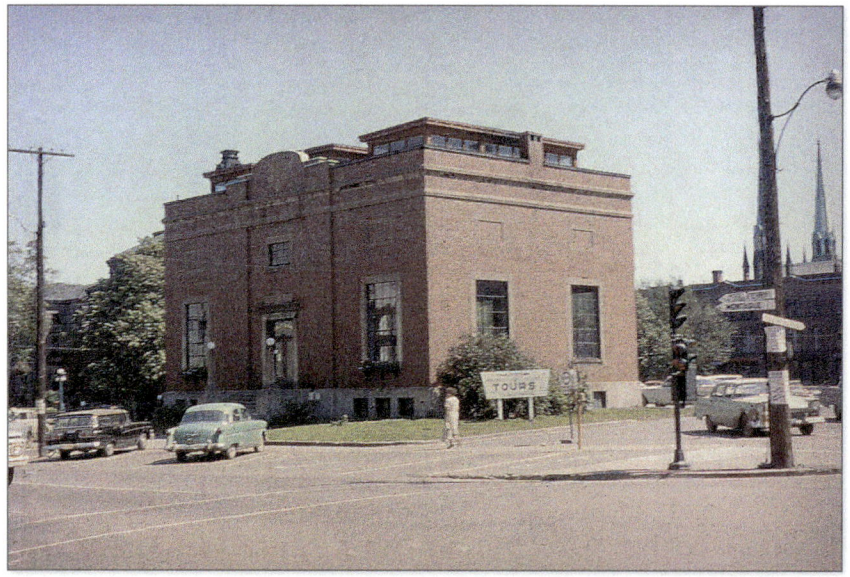

The Library, on the southeast corner of Queen and Grafton, was originally called the Harris Memorial Library and Art Gallery. It opened in 1930.

The Charlottetown Public Library and the Cabot Building were removed for the construction of the Confederation Centre complex. Demolition began on the library on December 17, 1963. ▪

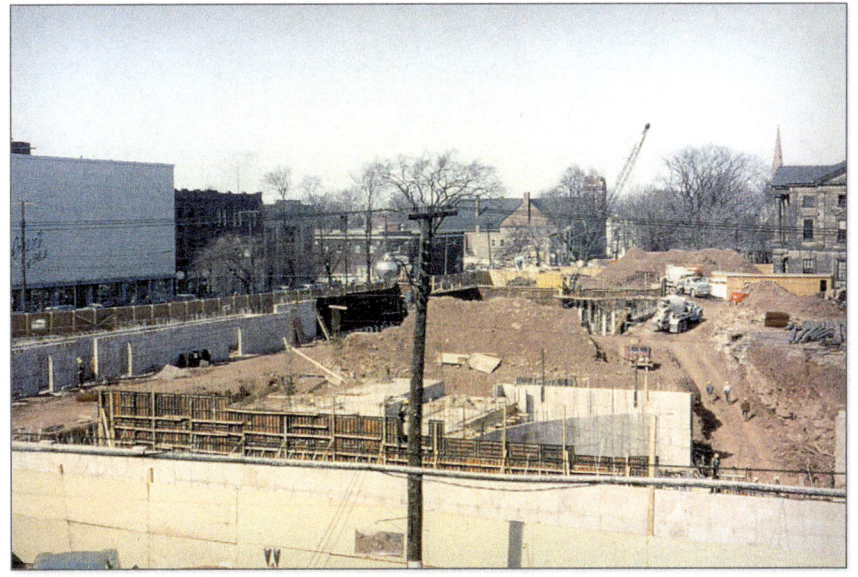

The Cabot Building, situated west of Province House, was completed in 1885 as the Charlottetown Post Office. This picture shows Jenkins Transfer moving the contents to the new Post Office located in The Dominion Building, on Queen between Sydney and Richmond.

With the removal of the Post Office and Public Library, work was well under way in May 1963 for the new Confederation Centre.

In the background from right to left is: Province House, Zion Presbyterian Church at Prince and Grafton, the Capitol Theatre at Great George and Grafton and the white-faced building - Holman's Department Store on Grafton Street.

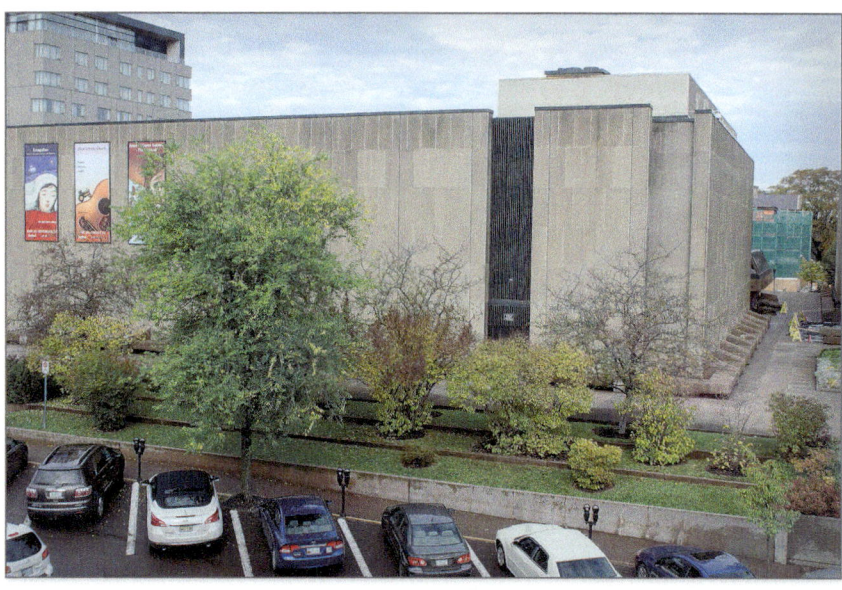

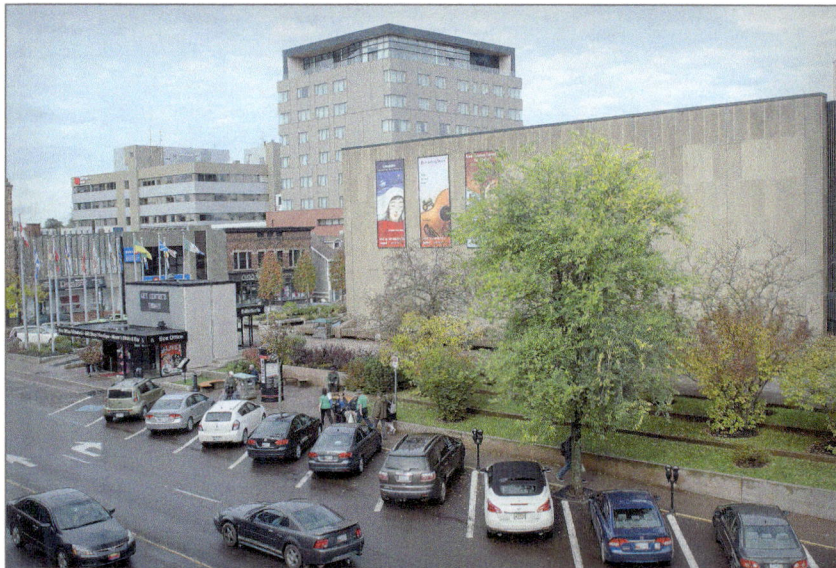

Some might say the concrete buildings that were opened in 1964 were not an improvement to the area. ■

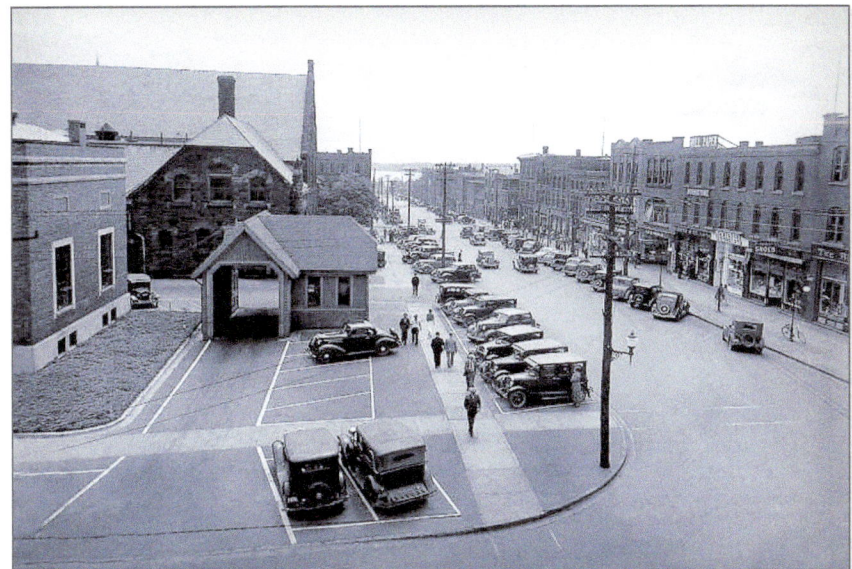

1930's: On the southeast corner of Queen and Grafton Street where the Confederation Centre main entrance is now, was the weight scales, with the Market building behind, and the Public Library to the left.

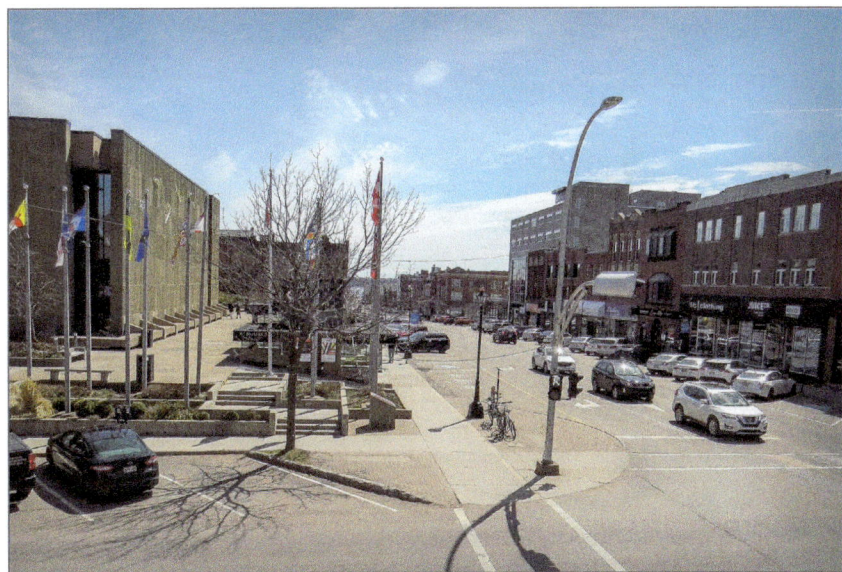

Current picture in 2022, looking south on Queen, shows the site today, with the entrance to the Confederation Centre of the Arts.

The next set of pictures is the block on Queen Street,
from Grafton to Kent Street.

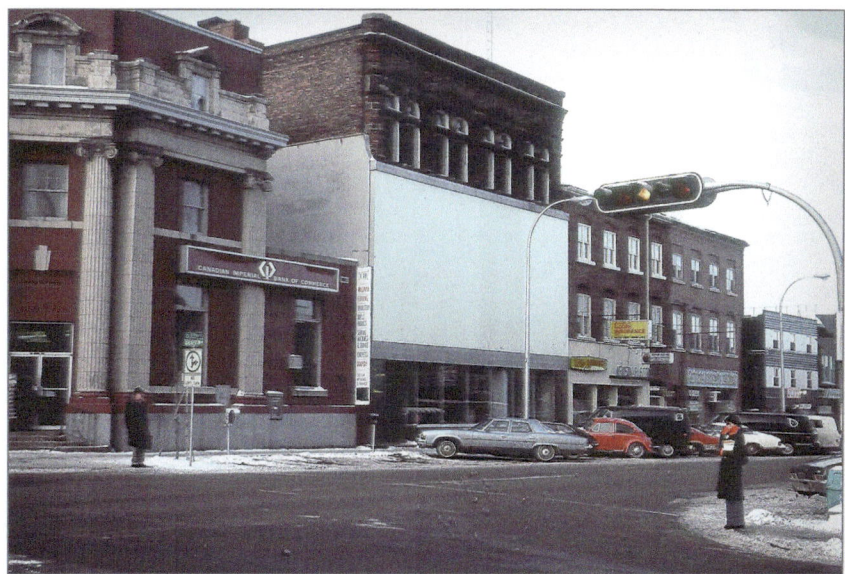

On the northwest corner of Queen and Grafton, J. D. MacLeod and Co. operated a family grocery store in 1887. By 1894, McKay Woolen mills had established on the corner. Note the large tree on the corner at the right where Hughes Drug Store was and now home to Cows Ice Cream. ▪

In 1906, following the merger of the Merchants Bank of Prince Edward Island with the Canadian Bank of Commerce, the amalgamated bank built a new building on this site. ▪

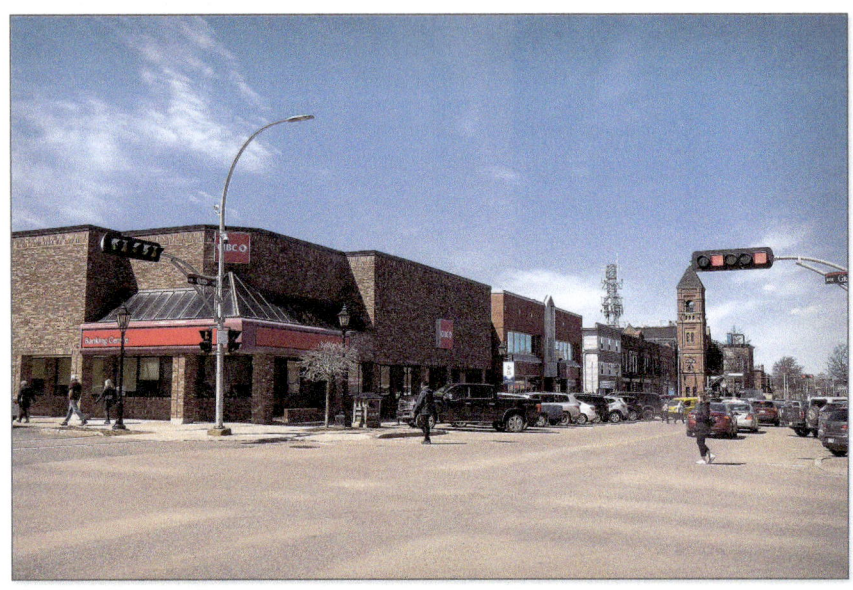

In 1982 the bank, now rebranded as CIBC, remodeled to its present look, as well as taking over the building to the right. (On June 01, 1961, Canadian Bank of Commerce and the Imperial Bank of Canada became CIBC, the largest bank merger in Canadian history)

CIBC, in 2021/22 unveiled a new look on all branches, teller machines, etc. which includes a bold and modern logo.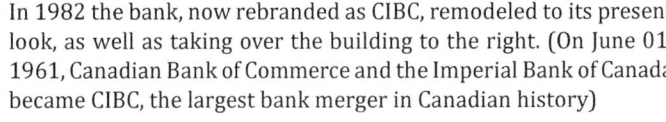

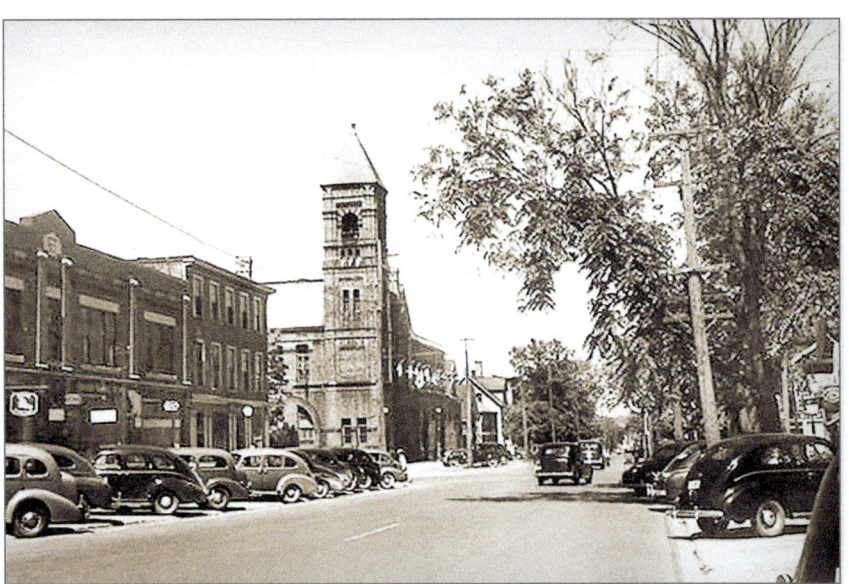

The east side of the Queen Street block between Grafton and Kent had lots of shade trees in the 1940's.

Picture taken in March 1979. On the far left is 180 Queen Street - Corney's Family Store. They later mover across the street to 175 Queen and closed for business in 2019. 180 Queen in 1937 was MacLean & MacFadyen Grocers.

The Bluenose Restaurant at 174-176 Queen was also known as the Schooner (note the schooner on third floor). The was also the site of the original Canton Cafe, which opened here in 1936. Wrights Shoes (Austin Wright) was at 164 Queen. Previously Wright's was at 175 Queen in 1937 and 125 Grafton in 1950. They later moved to 119 Queen Street in the former Moore & McLeod building, where it is recently closed. 164 Queen in 1937 was Gay's Grocery Store. ■

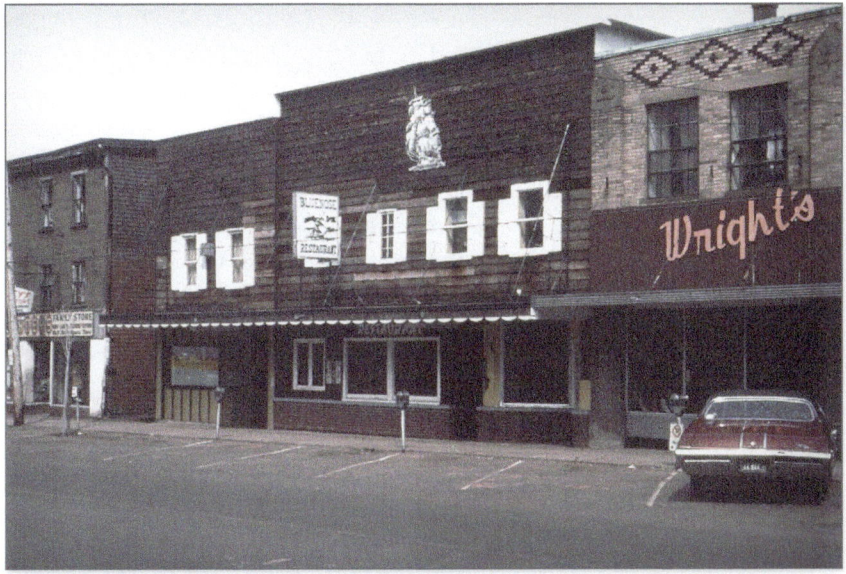

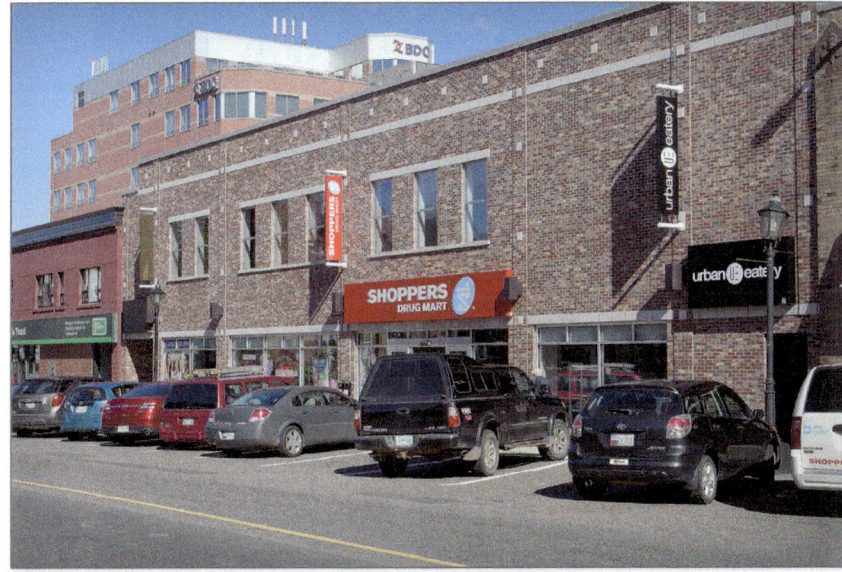

This block today contains Toronto Dominion Bank on the left, Shoppers Drug Mart in the center. BDC Place top center is on Kent Street and connected to this block by a pedway. ■

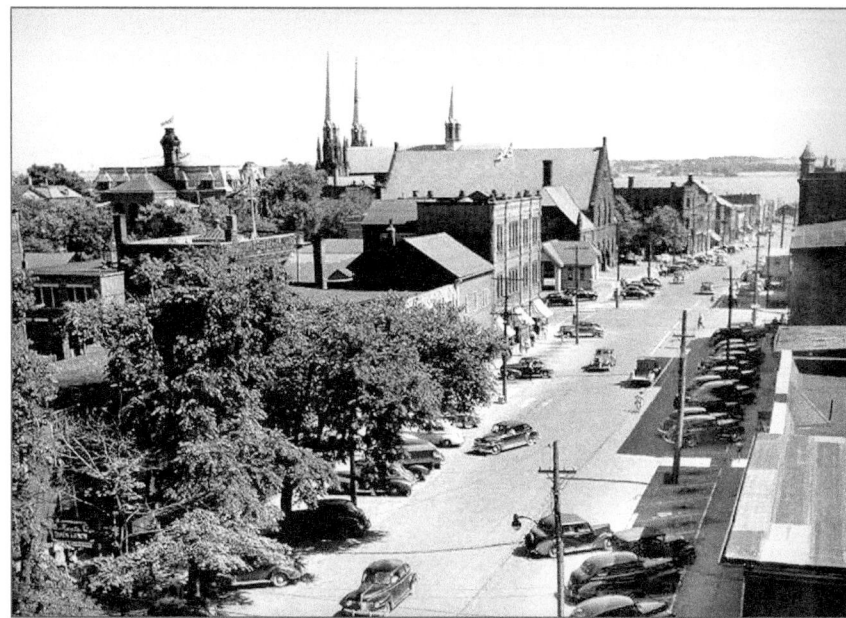

Taken from the tower of City Hall in 1940's, this picture looks southeast. Interesting to note again the trees on Queen Street. We see the tower of Cabot building (left of the basilica spires), as well as the weigh station on the southeast corner of Queen and Grafton. The Hughes Drug Store building is flying the British Union Jack flag. ▪

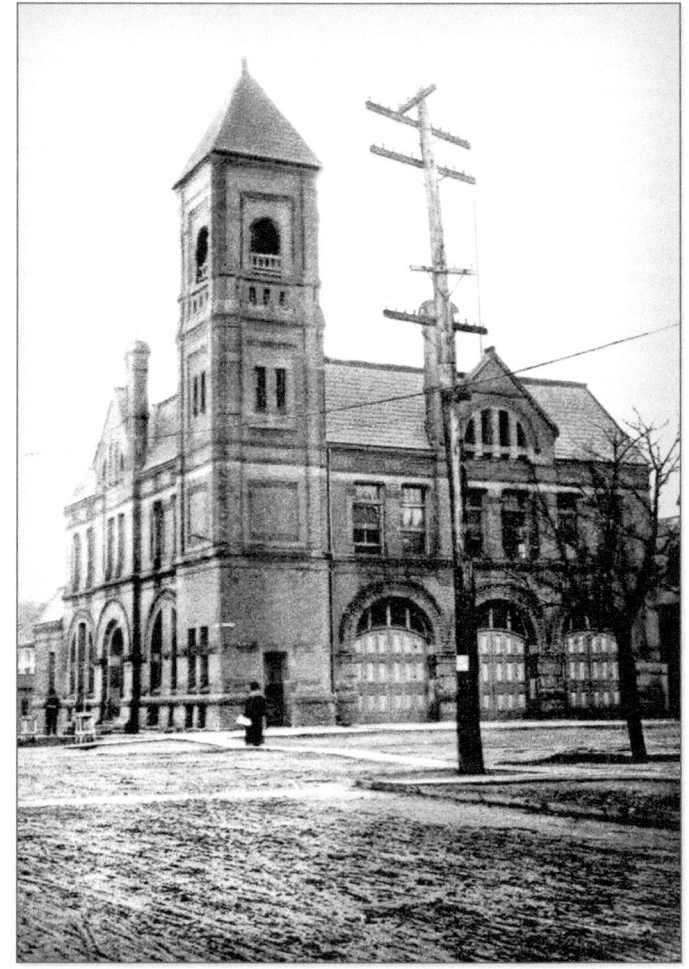

A picture from 1916: City of Charlottetown (previously Charlotte Town) was incorporated in 1855 with the name changed at incorporation. The City Hall was built in 1888. It was constructed by W. H. Fraser from a design by John Lemuel Phillips and Charles Benjamin Chappell. Originally the building held the police station and fire hall. It also housed horses for the fire wagons.

The three large facing doors were originally for the fire wagons, and later fire trucks. They are now windows and the main entrance to City Hall.

In the 1924-1925 McAlpine's Charlottetown Street Directory for Queen Street on the west side from Kent Street north listed: City Hall, City Fire Engine Hall, City Stables, City Hotel etc. ▪

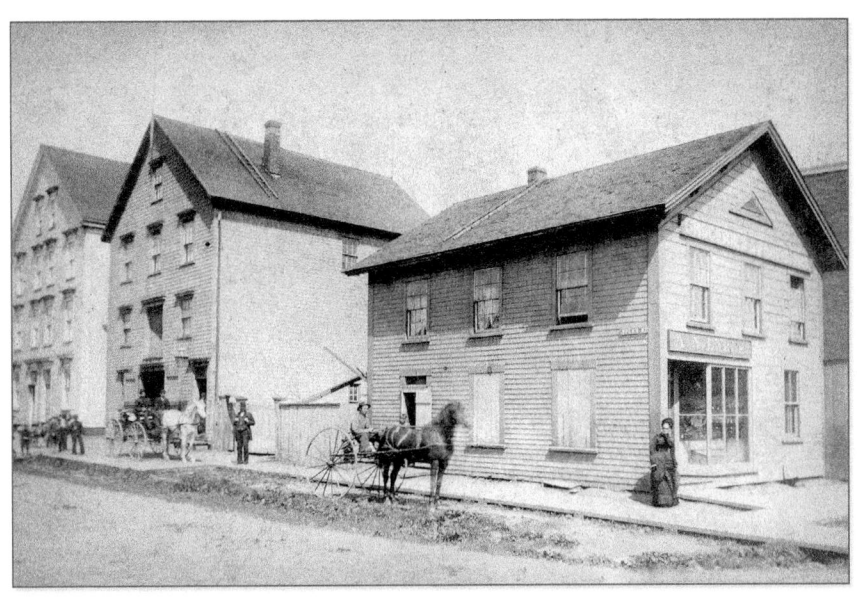

Queen Street looking northeast from Kent to Fitzroy. On the Northeast corner in 1870 was A. N. Large Groceries & Provisions. In 1887 Large built billiard Rooms, and was a Lager Beer bottler. By 1899 it was listed as A. N. Large Livery Stables.

A. N. LARGE,
BILLIARD ROOMS,
LAGER BEER BOTTLER,
AND MANUFACTURER OF
Soda Water, Ginger Ale, Lemonade, Sarsaparilla, Champagne Cider, Syrups, &c.
132 Queen, Cor. Kent Street, Charlottetown, P. E. I.

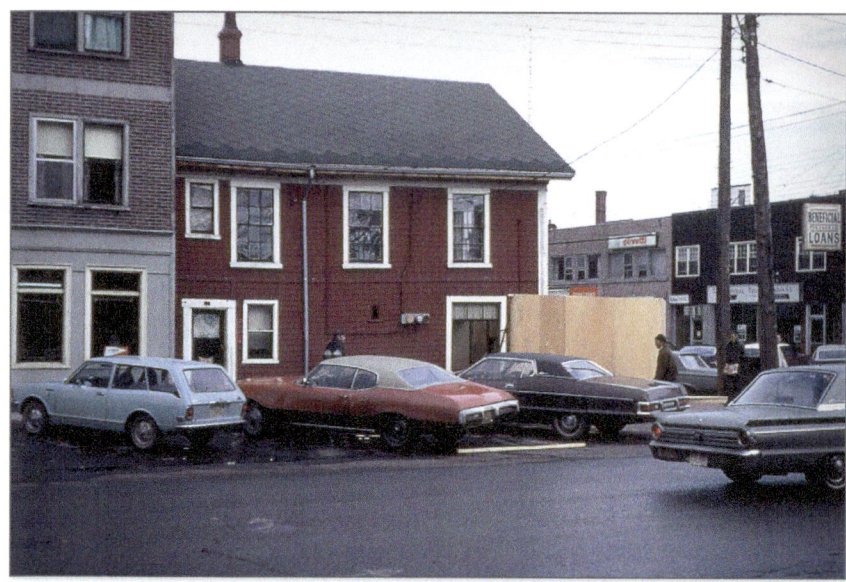

The building was still there until January 1973, when was removed and a new two-story building was erected. ■

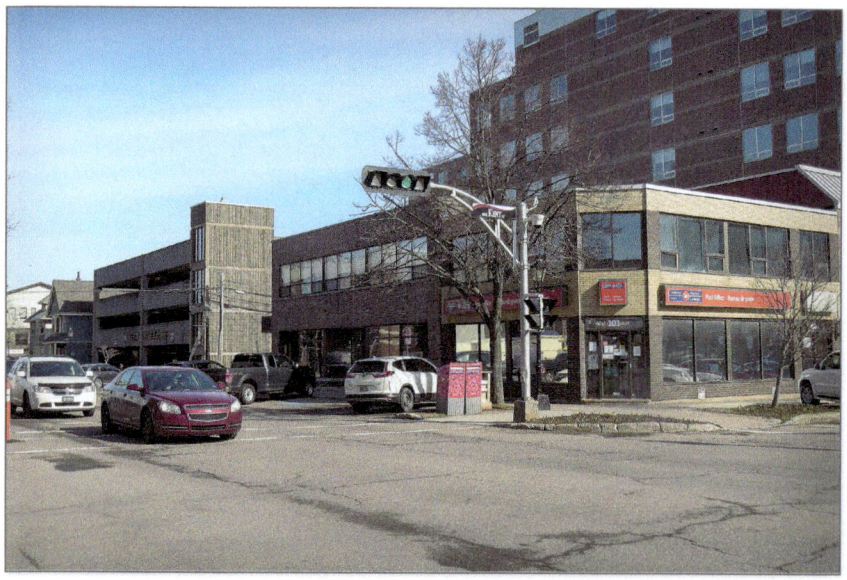

In May 2010 this corner was TD Commercial Banking offices. They moved to the second floor of the TD Bank across the street, in August 2010 after being here for two years. In October 2013, it became the main Charlottetown Post Office, having moved from the Dominion Building.

The law offices of T. Daniel Tweel are on the second floor. ■

Moving north to 208 Queen Street, the City water department operated a garage. Next was a Texaco station operated by Pete DesRoches. In 1972 it was Young's Texaco. The building on the right was: 202-204 Queen Street, the Charlottetown Clinic with: Dr. J. H. O'Hanley, Phys., Dr. F. A. MacMillan Phys & Surg., and Dr. K. A MacEachern, Dentist. Some of these doctors moved to the new clinic at 1 Rochford Street. Also in this building was the Charlottetown Labour Council and Blue Cross offices. Far left in this picture at 224 Queen Street was Dr. I. Rachmel and Dr. Harold Stewart. ▪

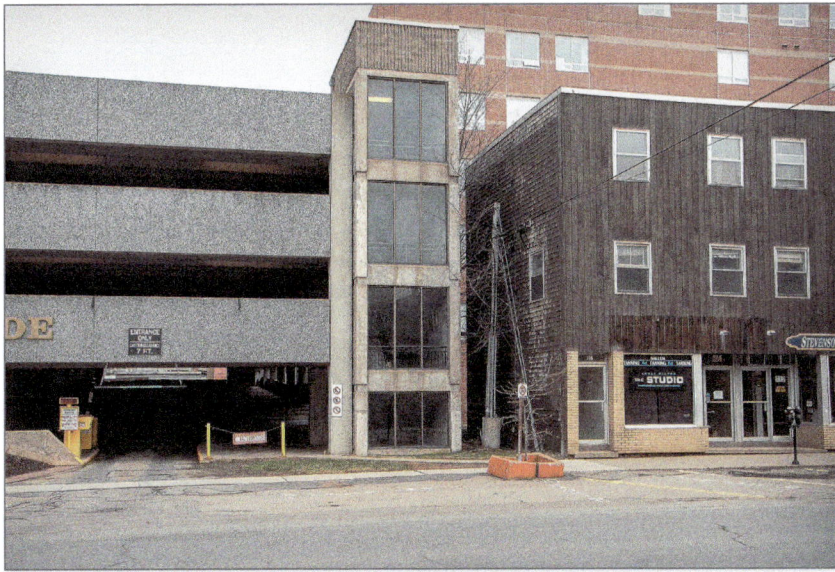

The City water building and the service station were removed to construct the Queen Parkade. It was opened on June 15, 1979 by Mayor Francis J. Moran and was designed to hold 338 cars. ▪

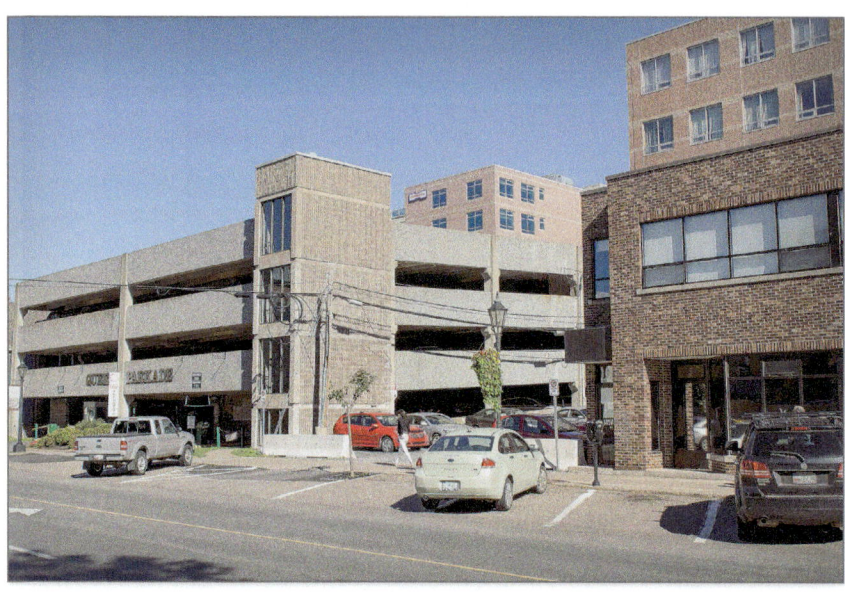

The building south of the parkade was removed in 2013 and is now a vacant lot.

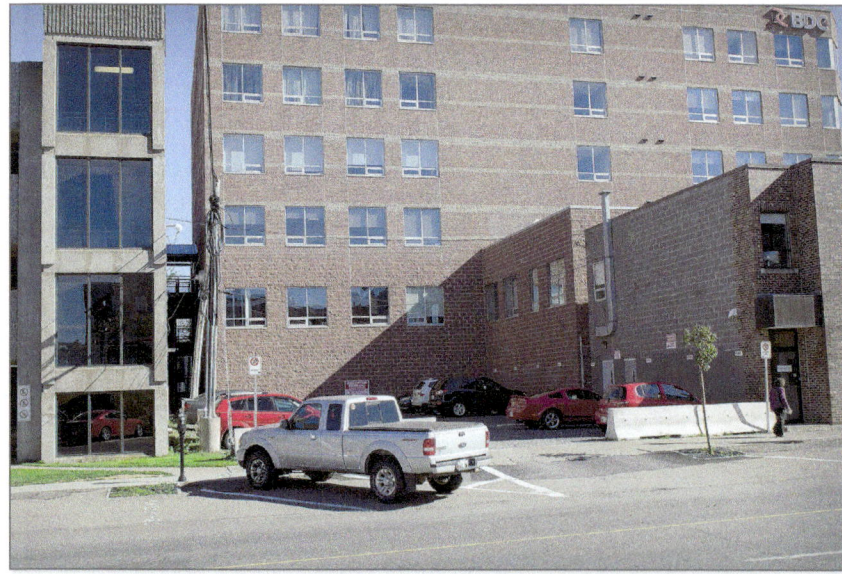

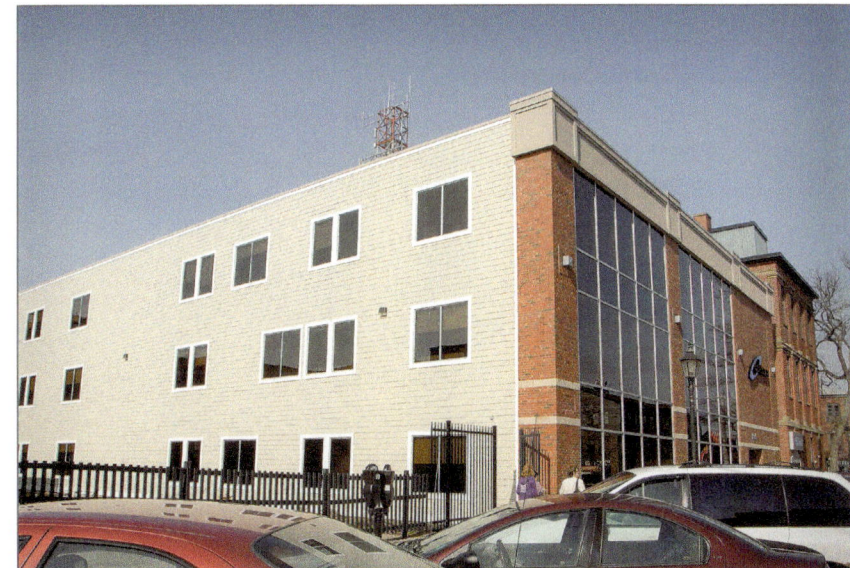

Across Queen Street, between Kent and Fitzroy, was the Queen Street Meat Market, opened in 1973. Note the fish hanging under the sign. This business was moved to University Avenue in 1978, and was still called Queen Street Meat Market. A new building was erected at 368 University Avenue and is now called Mike's Island Market. ▪

223 Queen Street: Ceridian opened in 2008 on the former City Hall Parking lot and site of former Queen Street Meat Market. The old Island Telephone Co. building is next on the right at the southwest corner of Queen and Fitzroy, having opened here in 1930. ▪

Grafton Street

Grafton Street runs west to east through the center of Charlottetown,
from West Street to the Hillsborough Bridge.

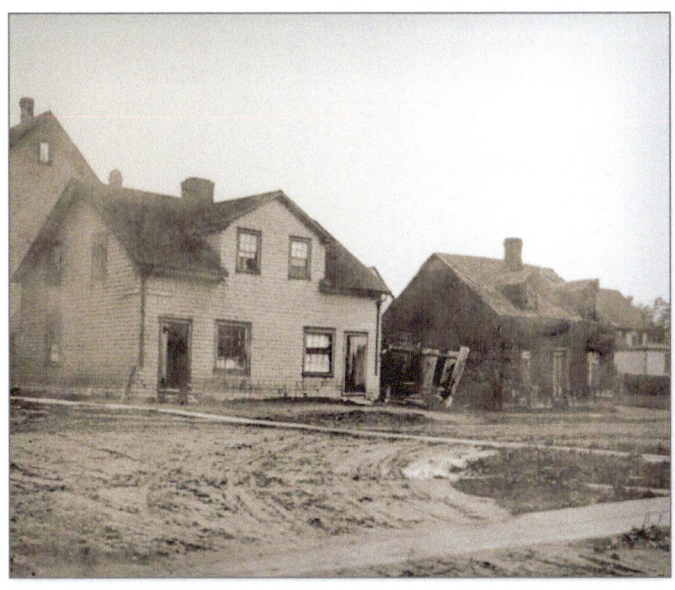

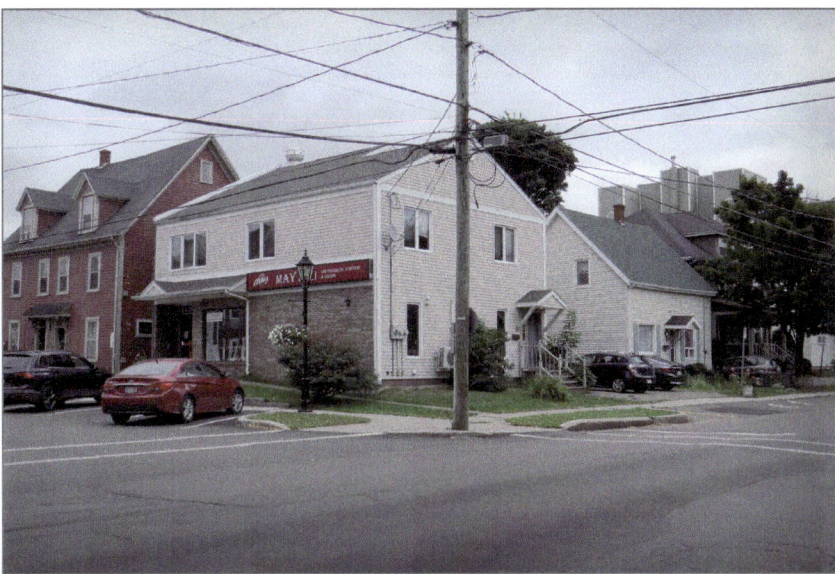

1904: The southeast corner of Grafton and Rochford. This is now the May Deli, Vietnamese Cuisine & Sushi.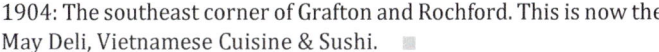

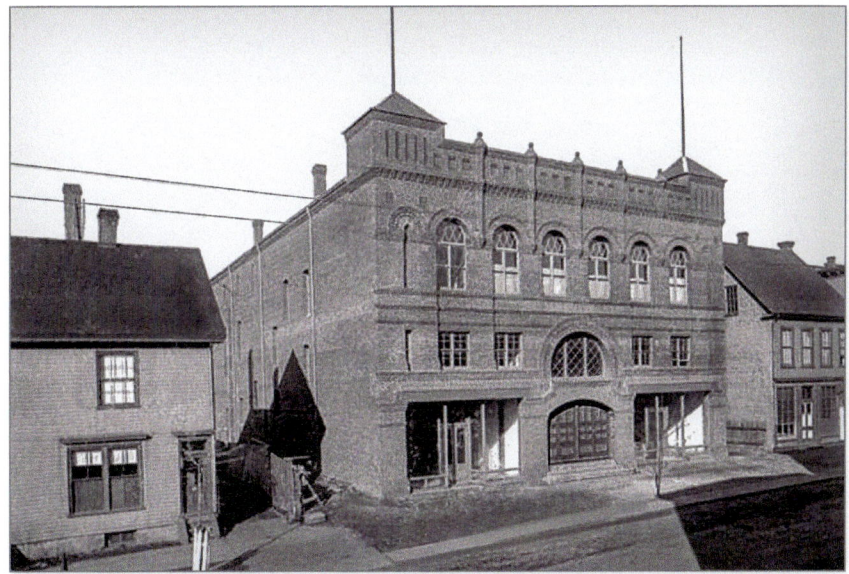

The Masonic Hall or Temple (sometimes called Lodge or Opera House) opened at 71 Grafton Street on November 2, 1893. It had a seating capacity of 1,000. The Hall was a three story building with lodge rooms on the upper two floors. [Cr: PARO Acc100/2]

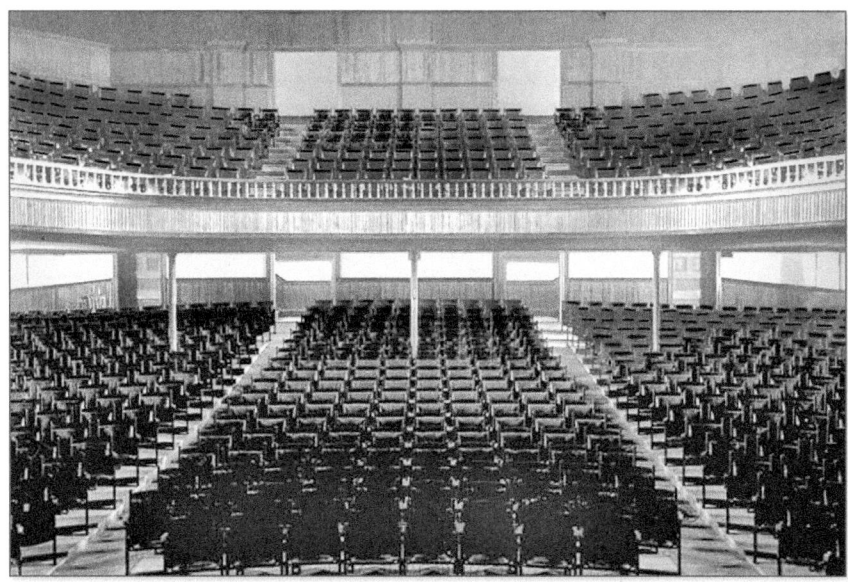

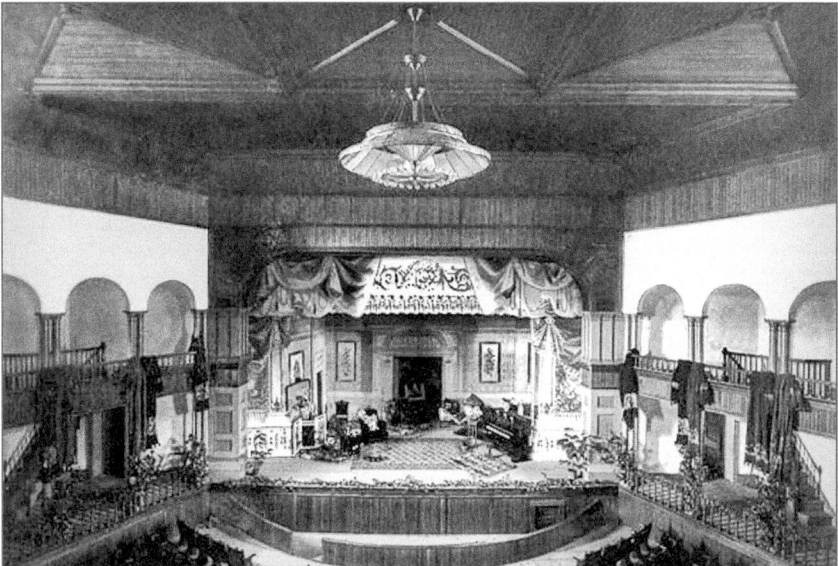

The Hall was a centre for live theatre, and political, religious and temperance speeches. When moving pictures arrived the Lodge was converted to the Prince Edward Theatre in 1919 to accommodate the new motion pictures phenonium.

The building was lost completely in a fire on December 14, 1955. It was replaced by a more modern building housing the Prince Edward Theatre, now home to H. L. Sear Insurance.

Before 1893, the Masonic Hall was on Richmond Street at the location of the Murphy's Community Centre (former Basilica Rec Center). That lot was sold on September 3, 1856 for the erection of the Queen Square Presbyterian Church.CR: PARO.

The aerial photo is c.1934, showing the whole block bounded by Grafton, Pownal, Kent and Queen. The large building second left of the Hall was the Legion Hall before they moved to 99 Pownal Street. The smaller house to the left of it with the three dormer windows is still there today. Interesting in this aerial photo is the number of barns behind most buildings taking up the whole of the center of the block. Transportation was by horse and buggy and the horses were housed and fed in that area.

The building on the far right is the Canadian Bank of Commerce (now CIBC) built in 1906. ■

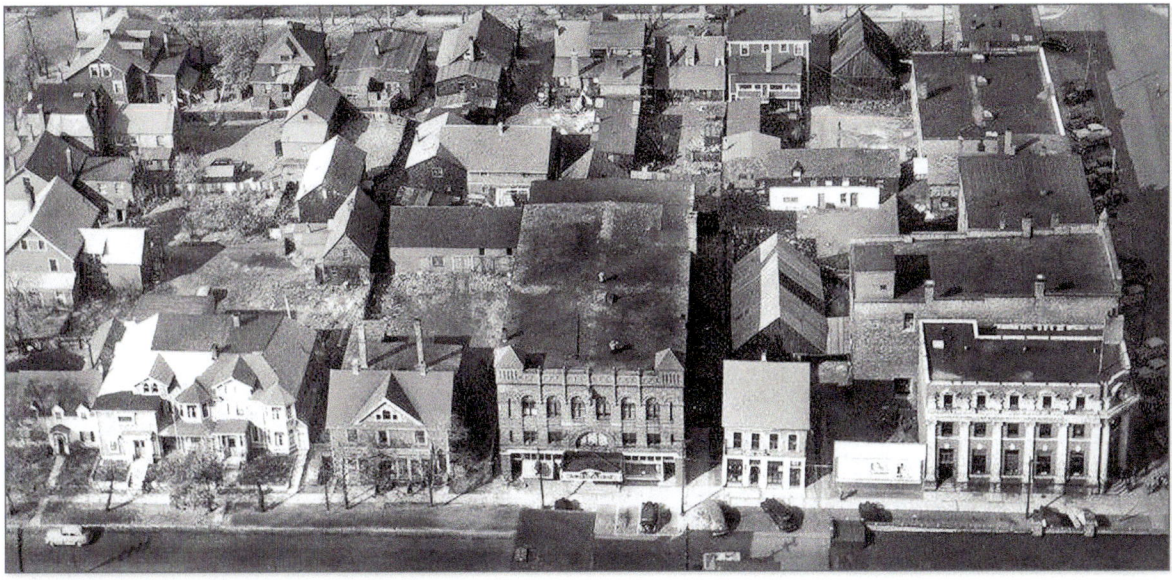

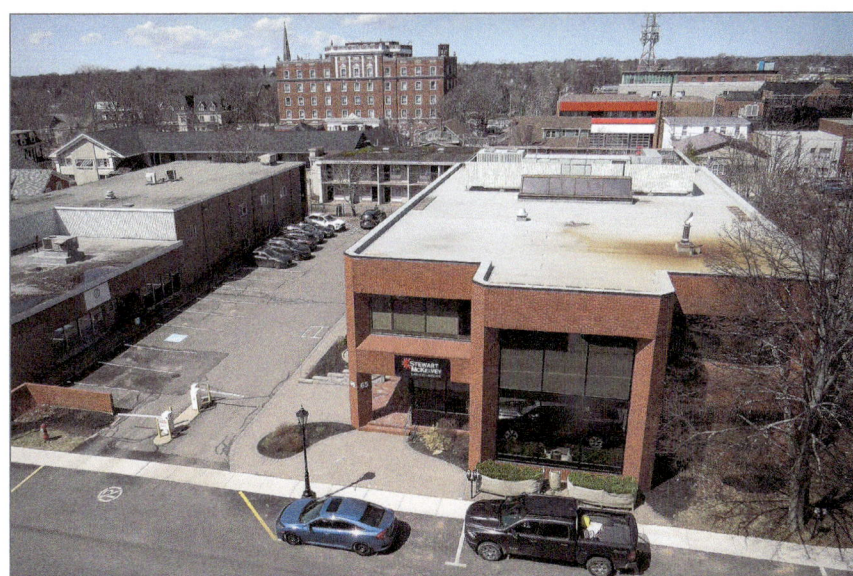

Taken from the balcony of Key Murray Law in 2022, showing the former location of the Masonic Hall as the building on the left, now Ironside Tattoo and Piercing, with H. L. Sear Insurance further left in the building at 57 Grafton Street. The center of the block is now taken up mostly by the Hotel on Pownal at 148 Pownal Street, formerly built as the Islander Motel Lodge. The brick building in the background is Rodd's Charlottetown Hotel on Kent Street. The brick building foreground right is the law offices of Stewart McKelvey. ■

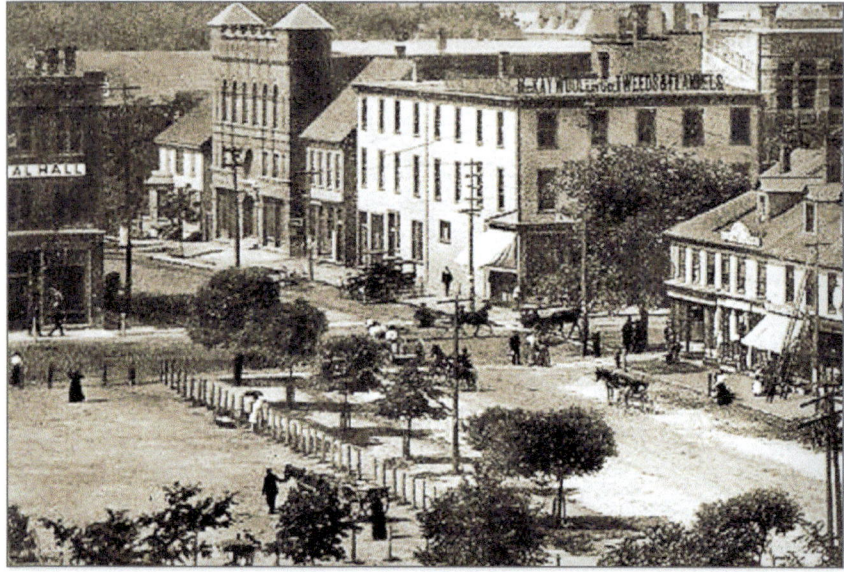

◀ This picture from 1893, looking northwest from Market Square shows the corner of Queen and Grafton with, from left to right: Medical Hall (present day MRSB), The Masonic Hall, McKay Woolen (present day CIBC) and Hughes Drug Store (present day Cows Ice Cream). ▪

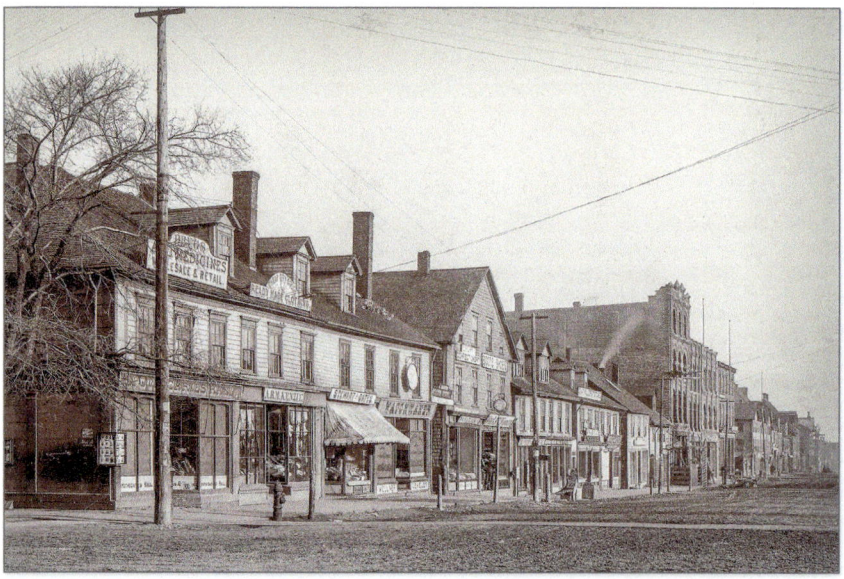

▼ Grafton Street from Queen to Great George c. 1898 (PARO), sometimes called Sunnyside. Note the fire Hydrant near the pole at left. This was installed with the first water System in 1888. The canon, still there today, almost hidden by the same pole, was placed there by Theophilus DesBrisay and dates from about 1860.

Some of the stores on this block were:

97 Grafton: Apothecaries Hall, built in 1810. Thomas DesBrisay was the original druggist, followed by his son until 1874. Dr Frank Beer and George E. Hughes continued the vocation until 1901, when George Hughes became sole owner in the new DesBrisay building. When it closed in 1986, it was Canada's oldest retail pharmacy at 176 years.

- 99 Grafton: A. B. McKenzie, Ready Made clothes
- 101 Grafton: Stewart & Gates
- 103 Grafton: W. W. Wellner, watchmaker (William W. Wellner)
- 105r Grafton: Robert Woolner, stabling and boarding house (r signified "rear")
- 113-15 Grafton: Adam Murray, harness maker
- 117 Grafton: A. W. Reddin, druggist
- 119 Grafton: G. H. Taylor, watchmaker (George Henry Taylor)
- 123 Grafton: W. P. Colwill, china and glassware
- 125 Grafton: Dr. J. H. Ayers, dentist (Josiah)
- 125 Grafton: Island Guardian Publishing Co.
- 133 Grafton: Haszard & Moore, printers, book binders (G. Herbert Haszard & Stewart C. Moore)
- 135 Grafton: Mark Wright & Co. Ltd. furniture manufacturer (one of his ads read: "furniture manufacturer, funeral director & bicycles")
- 139 Grafton: Simon W. Crabbe, hardware (Site of Bank of Nova Scotia today)

(Credit: H. B. Stirling collection PARO) ▪

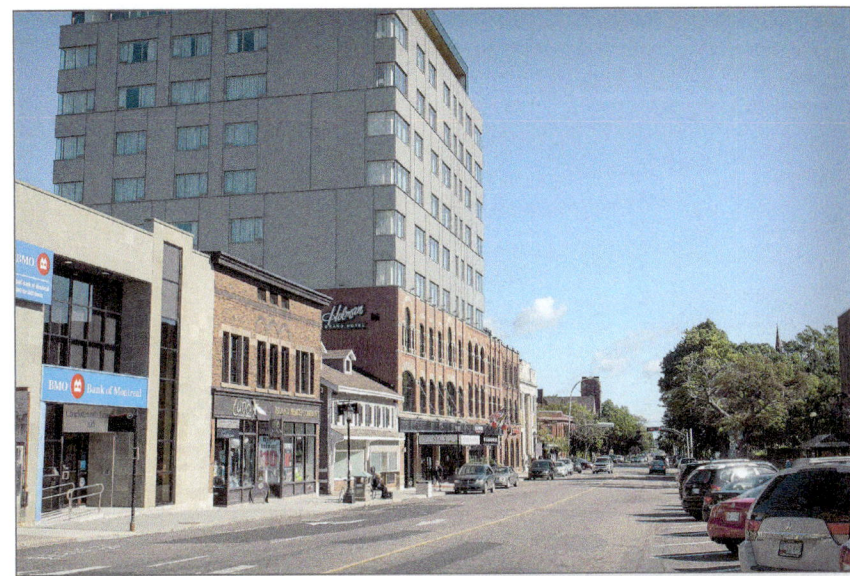

Grafton Street from Queen to Zion on Prince Street taken in 2013, with the prominent building being the Holman Grand Hotel. ▪

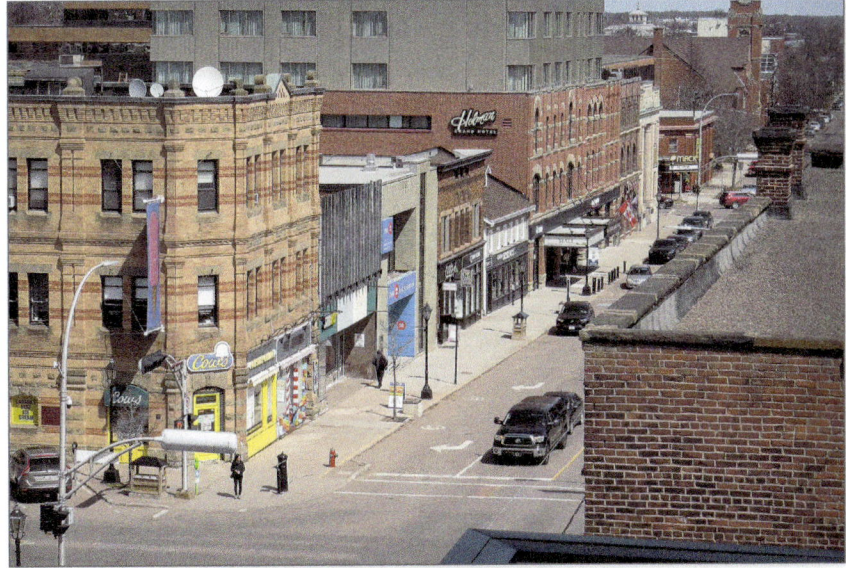

An updated version, from 2022, of this section of Grafton Street. This was taken from the office of Key Murray Law. at 80 Grafton Street. ▪

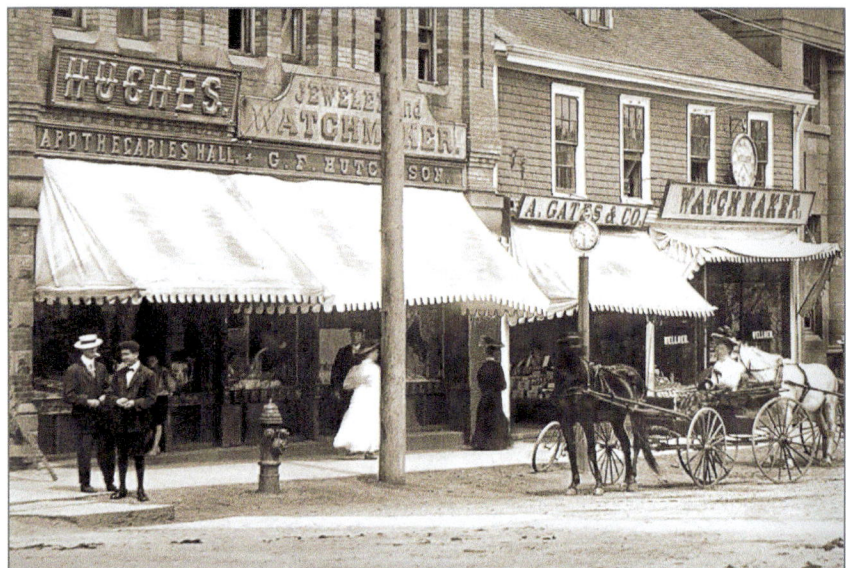

1909, showing the newly constructed DesBrisay building/Hughes Drug Store (built 1901), G. F. Hutcheson Watchmaker, A. Gates & Co. Store and Wellner Watch Maker, and the Bank of Montreal on the right. (Watchmaker was the term for Jeweller of today) ▪

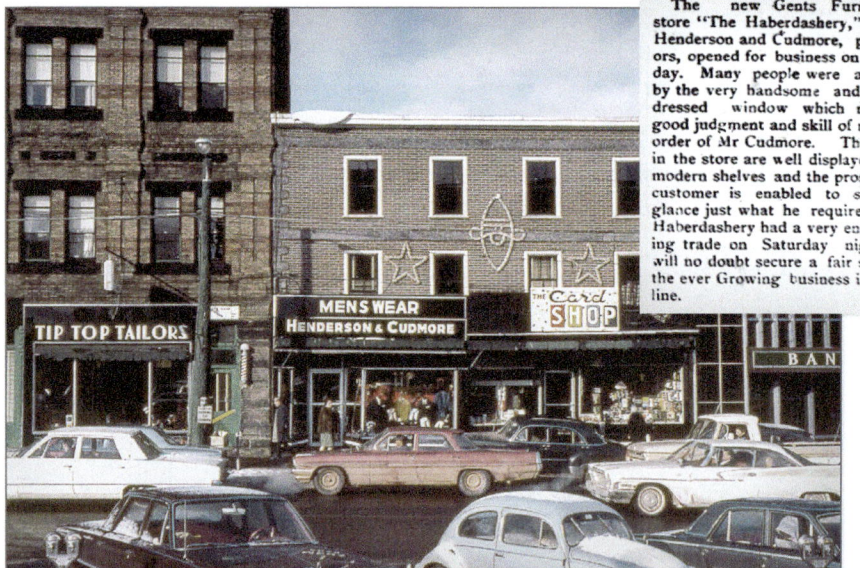

The new Gents Furnishings store "The Haberdashery," Messrs Henderson and Cudmore, proprietors, opened for business on Saturday. Many people were attracted by the very handsome and tastily dressed window which reflected good judgment and skill of no small order of Mr Cudmore. The goods in the store are well displayed from modern shelves and the prospective customer is enabled to see at a glance just what he requires. The Haberdashery had a very encouraging trade on Saturday night and will no doubt secure a fair share of the ever Growing business in their line.

From December 1966, this picture shows:
• 99 Grafton Street, Tip Top Tailors (which later moved in 2009 to the Charlottetown Mall and subsequently closed. Tip Top occupied one-half of the Hughes Drug Store building facing on Grafton. This building was constructed in 1901 as the Desbrisay Block.

• 101 Grafton Street: Henderson & Cudmore Ltd., The Haberdashery (Roy Cudmore and H. S. Henderson with Roy's sons Brian and Clive Cudmore later). The business first opened on April 4, 1914, closing in 2009, a total of 95 years.

• 103 Grafton Street: The Card Shop (W. W. Wellner Jewelers was still there in 1950)

• 105 Grafton Street: The Bank of Montreal dating from 1909, was remodeled from its original structure and officially opened by Premier Walter R. Shaw on May 12, 1964. ▪

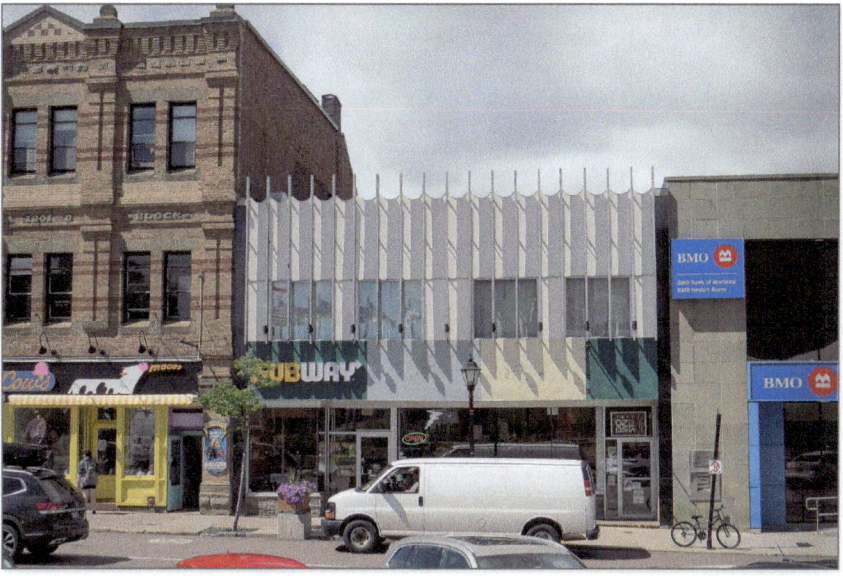

The former Henderson & Cudmore building and the Bank of Montreal were both upgraded. The former Tip Top Tailors was converted to a Subway, and in this picture, Subway moved to the former Henderson & Cudmore. Cows Ice Cream now occupies the former Hughes Drug Store on the corner. The Bank of Montreal, now showing its latest exterior renovation of 1990. ▪

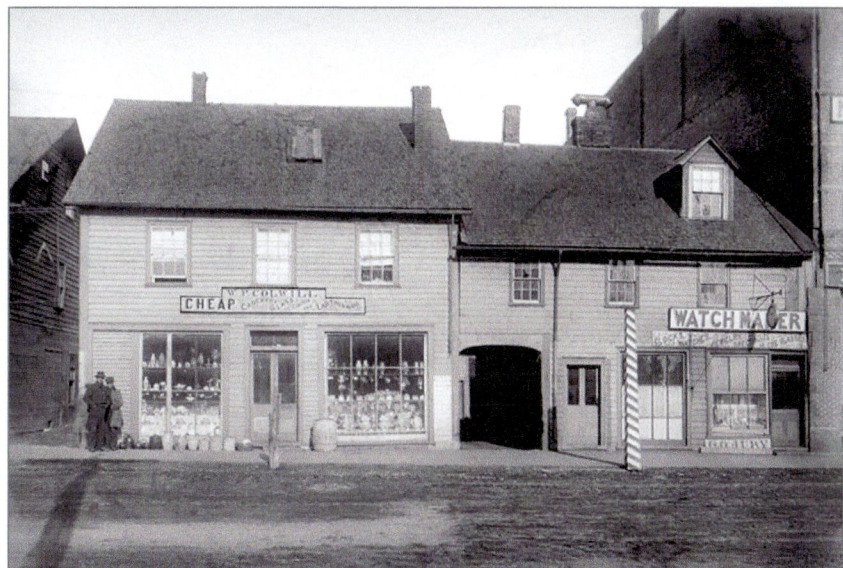

c.1898, with W.P. Colwell china and glassware. Note the entrance to the rear of the property for horse and cart. The brick building at the right is the site of present-day Holman Grand Hotel. ▪

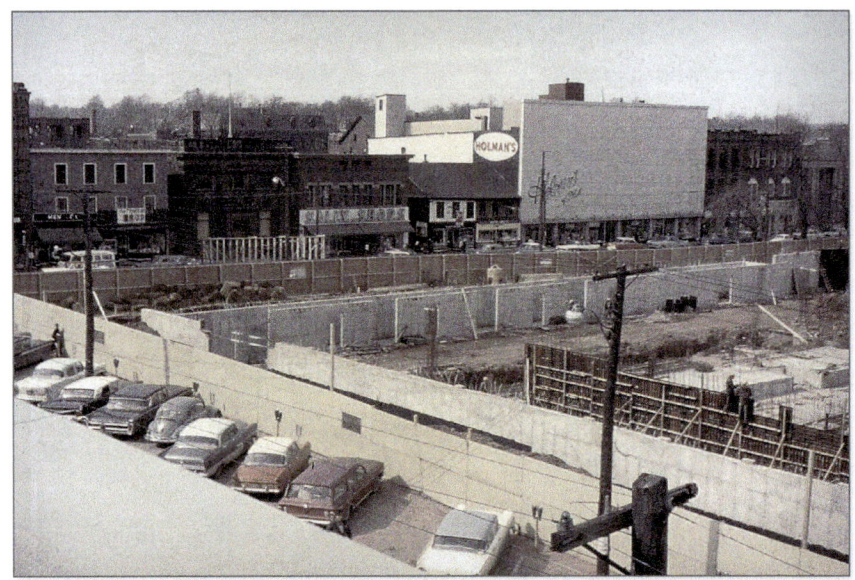

From May 1963, taken from Moore & McLeod's (G. M. Moore and S. A. McLeod) now Queen Square Centre and shows the Confederation Centre under construction. The Bank of Montreal, having opened on this site in 1909, is shown here under reconstruction. 111 Grafton Street: Atkinson's Clover Farm Store (Hiram C. Atkinson) is now Sally Shop. Their building was built in 1932. Eaton's had a food store here called Canadian Stores as well as their Catalogue office. They closed the Canadian Stores nationally in 1943, and Atkinson, their manager at the time, took over the store, under his own name until 1959.

Next door going right, was E. A. Foster Drugs. 121 Grafton Street was Taylors Jewellers (Roland G. Taylor at the time). This building dates from 1843 and is the oldest building on the block.

The white-faced building is Holman's of P E I ▪

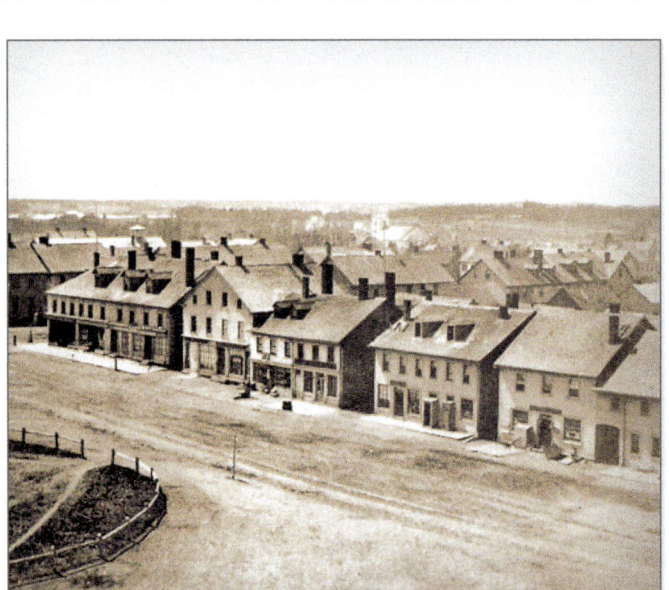

This picture looking northwest, c.1860 (PARO) shows the Grafton Street block from Queen (at the left) toward Great George. In the background we see the old Kirk of St. James at the corner of Fitzroy and Pownal. This church was constructed in 1826 and dedicated for worship on August 9, 1831. Also, you will note that City Hall was not yet build at the corner of Queen and Kent Streets. ▪

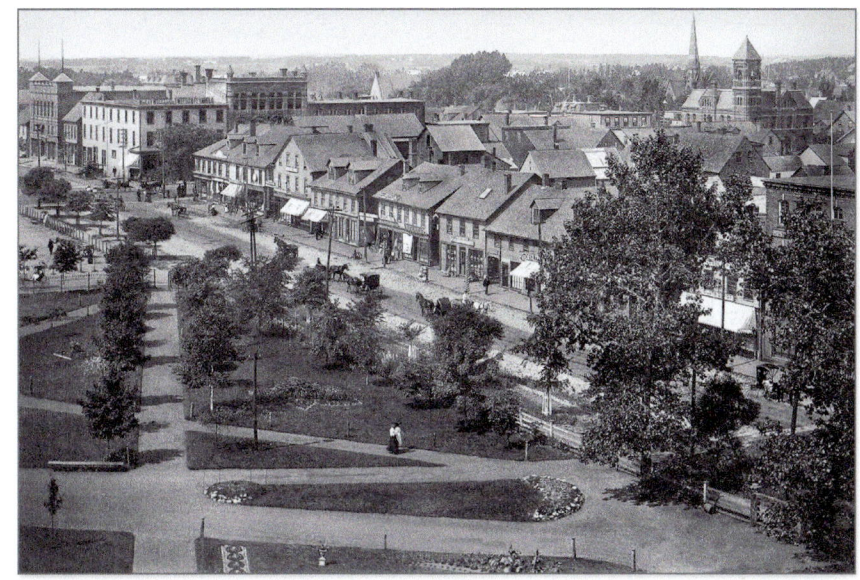

c.1893 (PARO) showing the present Kirk of St. James (the high tower left of City Hall). The corner stone was laid on June 7, 1877 with the church dedicated on October 20, 1878. City Hall, with the cornerstone laid on June 20, 1887 (Queen Victoria's Jubilee-50 years) and completed in 1888, is now shown in this picture. On the far left, on Grafton Street, is the Masonic Hall. (see details above)

Note the elaborate walkways and gardens in front of the Cabot Building. ■

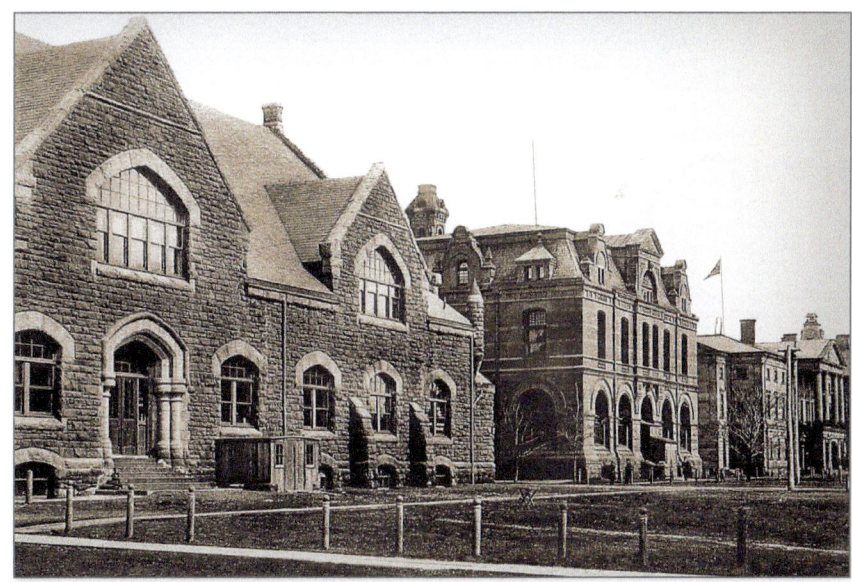

On the south side of this block, and extending to Church Street, are the four main buildings on Queen Square. Left to right, they are: The Market Building, Cabot Building, Province House and Coles Building. They are shown in this picture, from 1907 (PARO) looking northeast from Queen Street. The Market Building burned in a total loss on April 29, 1958. The Cabot Building was later removed to provide land for the Confederation Centre of The Arts, which opened in 1964. More detail on each building below. ■

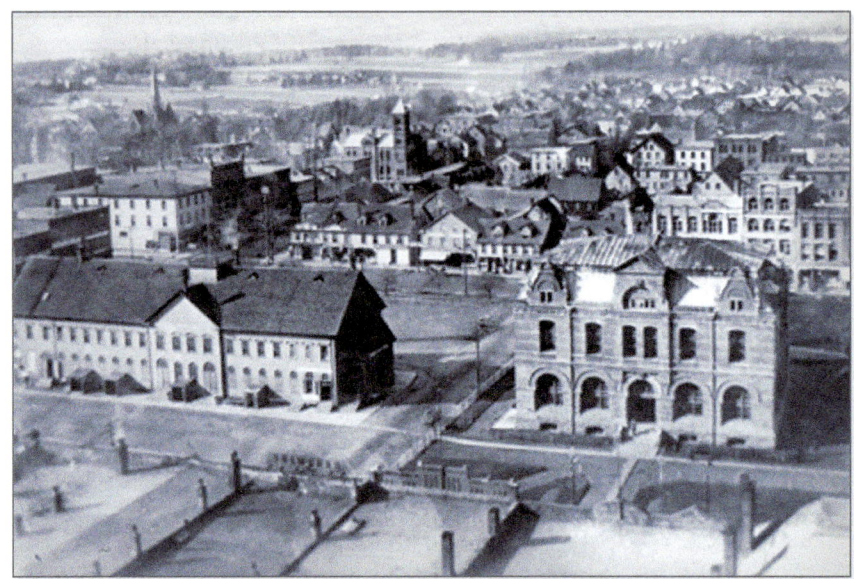

The Market building: Located on the west end of Queens Square, the Market had a long history in the city. The first market, built in 1813 was constructed where Province House now stands. It was replaced by a larger round structure in 1823. In 1867 a new 2 story wooden building was designed by Mark Butcher, cabinet maker. This picture shows the Market building, with the Cabot building beside from 1900 (PARO). This wooden Market building burned in 1902. ◼

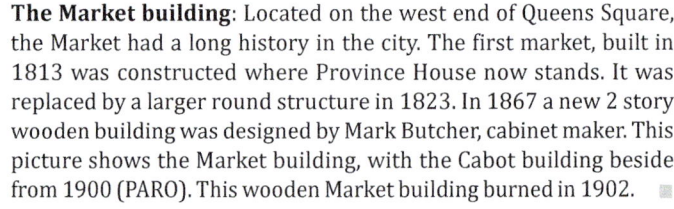

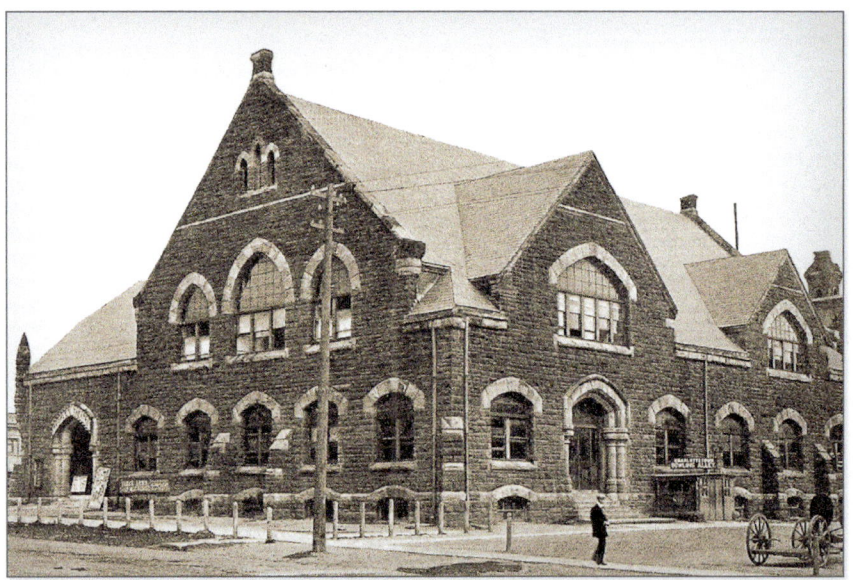

This picture c.1909, shows the new Market Building that was built in 1904. It was a brick and block structure, designed by William Critchlow Harris, a prominent Charlottetown architect. Note the sign above the door leading to the basement which reads: "Charlottetown Bowling Alley." The door at the far left with the curved arch reads: "Peoples Theatre." It was in operation upstairs from 1908 to 1920 and also known as the New Wonderland. Later it was the Empire Theatre as well being used by Little Theater Groups.

On the left in the background, is the new Bank of Montreal which opened for business in 1909. ◼

Unfortunately, this market building burned with a total loss on April 29, 1958. The Prince Edward Island Travel Bureau was located here, as well as the Island Motor Transport Terminal (the bus). In the east end of the building were Roop's Meat Market, the public market stalls, the city fish market and an egg candling station (candling - checking for development of the embryo inside the egg, so called because they originally used candle light) Cr: the *Guardian* April 30, 1958

On the right is the Cabot Building. ▪

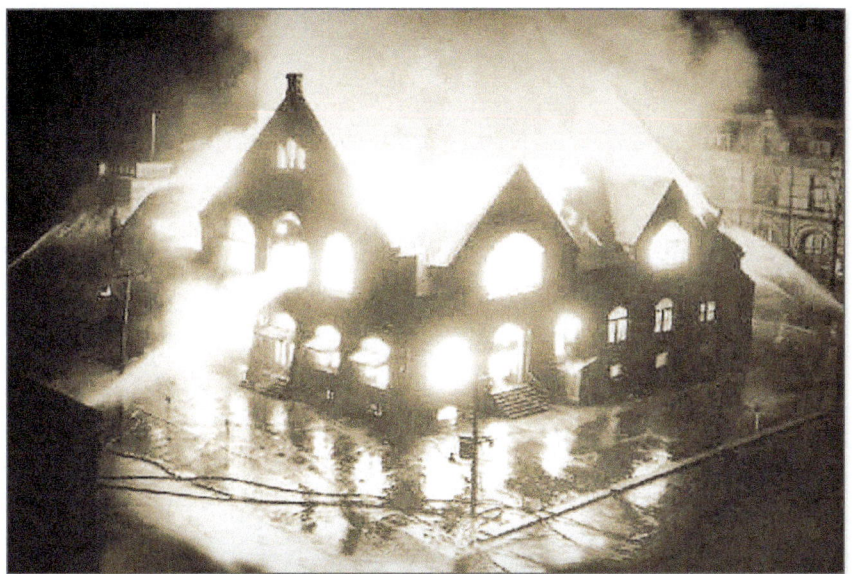

The Cabot Building: The fire that took out most of the buildings on Richmond Street from Queen to Great George on February 20, 1884 (see Richmond Street below), also destroyed the first brick and stone post office on Queen Square, built in 1871 at a cost of $15,000.

The new Post Office, the Cabot Building, starting on May 1, 1885, was completed in 1887 as the Charlottetown Post Office at a cost of $57,397. The edge of Province House is seen on the far right of this picture.

The Cabot Building was named after John Cabot who is credited with discovering the Island in 1497. ▪

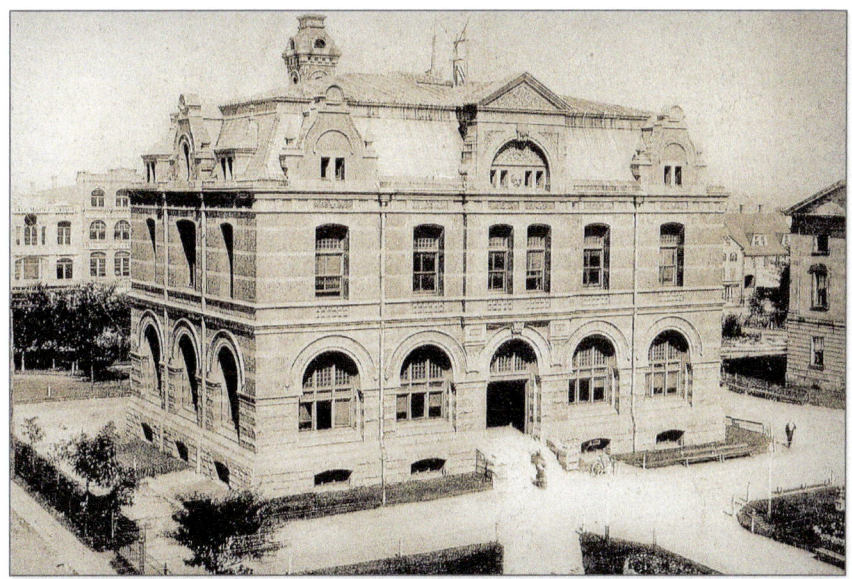

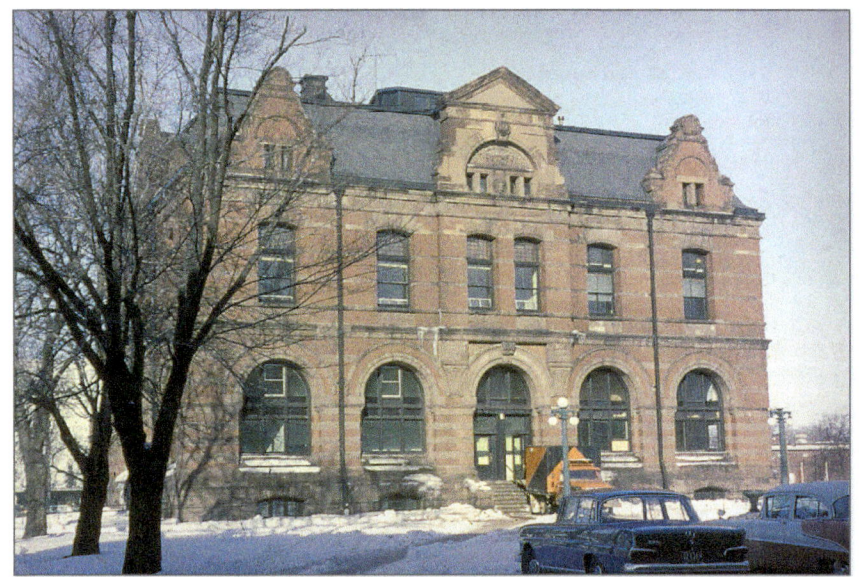

With the pending construction of the Confederation Center of the Arts, the Cabot Building was vacated by January 1, 1963 and demolished. Some Provincial Government offices were located here, including: the Education and Highways were moved to the Old West Kent School on Kent Street; Treasury to New Way Building at the northwest corner of Kent and Great George; Fisheries, Industry and Natural Resources and Motor Vehicle relocated to Queen Square School on the southwest corner of Richmond and Great George.

The Post Office then moved to new premises, in the new Dominion Building on the full block on Queen Street, bounded by: Sydney, Pownal, Richmond and Queen. ▪

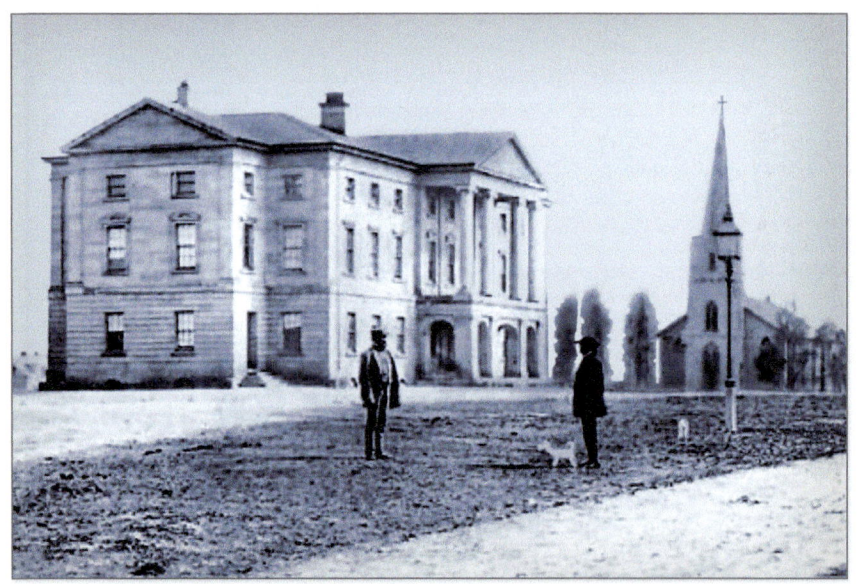

Province House: This picture c.1861 (PARO). This was the site, on September 1-7, 1864, of the Charlottetown Conference where the Fathers of Confederation sat down to start what was to be the Dominion of Canada. The building was designed by Isaac Smith, for which he was paid 20 pounds. The corner stone was laid in May 1843 and Isaac Smith was engaged as the supervisor. The cost at the time was 10,000 pounds, Isaac asked for 500 pounds for overruns but this was declined. The Legislative Assembly first met here in 1847. ▪

Province House was designated a nation historic site in 1973. The building was closed to the public in 2015 and extensive renovations were carried out to the tune of almost $100 million. While under renovation, the provincial assembly was relocated to the Coles building next door. ▪

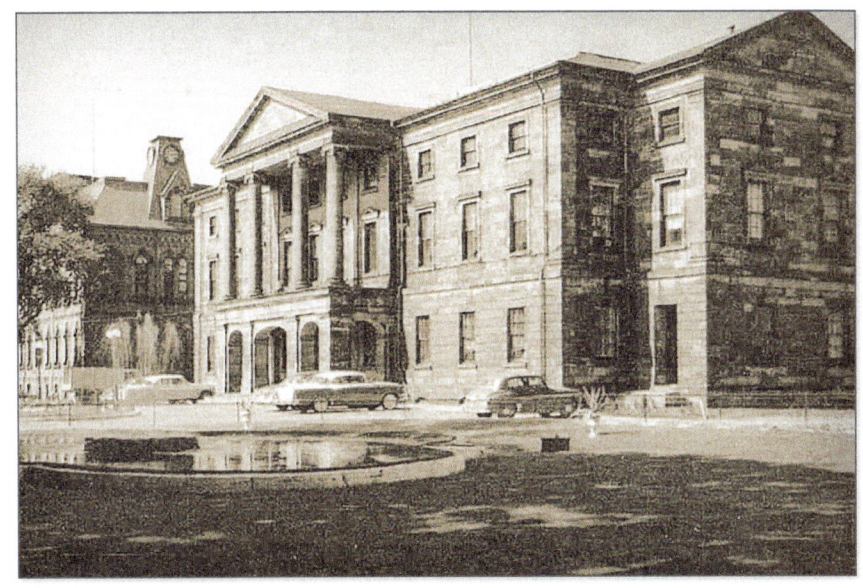

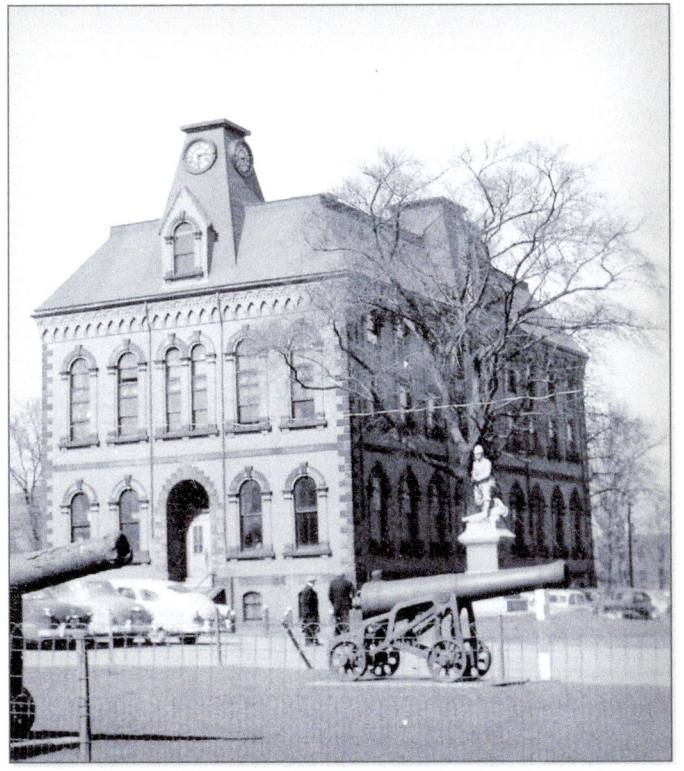

The Coles Building: The building constructed as the Law Courts Building, was built 1874-76. It was used as the Supreme Court.

The clock in the tower was lighted by gas in the overnight hours.

Following a fire in 1976 it was named after The Honourable George Coles (Sept 20, 1810- Aug 21, 1875). He was Premier of Prince Edward Island, serving three different terms (1851 - 1854, 1855 - 1859, & 1867 - 1869) as well as a father of Confederation. ▪

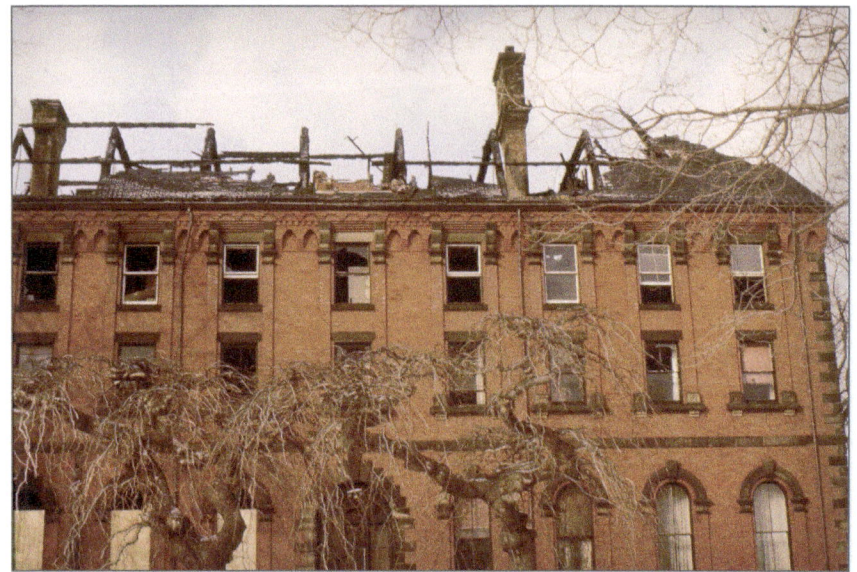

Unfortunately, in 1976, 100 years after it was completed, this building was destroyed by fire. The court was then moved to the new Sir Louis Henry Davies Law Courts Building on Water Street at Pownal. The Coles Building was restored and later used as offices with the Public Archives on the top floor. With Province House recently undergoing renovations, the House of Assembly was moved to the George Coles Building and the Public Archives moved to the Atlantic Technology Center on Great George Street at Fitzroy. This picture from the Frank M. Stewart Collection (PARO). ■

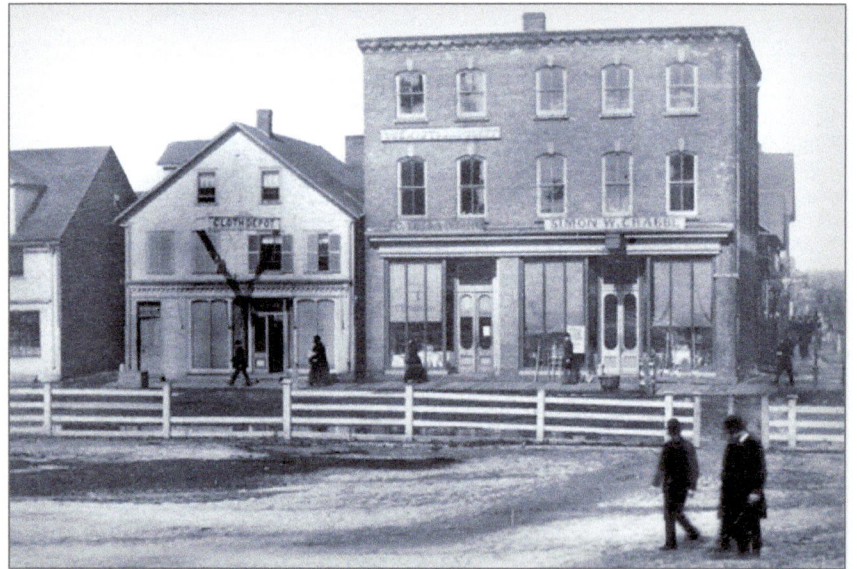

Crabbe Hardware, on the northwest corner of Grafton and Great George, was the only brick building on the Grafton Street block from Queen to Great George. Later Mark Wright removed the building on the left and built a brick building on site. PARO acc2301/247 ■

In 1896, the northwest corner of Grafton and Great George had Crabbe Hardware on the corner, with Mark Wright to the west. The building far left, was the future site of Holmans and later, the Holman Grand Hotel. The building on the Great George Street corner was later the Bank of Nova Scotia in 1921.

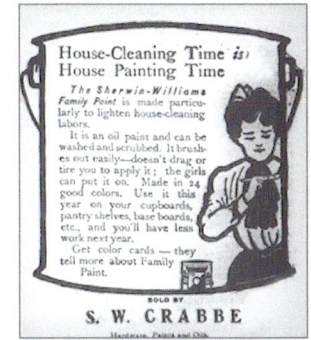

The building behind, upper left, with the mansard roof and the white sign is the W. E. Dawson hardware store on the northwest corner of Kent and Great George. Credit PARO Acc2702/s23/20

The ad from the *Guardian*, May 17, 1911, says in part the paint goes on so easily "the girls" can put it on. Women did not apply paint 100 years ago. ◼

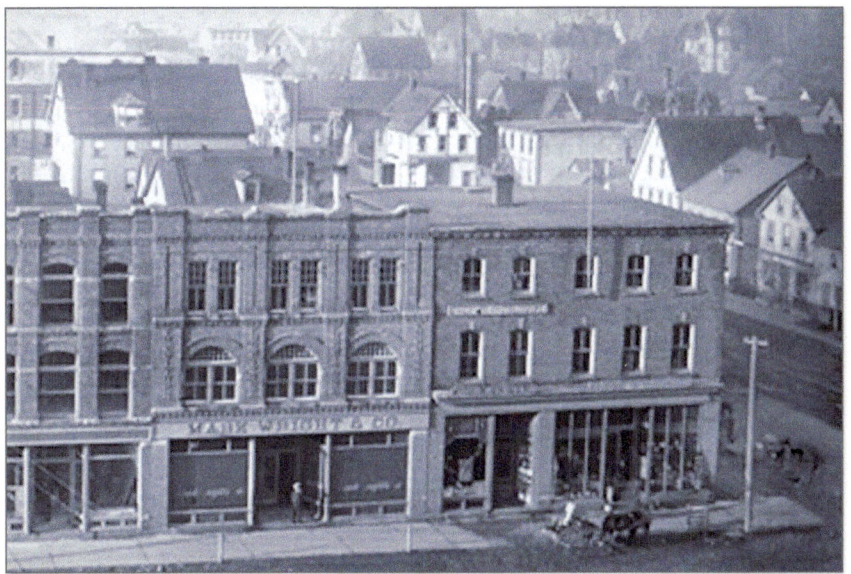

Looking west, c.1903 (PARO), from the corner of Great George we see: Crabbe Hardware, Mark Wright Furniture maker, up to the corner of Hughes Drug Store and beyond. Hughes Drug Store is the three-story block and brick building, after the row of wooden buildings. The next building, three story flat roof with the pole above it is McKay Ready Made Clothing on the northwest corner of Queen and Grafton. (see details under Queen Street section) Going left, the tall building with the pole is the Masonic Temple. ◼

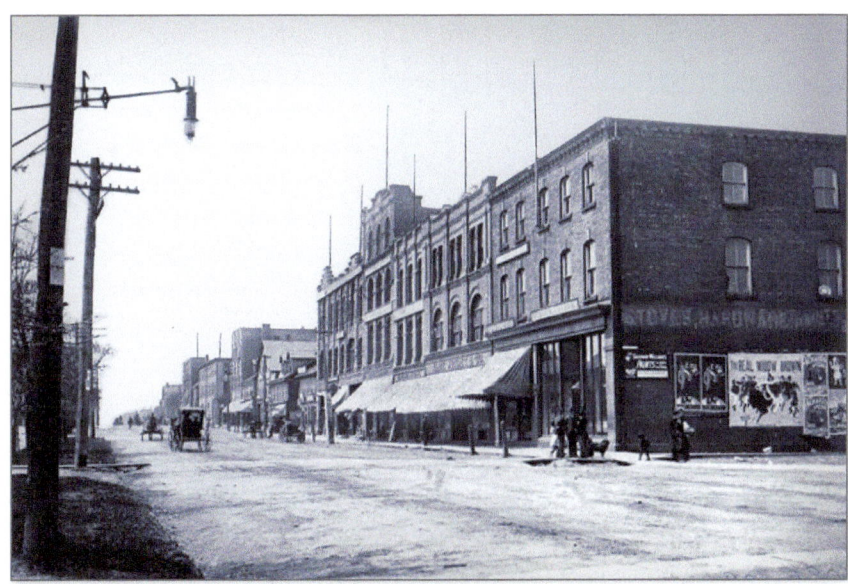

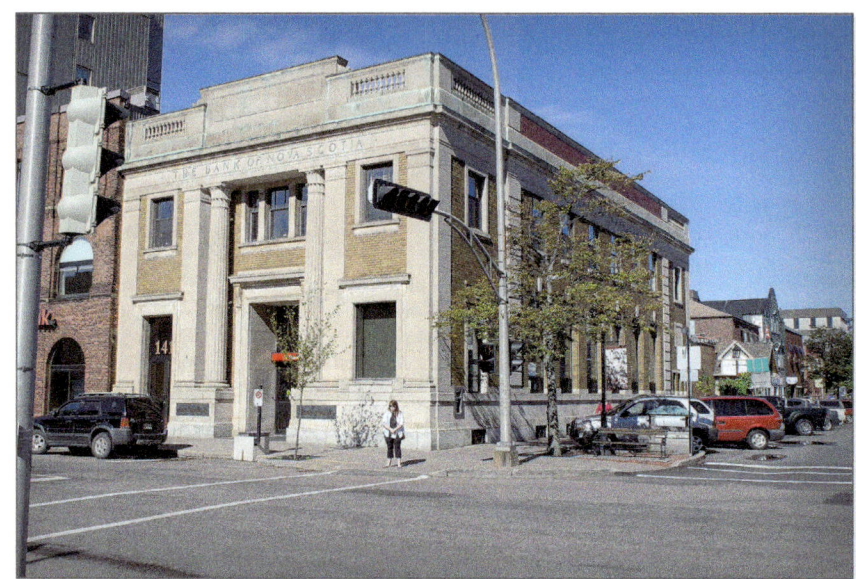

The Crabbe Hardware building was removed for the new Bank of Nova Scotia at 143 Grafton Street, opened in 1921.

High on the Grafton Street face of the Bank reads: "ANNO DOMINI MCMXXI"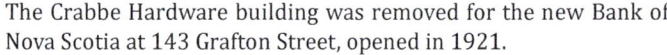

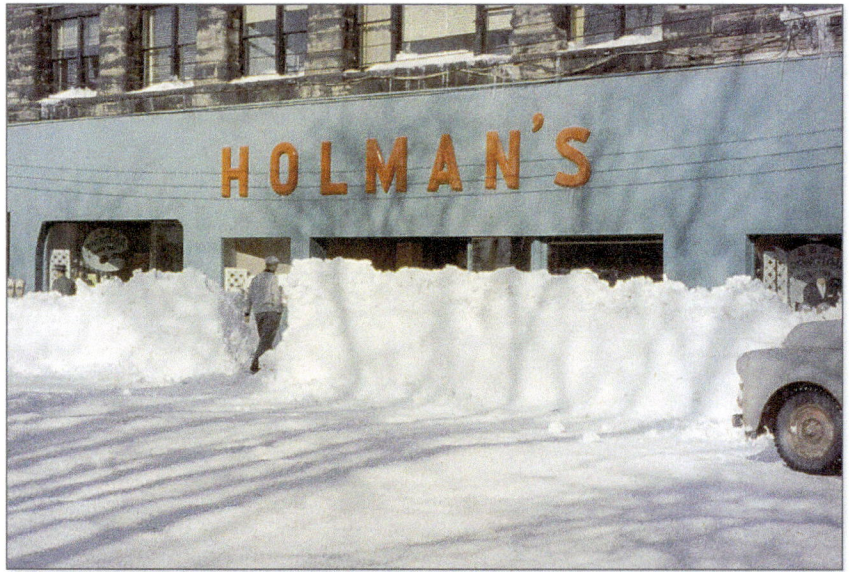

This photo from March 10, 1960 shows R. T. Holman Limited (Robert Tinson Holman). The ads in the windows are for "Springtime."

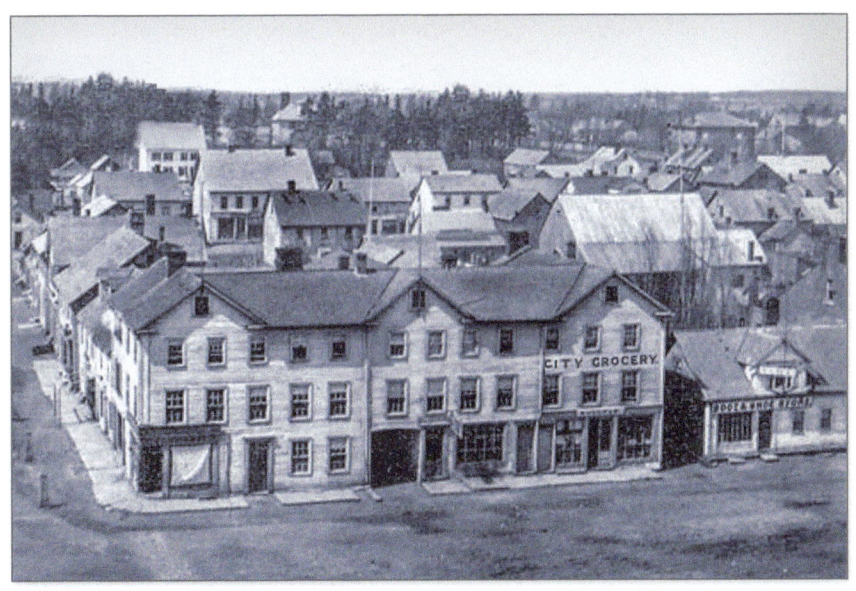

In 2011 the Holman Grand Hotel with Redwater Rustic Grill opened on this site at 123 Grafton Street. Incorporated in this construction was a facsimile facade of the first three floors of the original building on this site. ▪

Moving east to the next block, between Great George and Prince, we see, c.1860 (PARO), the corner building far left where the MacKenzie Theatre (The Mac) now stands. This corner used to be the Capitol Theatre, showing movies.

The heavy stand of trees, back center is the present-day location of First Baptist Church on the northwest corner of Prince and Fitzroy. ▪

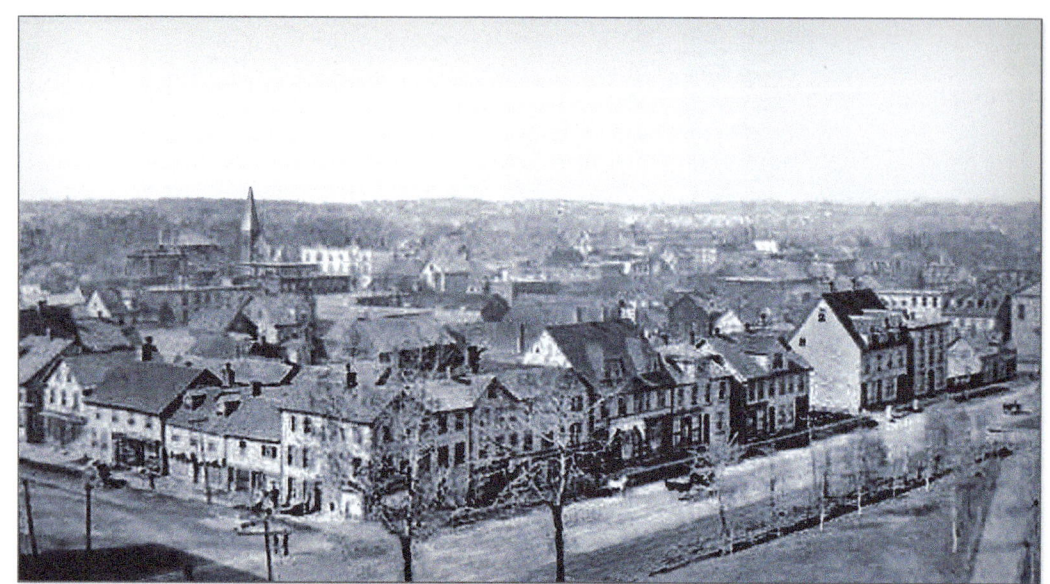

c.1895 (PARO), taken from the top of the Cabot Building (old Post Office), showing the full block of Grafton Street from Great George to Prince. The building at the far right is the Athenaeum (see write up under Prince Street below). The small building to the left of this, and across Prince Street, was removed in 1911 for the construction of Zion Presbyterian Church. The tower to the left at the back is the old First Baptist Church on the southeast corner of Prince and Fitzroy Streets. It was opened for worship on January 11, 1891. ■

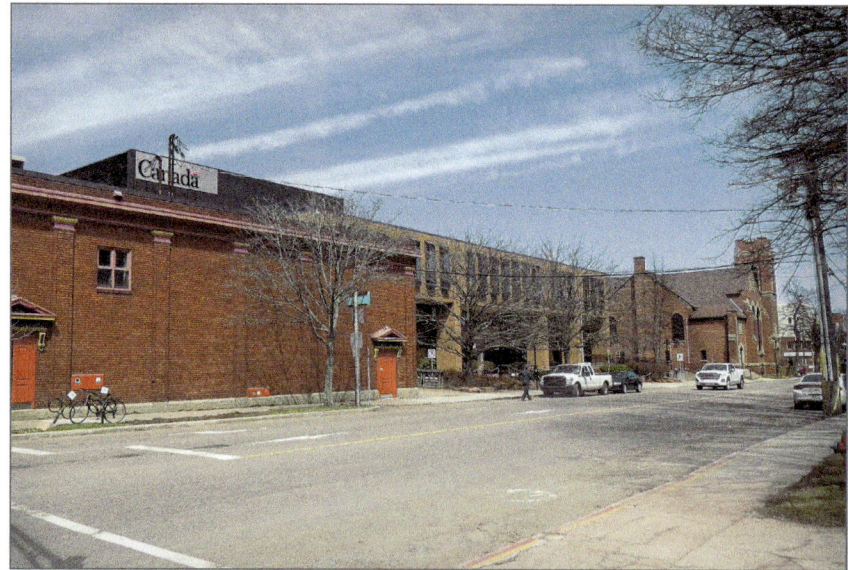

Present day picture shows the MacKenzie Theatre, Veteran Affairs Building and Zion Church ■

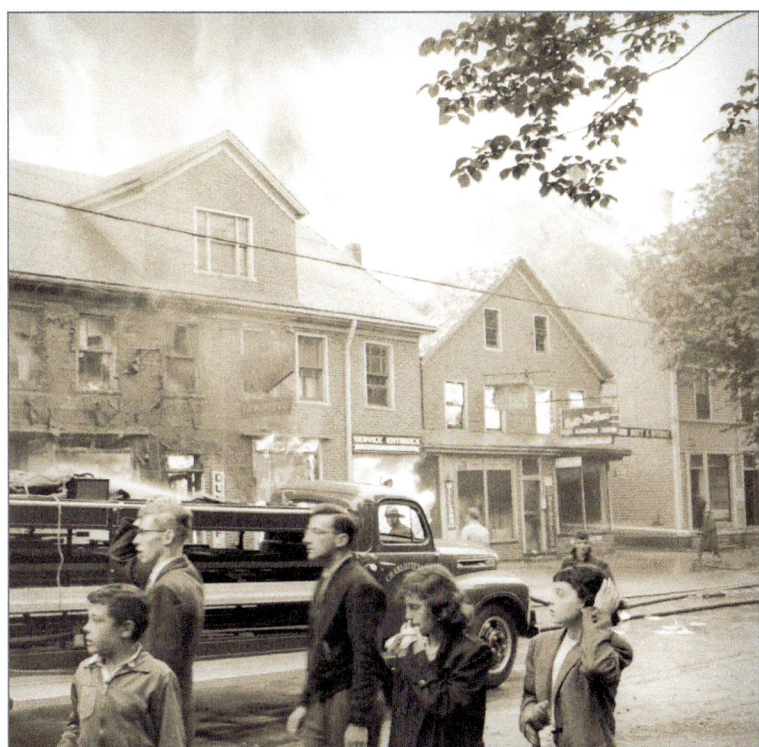

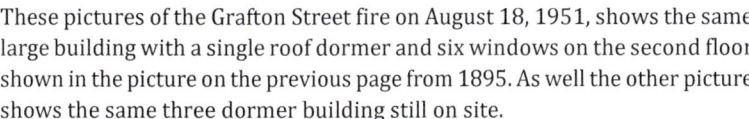

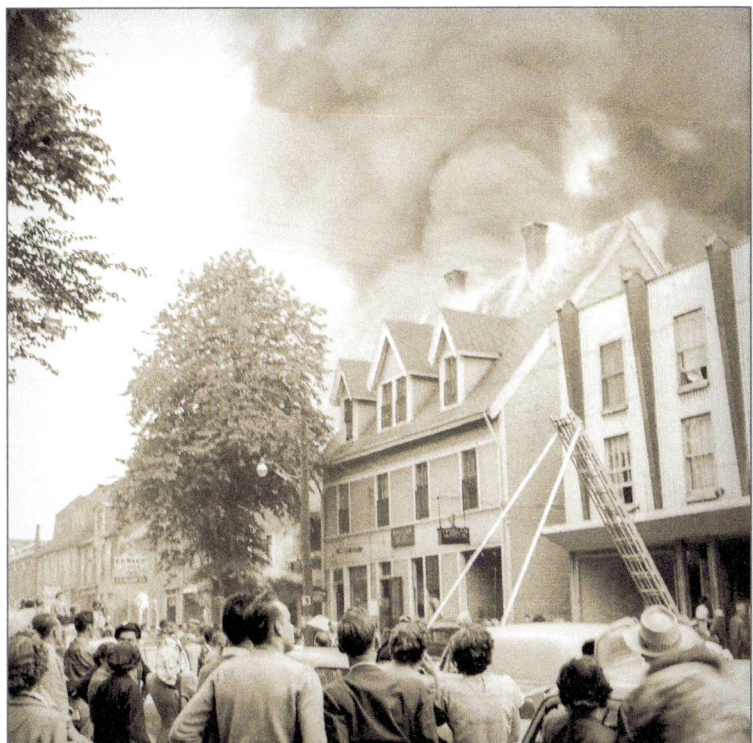

These pictures of the Grafton Street fire on August 18, 1951, shows the same large building with a single roof dormer and six windows on the second floor shown in the picture on the previous page from 1895. As well the other picture shows the same three dormer building still on site.

The pictures show F. R. McLaine's Dunlap sign. F. R. (Rankin) McLaine Plymouth Chrysler dealership at 169 Grafton Street as well as Batt & MacRae at 171 Grafton Street were a total loss in the fire. George Batt & Elmer MacRae (Elmer was Mayor of Charlottetown from 1972 - 1975) left Palmer Electric to start their own automotive electrical parts and service business. Following the fire they moved to 91 Euston on the northeast corner of Upper Queen (Present day DALMAC/ former Kwik Kopy). F. R. McLaine moved to the northwest corner of University and Belvedere following the fire (present day Petro-Canada Service Station). The fire took out all buildings on Grafton except both corners, the center of the block, as well as Horne Motors on Kent Street.

These pictures were taken by Vic Runtz, editorial cartoonist for the Guardian 1948 - 1958. ■

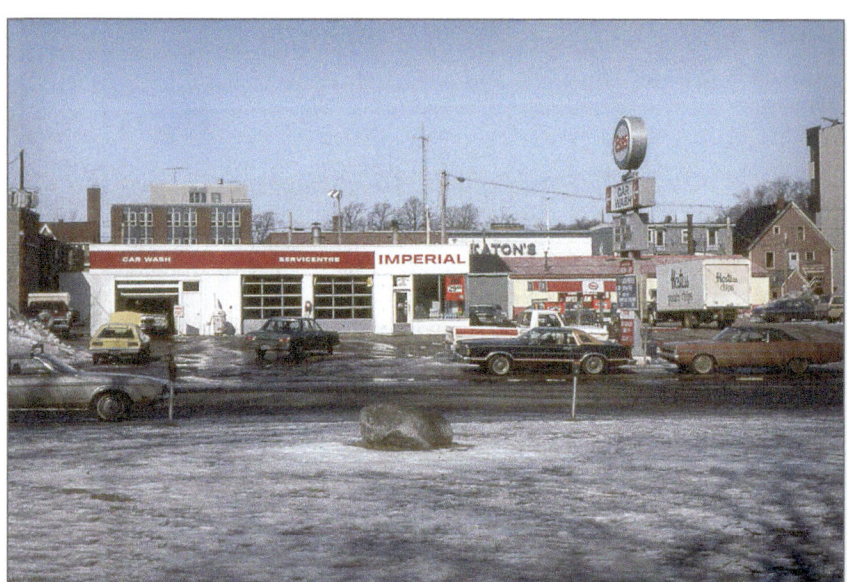

◄ 163 Grafton Street: Following the fire, David A. Mosher operated an Esso Service Station & Carwash, from this picture of March 1979. Earlier in 1958, the station was run by Edgar Hayes

Note through the block, Eaton's on Kent Street, that location now being a parkade. ▪

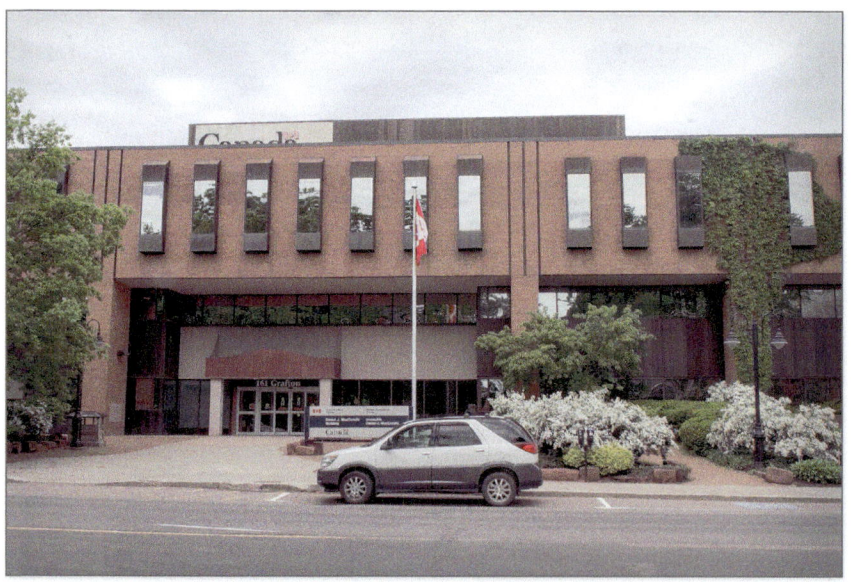

◄ ▲ The Service Station was removed in 1983 for the construction of the Daniel J. MacDonald Building, Veterans Affairs Canada at 161 Grafton Street. The corner stone was laid on June 15, 1983 by Prime Minister Pierre Elliott Trudeau. ▪

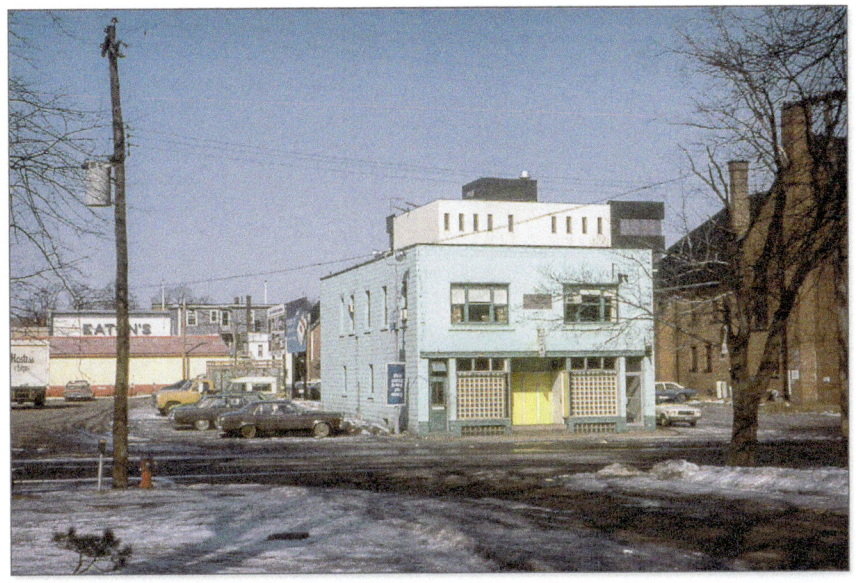

175 Grafton Street: The new Whelan Memorial Building containing the Benevolent Irish Society (BIS) Hall. Constructed after the fire in 1951, it was removed for construction of the new DVA Building.

The building was named in honor of Hon. Edward Whelan, one of the Fathers of Confederation, and former president of the BIS.

This site in 1899 was the Empire Hotel and then Strathcona Hotel from 1914 to 1937.

The second picture shows the east section of the DVA building with the entrance to the underground parking garage.

The building on the right in both pictures is Zion Presbyterian Church. ■

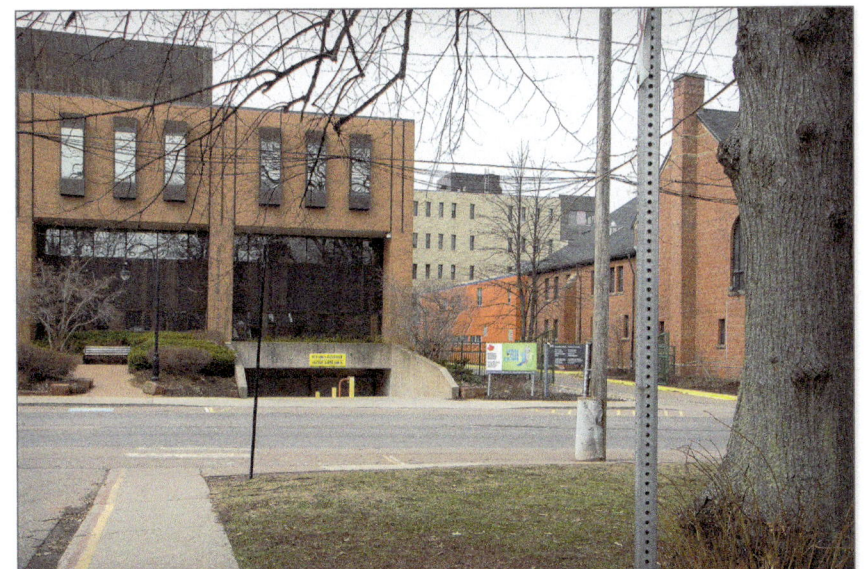

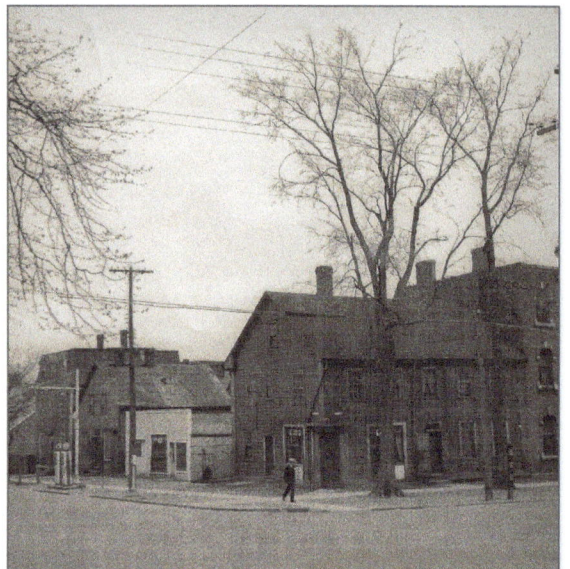

The next four pictures show the transformation on the southeast corner of Prince and Grafton. The first picture shows an original service station at this corner c.1920. Note the gas pumps between the sidewalk and the street.

This corner was listed as: 1900 as John McIntyre, shoemaker; 1914 as Philip Curley's Meat Shop; 1924 as McLaine Service Station; 1937 as Beer's Service Station; 1950 as Pete's service Station, then Blairs Irving and then in 1979 as Robertson's Irving Service Station. The site was cleared to make way for a new condominium started in September 2010. The building to the right at 120-124 Prince Street was built in 1872 by John Quirk, a baker. It is still there today. ■

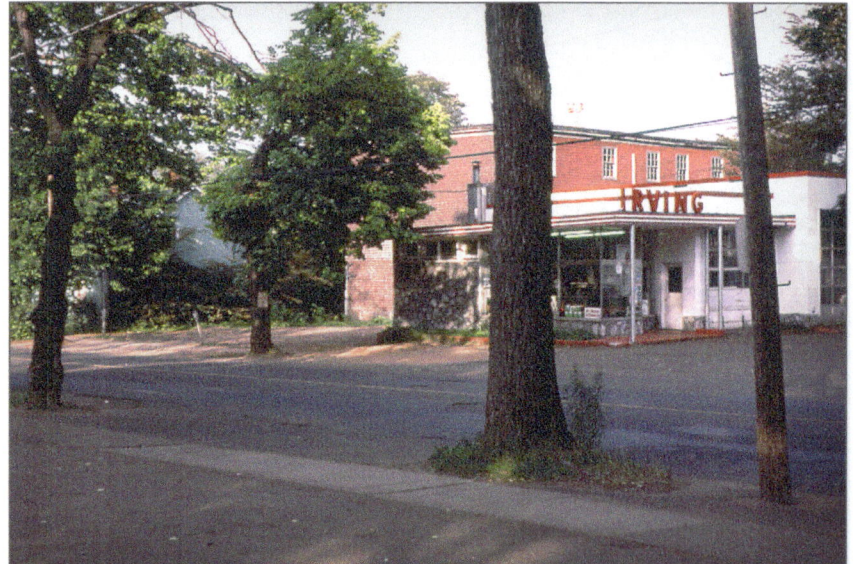

From 1979, showing the service station at 130 Prince Street.

The red three-story building behind the service station was Hickey Nicholson Tobacco Co. Ltd listed at 119 Prince Street. Hickey Nicholson was founded in 1860 and operated under that name since 1882. They were originally located on Lower Queen Street. ■

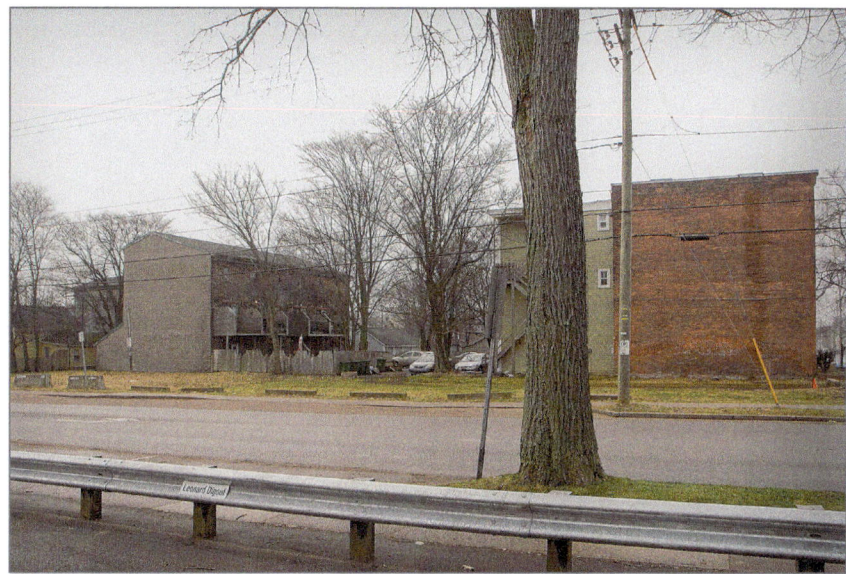

This corner was since a vacant lot on the southeast corner of Grafton and Prince Streets in 2010. ▪

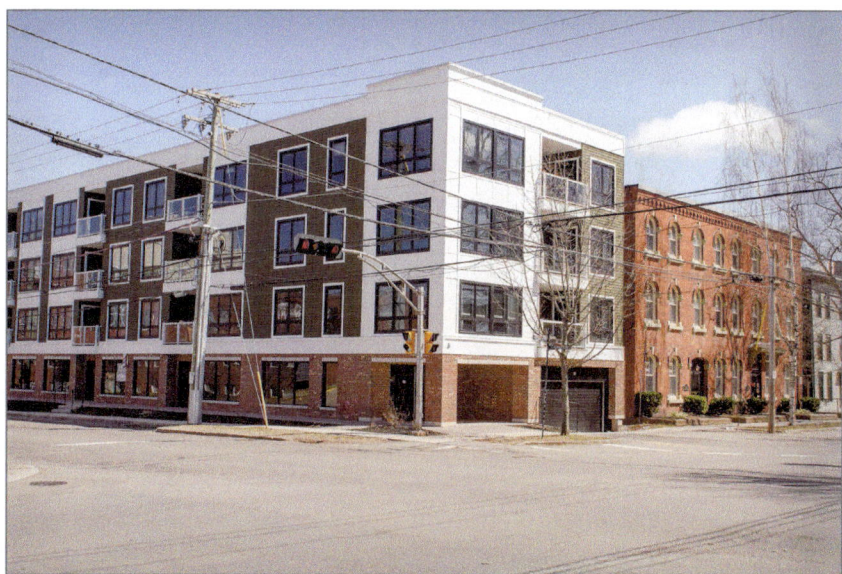

The construction started on the condominium in 2014 and finished some 3 years later. It contains the first floor as commercial, with three upper floors of condominiums with underground parking. ▪

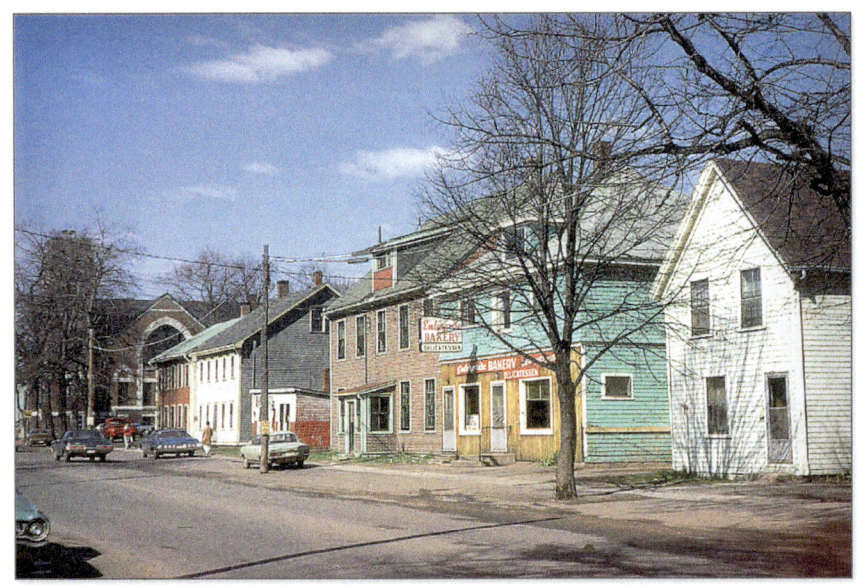

Looking west on the north side of Grafton Street toward Zion Presbyterian Church on Prince Street, this first picture was taken in April 1974. 203 Grafton, the green building, was the Enterprise Bakery & Delicatessen (in 1937 it was Hynes Bakery). ▪

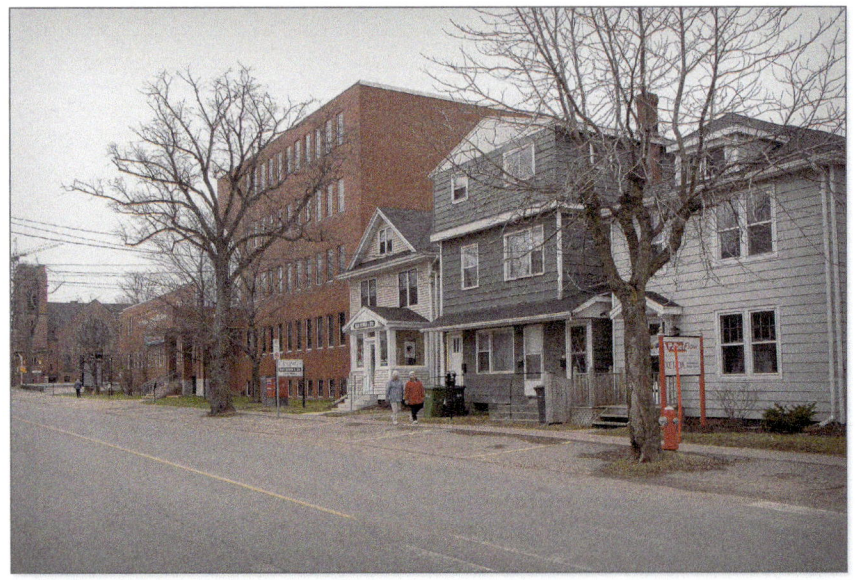

The same shot from 2013 shows the Polyclinic, which opened July 1, 1986. The Polyclinic was originally at 186 Prince Street, having opened there in 1925. In 1946 they moved to 170 Fitzroy Street, on the south side between Prince and Hillsborough Streets. That building was since renovated and is still there today. ▪

Remember when Milton's Old Spain was a great meeting place

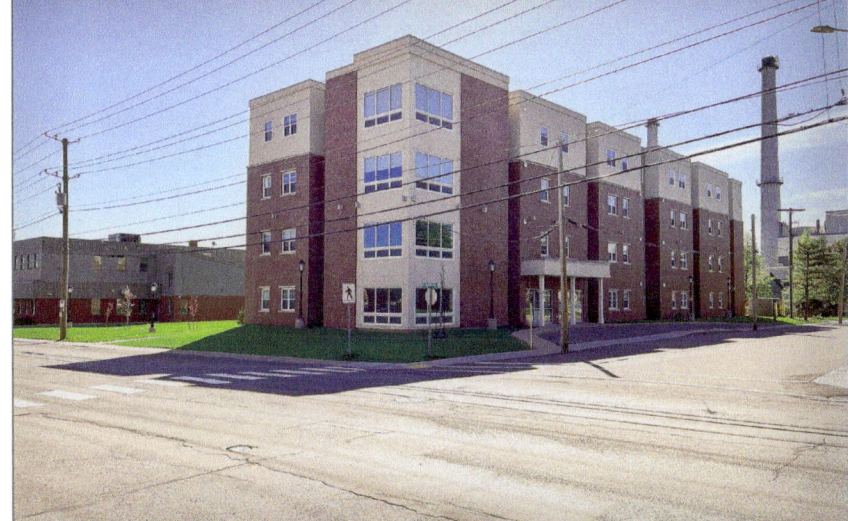

On the southeast corner of Grafton and Cumberland, George Bassett operated a store until 2016. George bought this building in 1961. The previous store keeper was Victor McKarris who was renting the premises. In 1959 this was listed as: 302 Grafton Street, Victor Mc-Karris, Grocer. ■

This corner and houses on both sides on Grafton and Cumberland streets were removed in 2017 to make way for a new residence for Holland College.

The building at the far left in both photos is the Summit Centre - Maxillofacial Surgery of Dr. Gregory A. Mitton. On the right are the stacks at Maritime Electric. ■

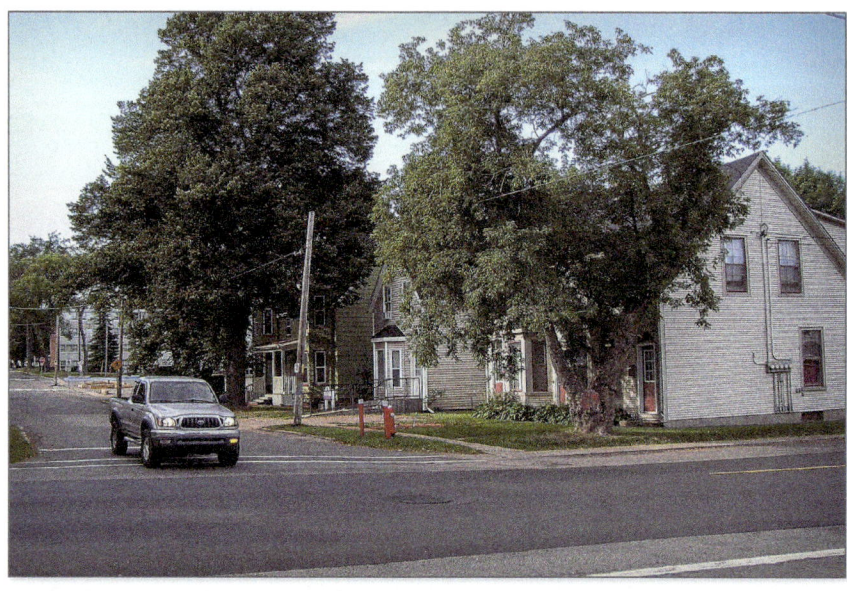

The buildings on the block bounded by Kent, Edward, Grafton and Cumberland were removed in 2013 to make way for the new CAST building (Center of Applied Science and Technology) and CCE building (Center for Community Engagement) leaving only the existing residence, Glendenning Hall in place at Edward and Grafton. (CCE was subsequently renamed MacMillan Center for Community Engagement). The first picture is looking north up Cumberland from Grafton Street. The second is looking northeast along Grafton Street from the corner of Cumberland and Grafton. ▪

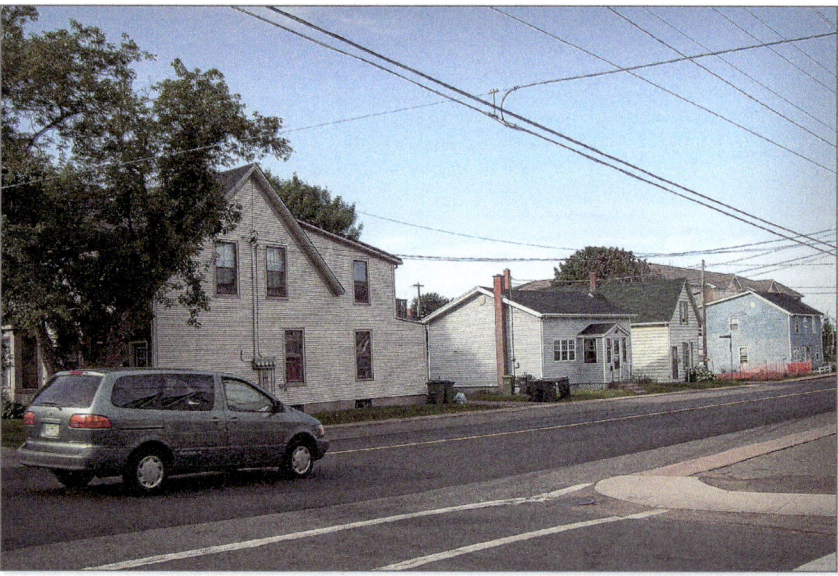

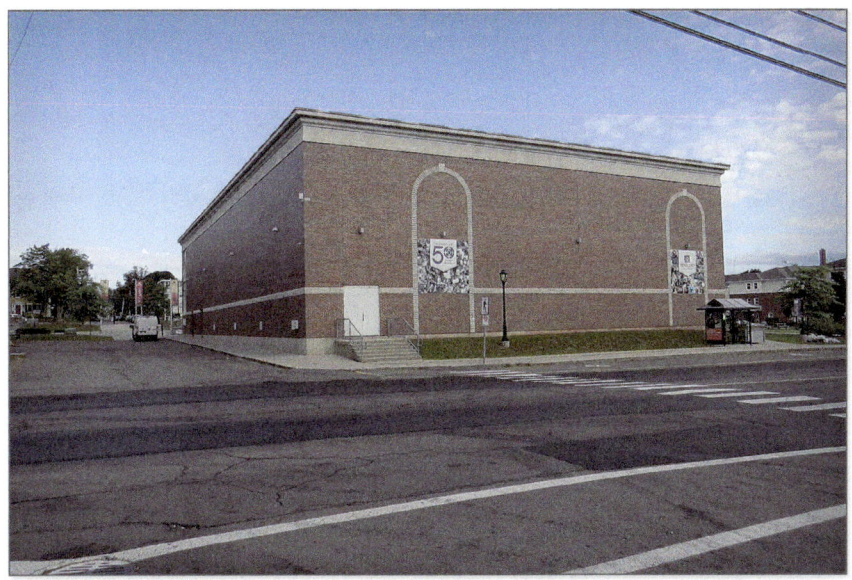

This picture taken in September 2022 shows the same site today with the CCE taking up the site. Cumberland Street no longer runs through to Kent Street, and is now just for local deliveries.

The Holland College residence, Glendenning Hall, is far right at the northwest corner of Grafton and Edward.

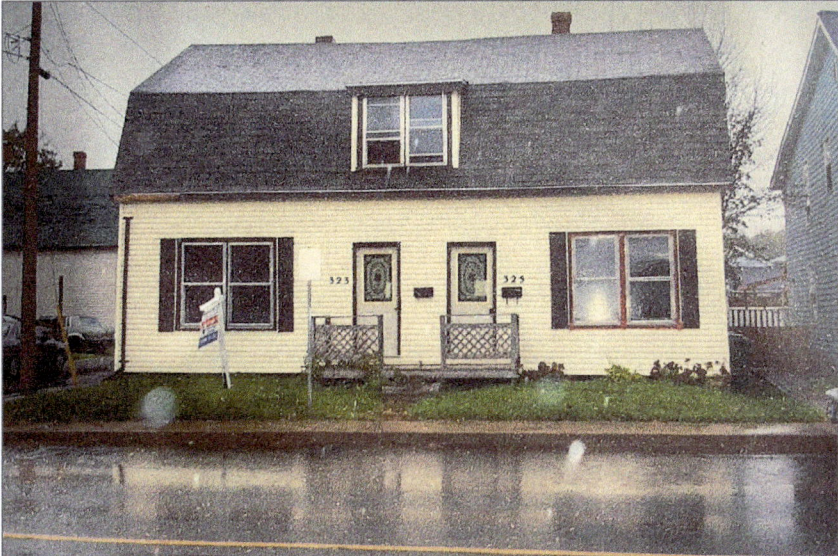

323 - 325 Grafton Street: This duplex was on the northeast corner of Grafton Street Lane. and one of the first to be removed.

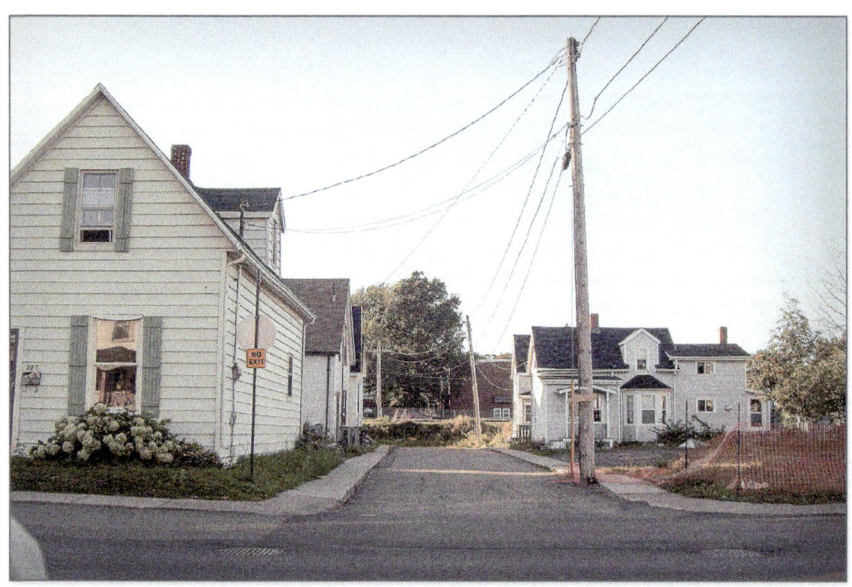

Grafton Street Lane was a 1/2 block long lane that went north into the center of this block from Grafton Street. ▪

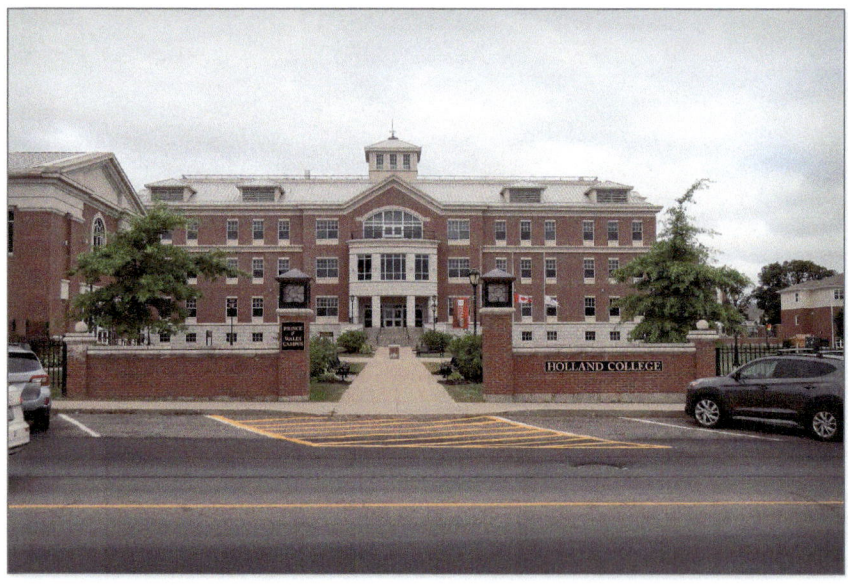

The current picture shows the same location now leading to the CAST building of Holland College, with the CCE on the left, and Glendenning Hall on the right. ▪

Looking east from 1957, on Grafton Street at Edward Street. The train tracks ran on the east side of Canada Packers. Everything in this picture is gone. The tracks, the signal warning (look and listen), the Texaco station, and the petroleum storage tanks. There were three service stations from here to the bridge.

From this point eastward, Grafton Street was traditionally called Grafton Street East, in phone book addresses, advertisements and stationery.

Cr: Frank M. Stewart Collection, City of Charlottetown Archives. ▫

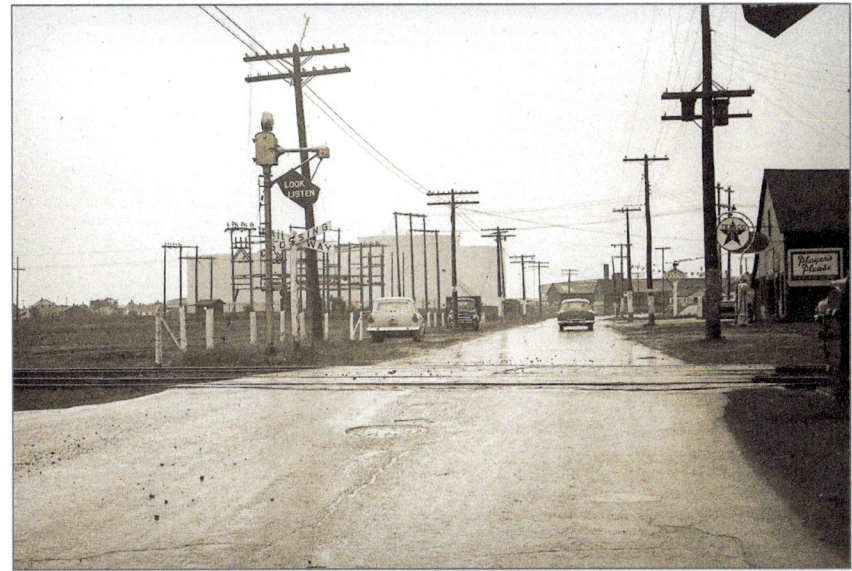

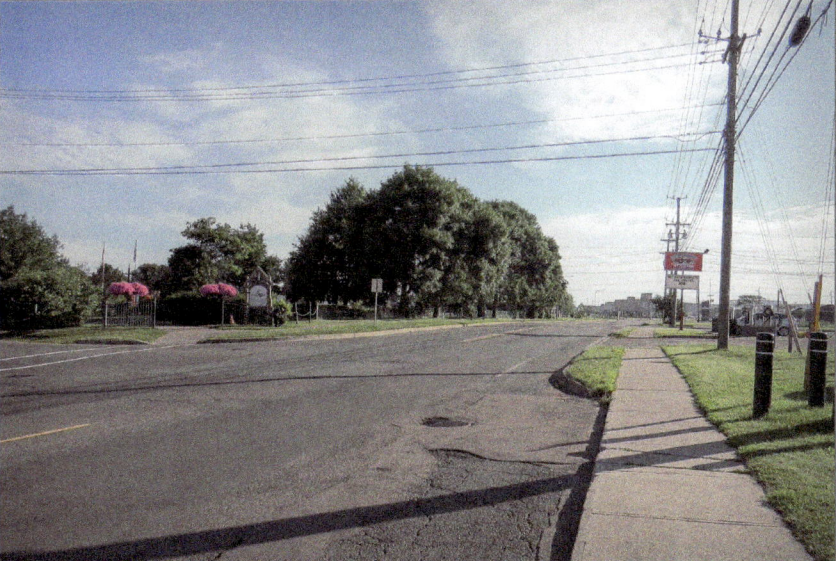

This area now contains the Joseph A. Ghiz park on the left with Holland College parking and Wash World on the right. ▫

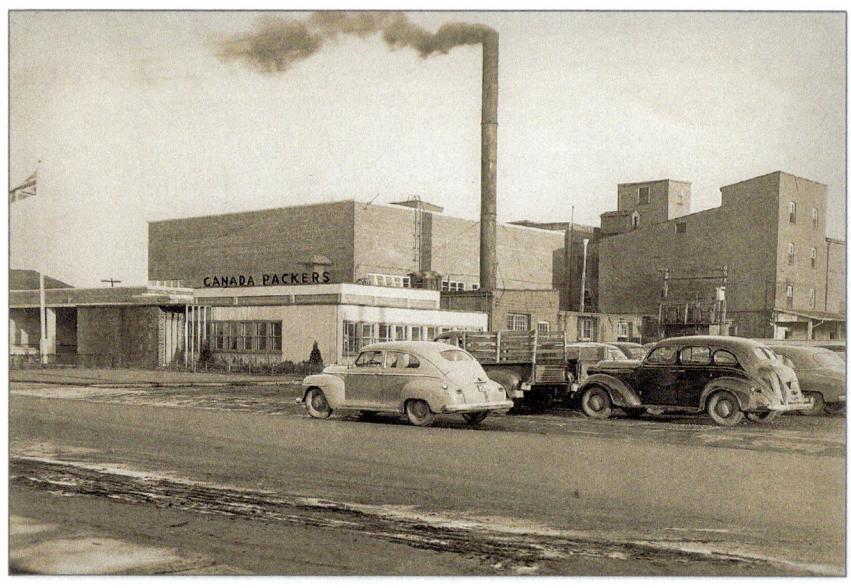

Canada Packers Limited was formed on June 10, 1927 with the merger of Harris Abattoir Co., Gunns Ltd., Canadian Packing Co. and William Davies Company.

On Prince Edward Island, Harris Abattoir Company was listed as early as 1910, with their location at 88 Queen Street. An ad on November 07, 1918 listed a request for "20 more women for plucking chickens."

In March 1903, Davis and Fraser of Halifax created a joint stock company in Charlottetown to enter the abattoir business. Their original location was on Kent Street, moving to Grafton Street East in 1915. This business operated successfully until November 29, 1946 when a fire severely damaged the building, resulting in the death of one worker. Canada Packers purchased the plant in 1947, having originally been at 1 Prince Street, below Water Street. They set about to construct a new modern slaughter house and processing plant.

This site is now the parking lot, south of Grafton Street, for Holland College and the Wash World car wash. ∎

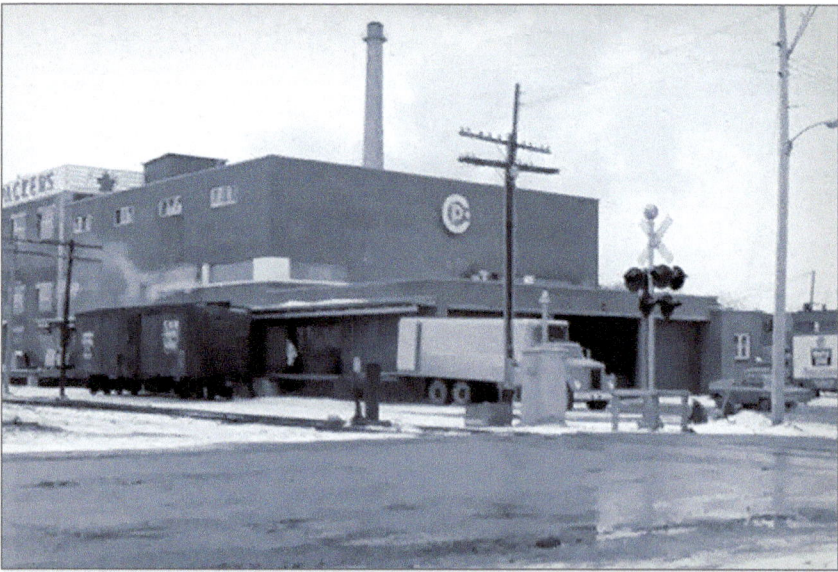

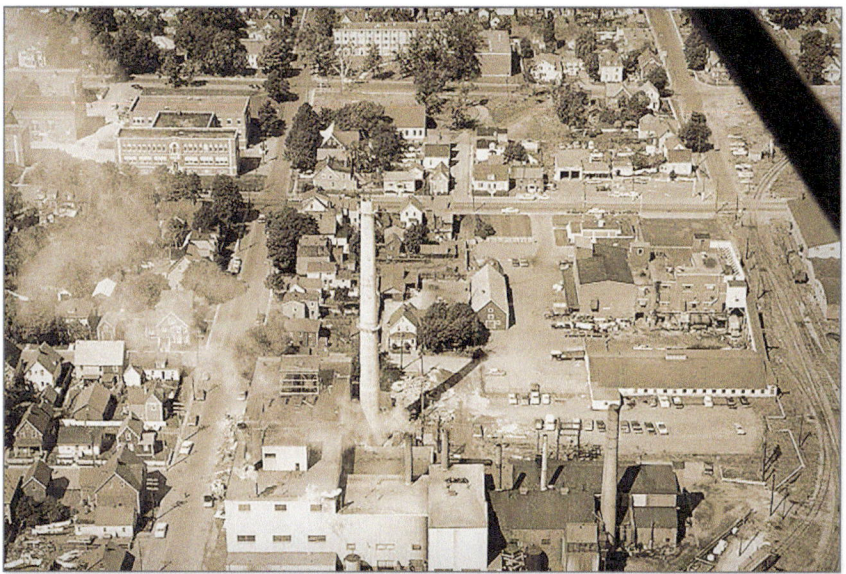

Grafton Street Lane can be seen just to the right of the top of the stack for Maritime Electric. The tracks from lower right up the right side pass Canada Packers on their way through to what is today Joseph A. Ghiz Park. Cumberland Street is a through street by Holland College. The extensive buildings to the right of the track comprise Canada Packers. Just north of that and across Grafton Street is a service station on the corner of Grafton and Edward Street.

Credit: from the Maritime Electric Collection.

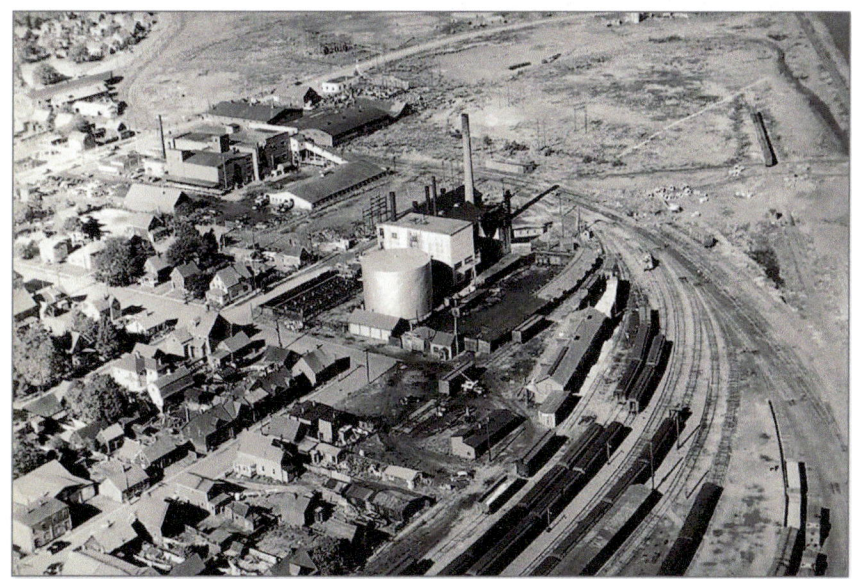

This picture, from 1956, shows the multiple tracks from the train station on Weymouth Street curving to the left behind Maritime Electric and passing by Canada Packers, before becoming a single line through what is today Joseph A., Ghiz Park. It looks like the pads for the Esso storage tank are in place, north on Grafton Street East.

Credit: from the Maritime Electric Collection.

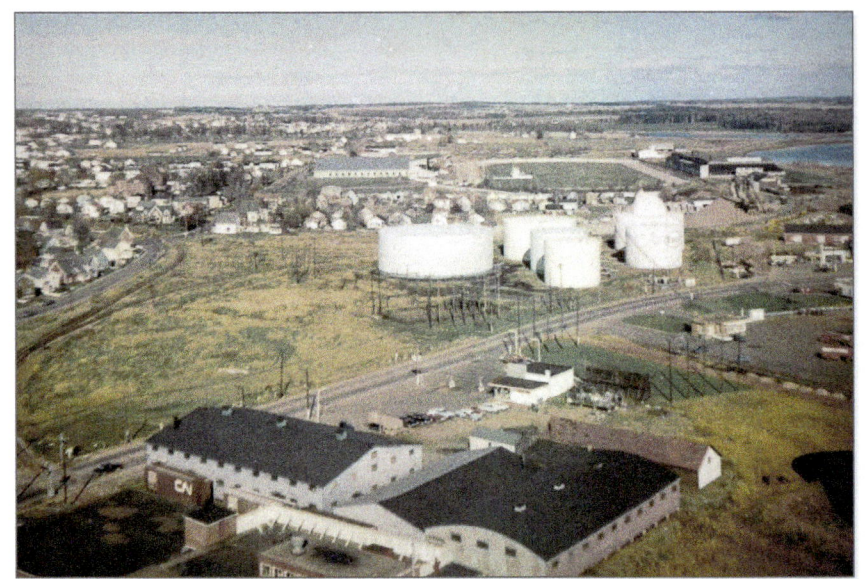

Once you pass the train tracks east of Canada Packers, Grafton Street became Hillsborough Bridge Road as listed in the 1950 Provincial Directory. The large building next to Canada Packers was Carters Storage. Then MacMillan's Service Station. the Canadian Oil Company (later Imperial Oil/Esso), McColl Frontenac Oil Company (bought out by Texaco Canada).

This picture, looking northeast, was taken in 1979 from the top of the 200 foot stack of Maritime Electric by Ralph Stewart. Lower left is Canada Packers, with the Imperial Oil (ESSO) tank prominent in the center of the photo. The green space at the left is the location of current day Joseph A. Ghiz park. Above the tank farm you can see the raceway of the Charlottetown Driving Park and exhibition grounds. Above this and to the right, the green space across the water is Belvedere Golf Course.

Cr: Frank M. Stewart Collection, City of Charlottetown Archives.

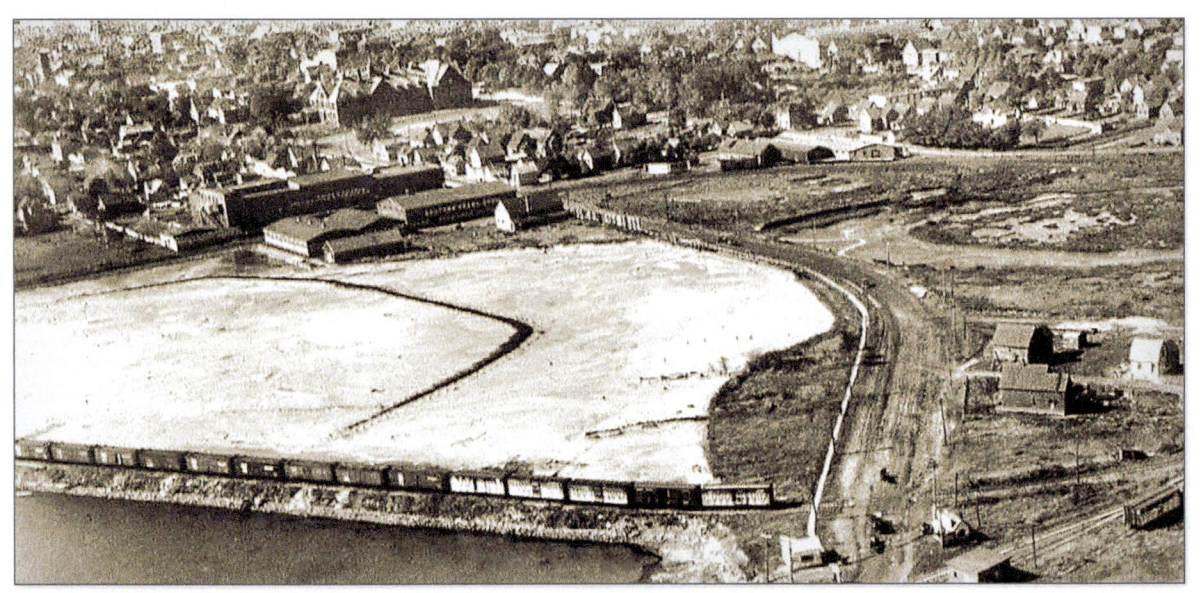

This picture from 1931 has the train on the tracks at the bottom following what is now Water Street to the bridge. The white faced, peaked building top center is the Charlottetown Forum constructed in 1930. The old Prince of Wales College that burned in 1932 is seen in this picture.

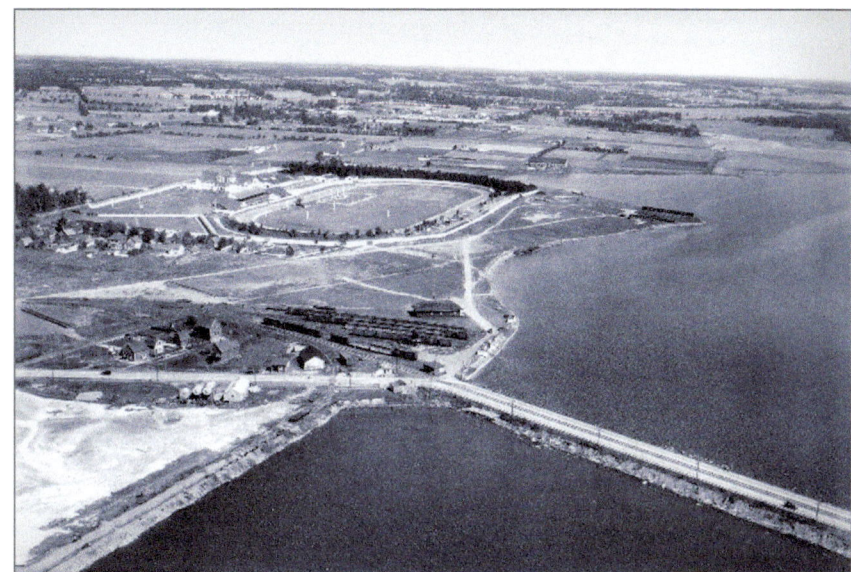

From 1935. Before the fertilizer Plant and Government Garage. This photo shows tracks leading the Hillsborough Bridge. You will note the race track does not have light poles around it, which were not installed until 1947. ▪

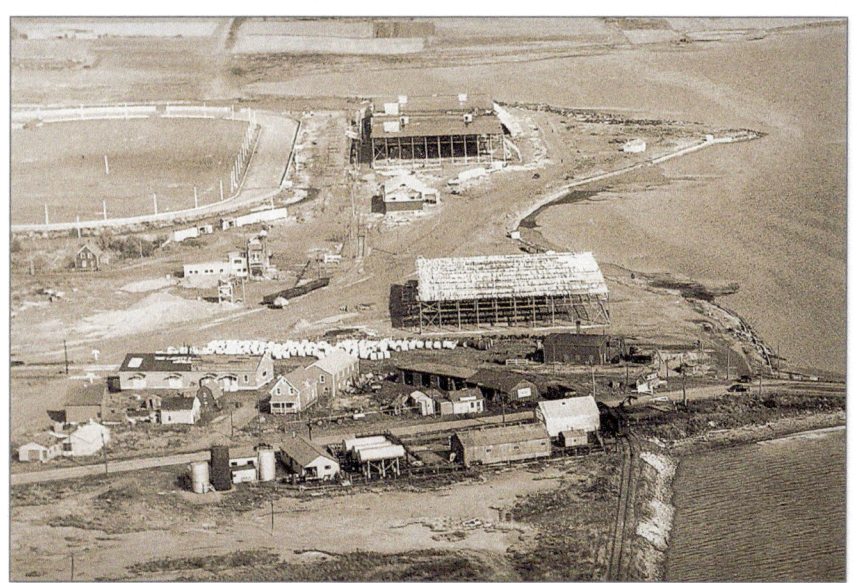

Taken in 1948 showing the Government Garage under construction, with the fertilizer plant above also under construction. The road leading to the right is to the Hillsborough Bridge. Riverside Drive east along the water and Water Street Parkway west into town, both present day starting at the bridge, were non-existent at that time.

The building on the north/ upper side were listed as: East End Wood-workers Company, an unoccupied house and then Weeks Coal Yard with the four large bay doors. Weeks Coal Yard is the present day location of Tim Hortons. ▪

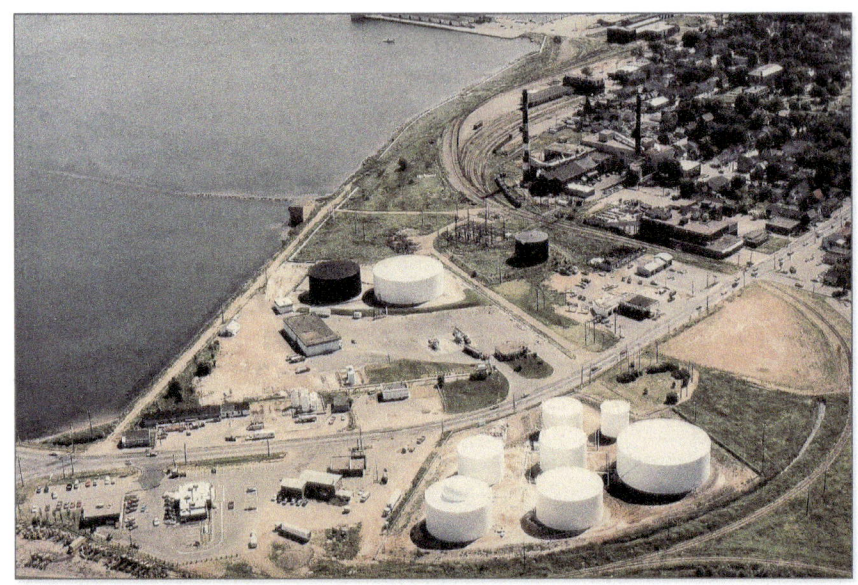

This photo shows the various service stations on Grafton Street East. Tim Hortons was in operation near the end of Grafton Street. They had counter service with no drive thru. Canada Packers, center right, was in operation. The potato shipping wharf top center is there today, but is now a welcome center for cruise ship tourists. ◼

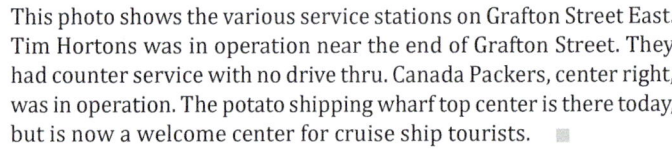

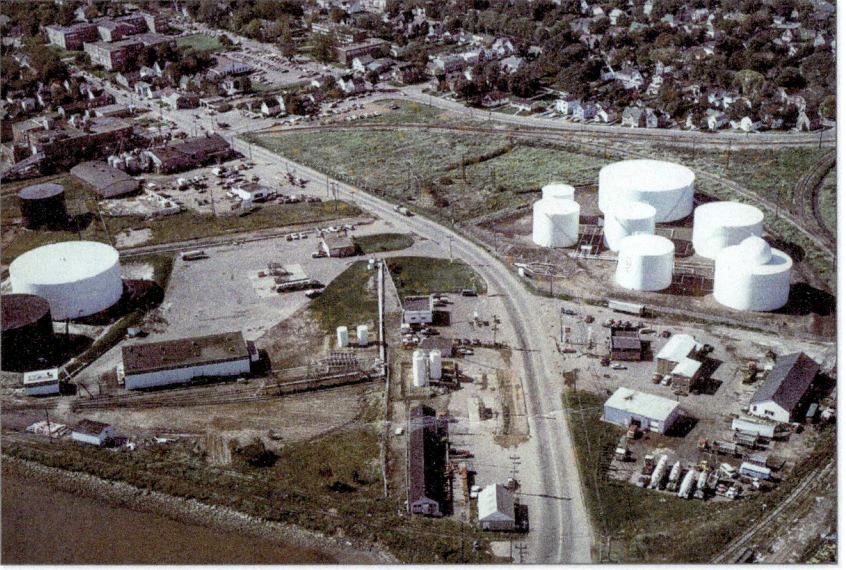

This photo from 1979. Top center in this photo is the old Charlottetown Forum on Fitzroy Street, with the white peaked facade. Below that is Montgomery Hall, of Holland College. The cars in the lot south of the hall is the parking lot for Allison McLeod Ltd., Pontiac, Buick and GMC Truck dealer. The northwest corner of Grafton and Edward had a service Station. Across Edward Street to the right, Joseph A. Ghiz park was a vacant lot.

The train tracks at the bottom right are heading to the Hillsborough Bridge.

This photo highlights the Esso Tank farm which was on both sides of Grafton Street.

Cr: Frank M. Stewart Collection, City of Charlottetown Archives. ◼

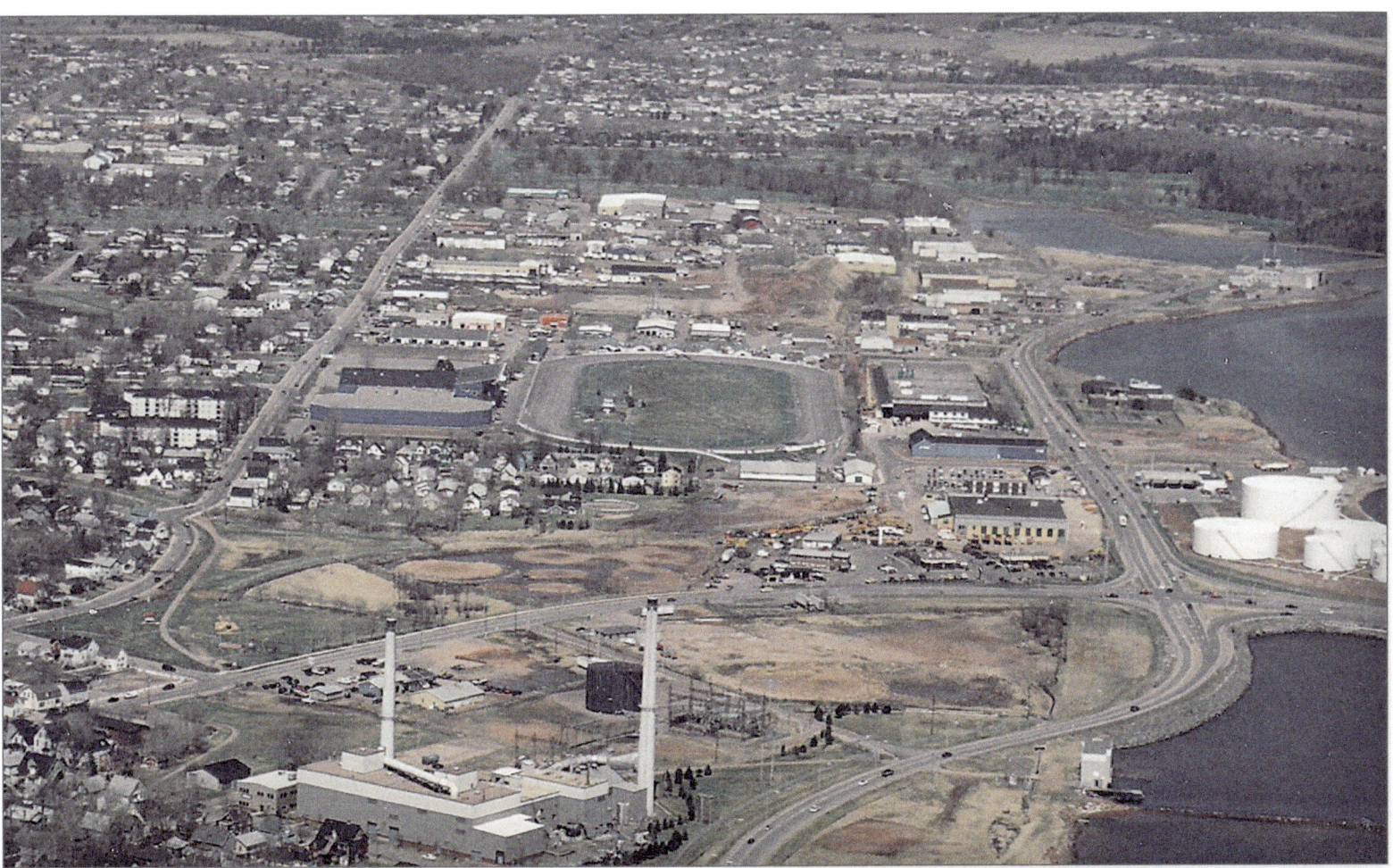

Photo from Creed's Petroleum collection, showing the tank farm completely gone. At the right is the Irving Oil tanks which supply all brands. The Joseph A. Ghiz park is not yet in place as the track base still runs through this area. Water Street Parkway through to the hospital is completed. ■

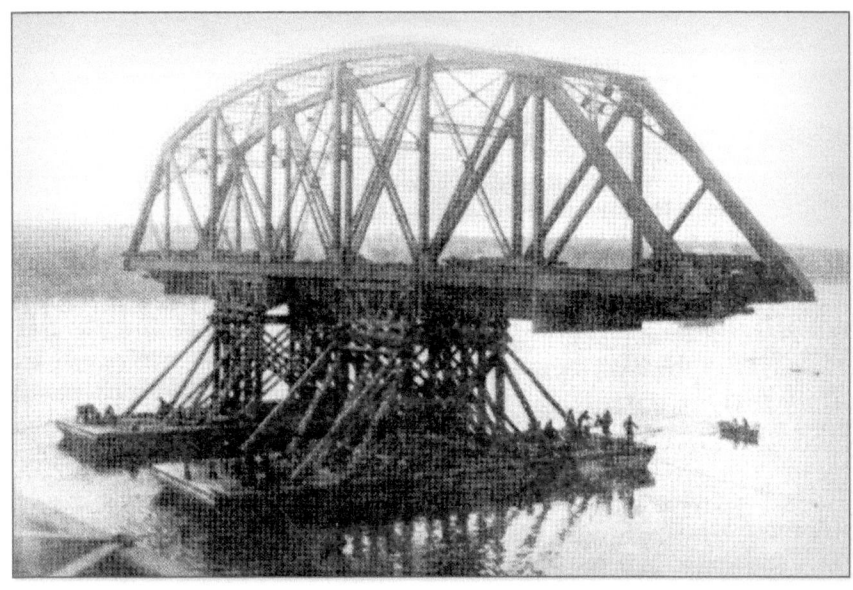

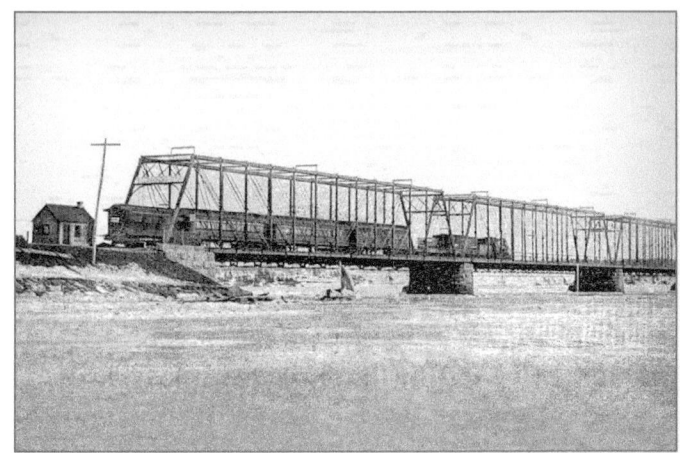

▲ From 1910 showing a train on the bridge travelling south from the Charlottetown side. The building at the entrance to the bridge on the left is the caretakers shack. ▪

◄ As Grafton Street flows naturally to the Hillsborough Bridge, I have added a few pictures of the bridge under construction in 1905. The bridge was talked about as early as 1893 to allow the trains to travel conveniently to Murray Harbour, without having to travel to Mt. Stewart. These pictures show the sections of the bridge being moved into place.

The first unofficial crossing of the bridge was on November 1, 1905 by W. T. Huggan, accountant of the Prince Edward Island Railway. ▪

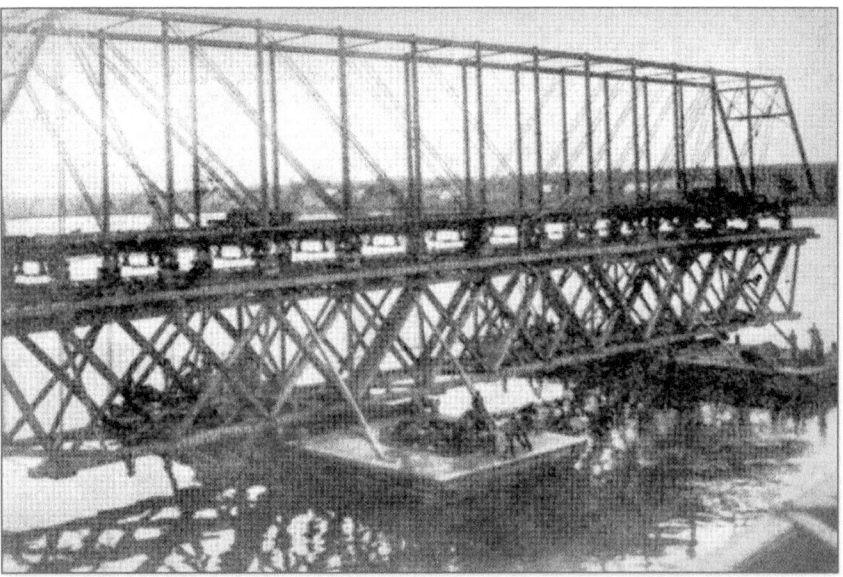

These pictures from May 11, 1959, were taken from Stratford. Note the center span opened to allow boats to travel up the Hillsborough River. This single lane bridge was built in 1905 from iron spans from two bridges in Miramichi, New Brunswick that were built some thirty years prior. Miramichi had just received a new bridge to accommodate the heavier Maritime rail traffic. The bridge owner here and in Miramichi bridges were both owned by the same rail company. This bridge across the Hillsborough River was to accommodate rail traffic for the Murray Harbour branch line. It was later used by automobiles.

By the mid 1950's this bridge could no longer support train traffic, and a new bridge was under construction as shown in these photos. The new bridge opened in 1963 for vehicles only, following improvements to the Trans-Canada Highway system on the Island. This was a two lane bridge and later widened in 1998 to four lanes by the same company (Strait Crossing Joint Venture) that constructed the Confederation Bridge at Borden Carleton to New Brunswick.

In 2021 the province built an active transportation Corridor on the west side of the bridge. This allowed walkers, runners, bikes and strollers to travel across the bridge without interfering with the traffic. ▪

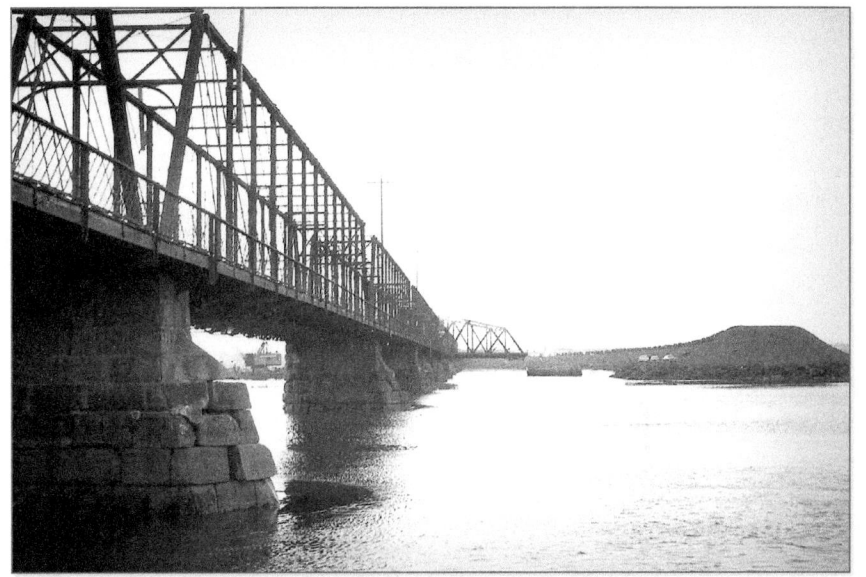

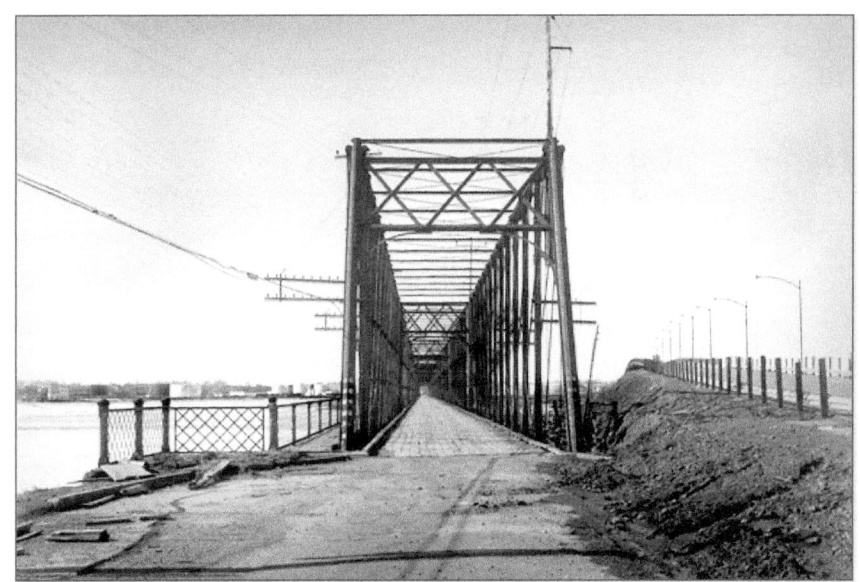

Richmond Street

Richmond Street starts at West Street and extends eastward to end at Cumberland by Maritime Electric power plant. It is a one-way street going east except for the block between Pownal and Queen.

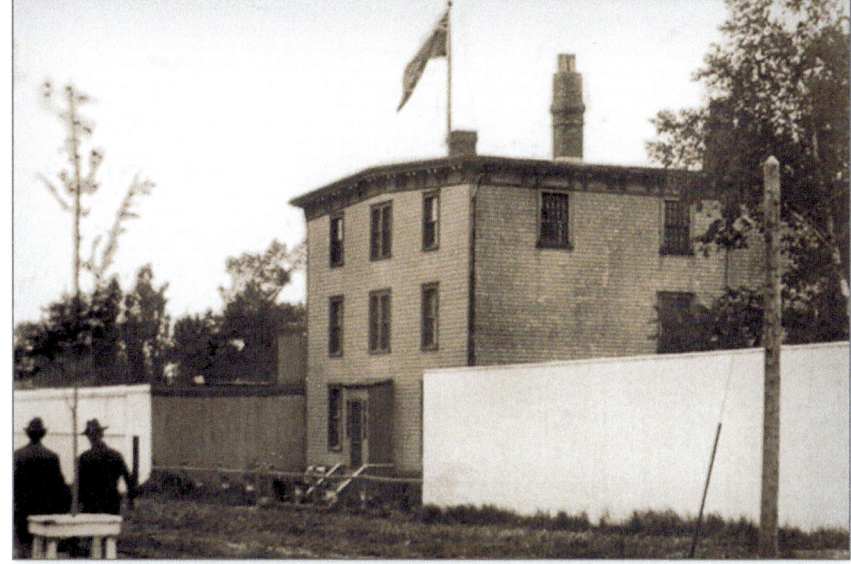

At different times called Jail Square, Connaught Square and Pownal Square, it housed the Jail from 1830 to 1911. Following the move of the jail in 1912, the square was the site of the J. H. Eschman European Railway Circus in August 1914. It advertised Aerialists, Acrobats, Clowns, an Elephant and Tamed Animals. ■

On November 8, 1910 tenders closed on a new jail, however it was not opened for intake until April 6, 1912. Following the movement of the Jail in 1912, and the demolition of the old jail, the square was renamed Connaught Square in honour of the visit of the Duke of Connaught and Strathearn (1850-1942) who was Governor General of Canada (1911 - 1916) and the third son of Queen Victoria. Although renamed, many still call it Pownal Square.

This building on Longworth Avenue, St. Peters Road, Mt. Edward Road intersection was most recently a Pizza Delight location. The original name "County 1911 Jail" is still evident on the building over the main door. The last hangings in Charlottetown took place here in 1941.

In 1977 a new jail was announced at Sleepy Hallow. The present jail is at 580 Sleepy Hallow Road. ■

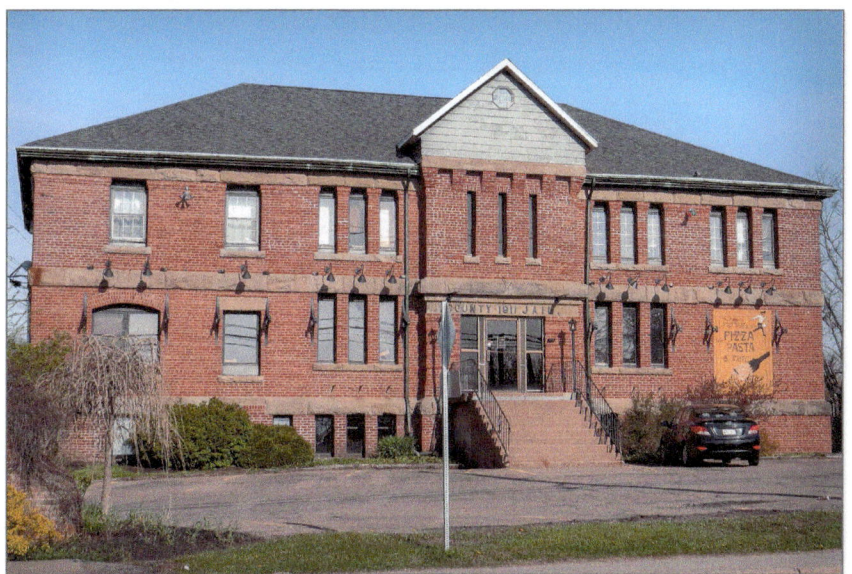

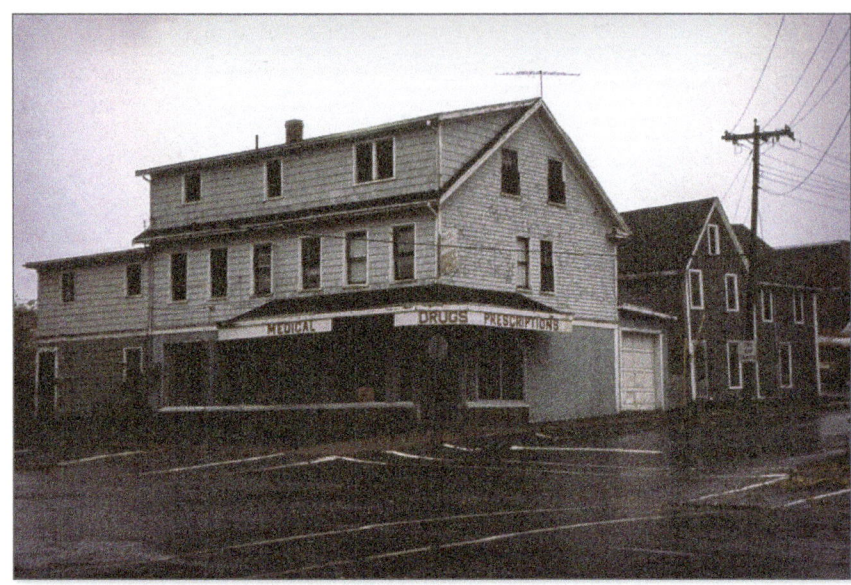

86 Pownal: Taken in October 1979 on the northeast corner of Pownal and Richmond, the Medical Pharmacy (J. A. MacLellan). This building in 1950 was Albert Kay's Grocery Store. ▪

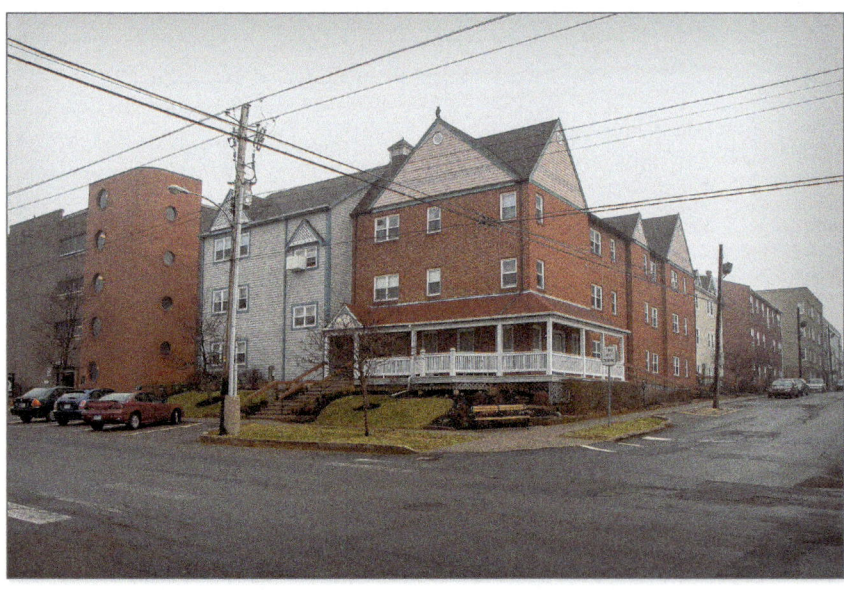

Today it is 90 Pownal Street, Pownal Square Co-op. ▪

The Richmond Street block from Queen to Great George on the south side was originally all wooden buildings and contained three-quarters of all the doctors and lawyers offices in Charlottetown. The Grafton Street block of businesses between Queen and Great George was called Sunnyside. Some of the merchants on the Richmond Street blook called their block Cheapside.

The picture c.1870 looking east with the spire of the Queen Square Presbyterian Church (erected 1860) on the far left, where Murphy's Pharmacy Community Center is today. Cr: PARO ■

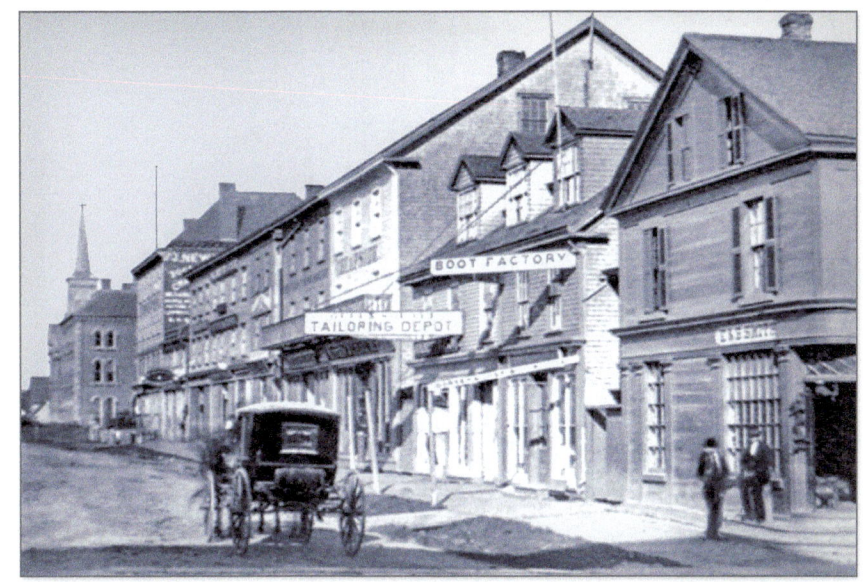

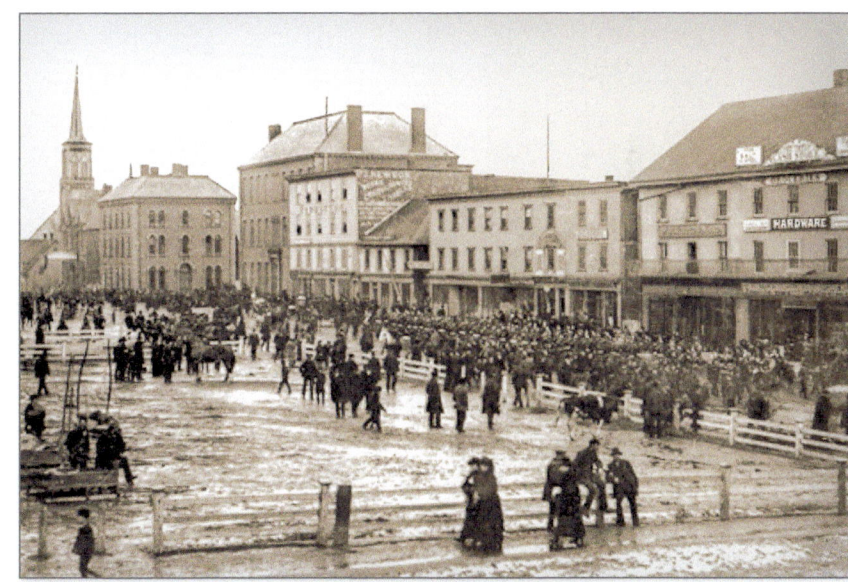

Taken from Queen Square/Market Square looking southeast. The two, three story brick buildings with the mansard roofs are: Queen Square School on the southwest corner of Richmond and Great George and the Bank of Nova Scotia on the southeast corner. The latter was built in 1872 as the Union Bank. In 1883 the Union Bank amalgamated with the Bank of Nova Scotia, which occupied this building until the Bank of Nova Scotia build their present building in 1921 at the northwest corner of Grafton and Great George. Cr: PARO ■

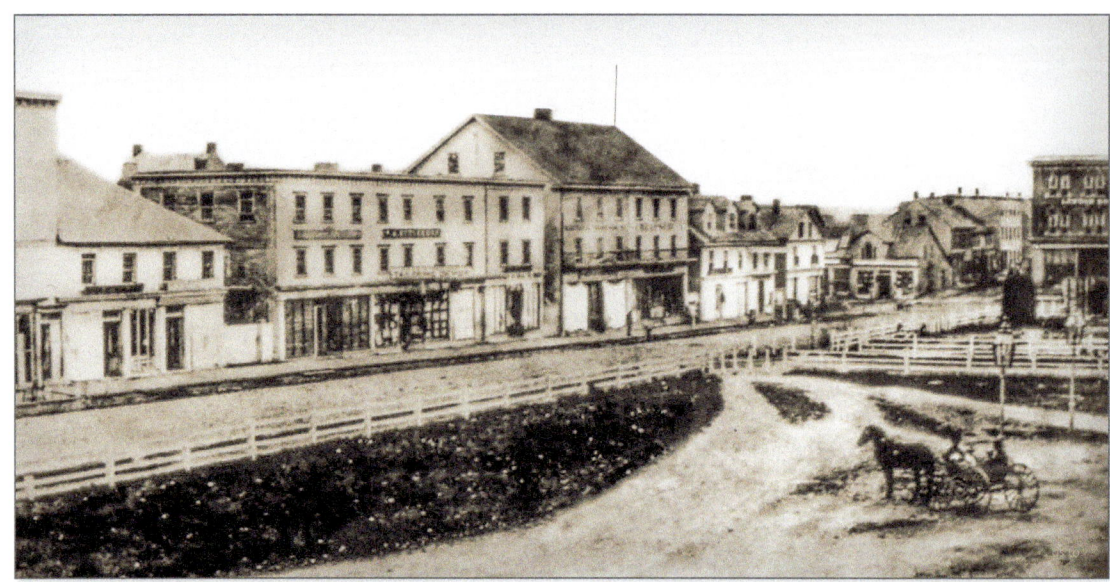

Looking west from Queen Square to the corner of Richmond and Queen Street. The three-story brick building at the right in on Queen Street. ▪

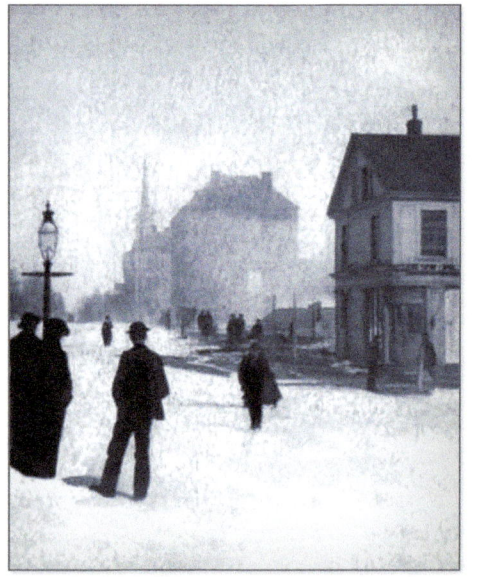

This Richmond Street block above was destroyed by fire on February 19 and 20, 1884. The only buildings left standing were on either end of the block. The west end of the block was a small shop and private residence. The east end of the block was St. Patrick's Hall, part of Queen Square School. The fire started with an overturned kerosene lamp at Kennedy Confectionary.

Almost immediately, the rebuilding effort began, with brick and stone the standard for all the new buildings. ▪

This picture, c.1895, again shows the same block from Queen to Great George as seen on page 81, with the spire of the Presbyterian Church at the left.

This block was rebuilt with three story brick and block buildings starting in 1884. This block of new buildings have stones high on the face that read from Queen Street: on the corner Stamper 1892, unidentified building, Brown Block, unidentified building, Cameron Block 1884, Morris Building 1890 and Newson Block.

After the fire Prowse Bros occupied the corner at 100-102 Queen Street and 126 Richmond Street as they fronted on both streets.

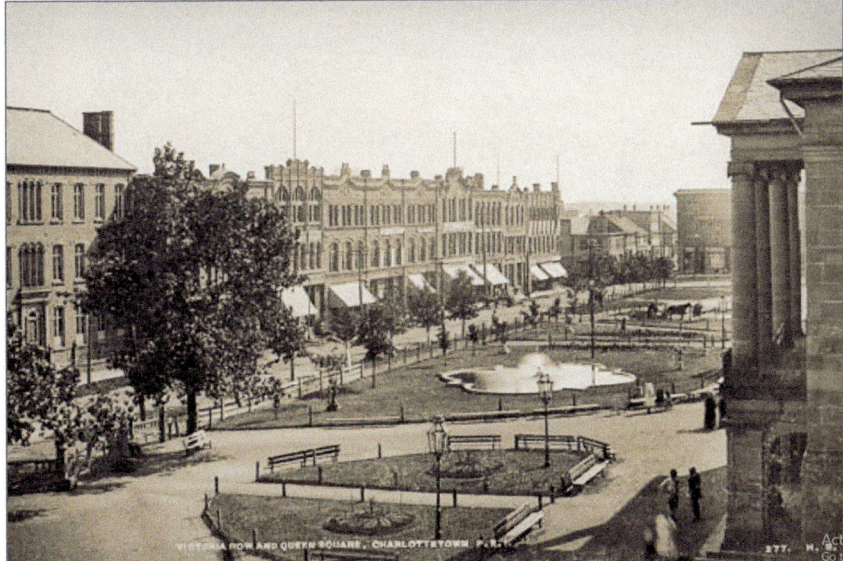

The block from Great George to Queen Street as in the last picture, this time looking west from the Coles Building. The building on the left with the mansard roof is Queen Square School.

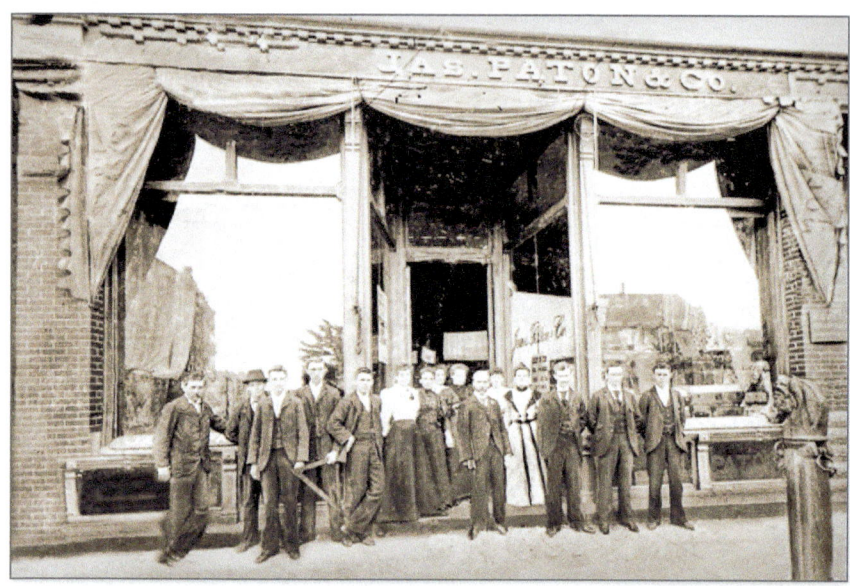

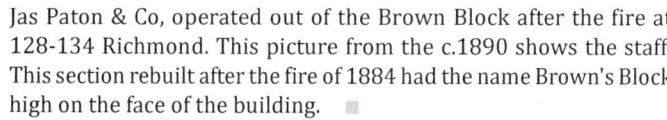

Jas Paton & Co, operated out of the Brown Block after the fire at 128-134 Richmond. This picture from the c.1890 shows the staff. This section rebuilt after the fire of 1884 had the name Brown's Block high on the face of the building.

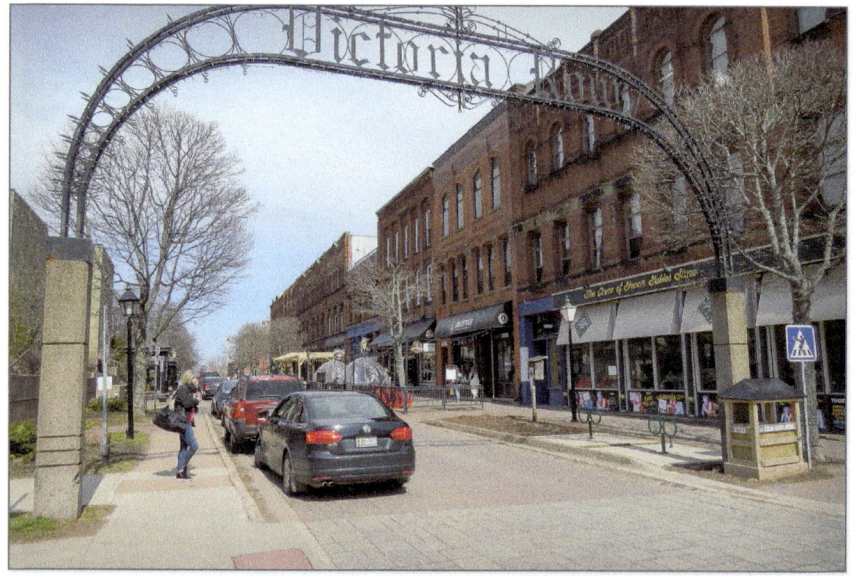

Photo taken from July 2022 is of the same block, Queen to Great George, and is commonly called Victoria Row. This section of Richmond Street is closed off to vehicular traffic in the summer and allows pedestrians to visit the various shops and eating establishments.

This picture of Prowse Bros c.1890 on the southeast corner of Queen and Richmond. They were established in the 1880's by Lemuel Ezra Prowse and later joined by his brother, Benjamin Charles. Their business grew with a combination of keen buying and great marketing. They called themselves the "Wonderful Cheap Men", and appealed to the middle income Islanders. Both brothers were active in civic, provincial and national politics. Lemuel with the Provincial Legislative Assembly; Benjamin was city councillor, mayor and was appointed to the senate on May 5, 1911. Ezra's son Thomas William Lemuel Prowse later ran the business. T. W. L. Prowse was mayor of Charlottetown 1930 to 1932, was elected to the Provincial Legislature and in 1950 became Lieutenant Governor of Prince Edward Island.

The Bank of New Brunswick, Atlantic Canada's first chartered bank, established an office here in 1901 in the corner with the R. K. Jost (previous tenant) sign over the door. ▣

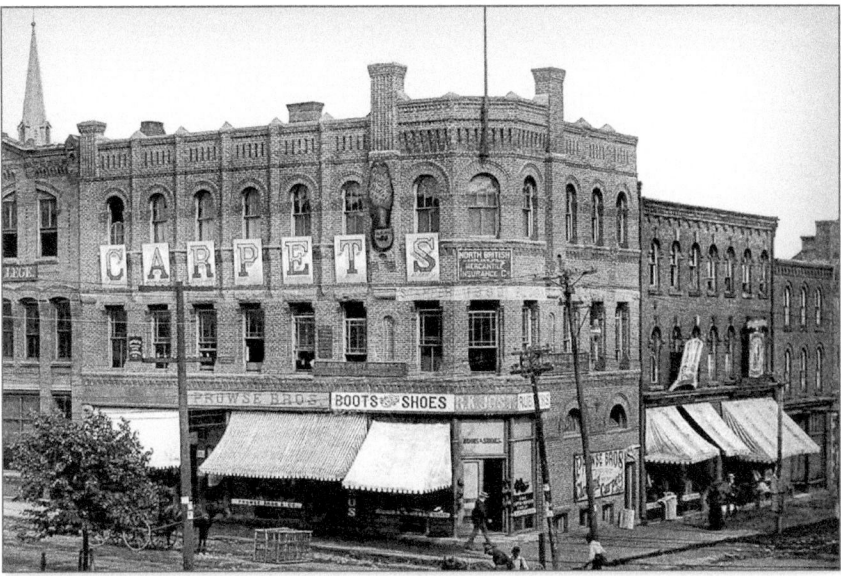

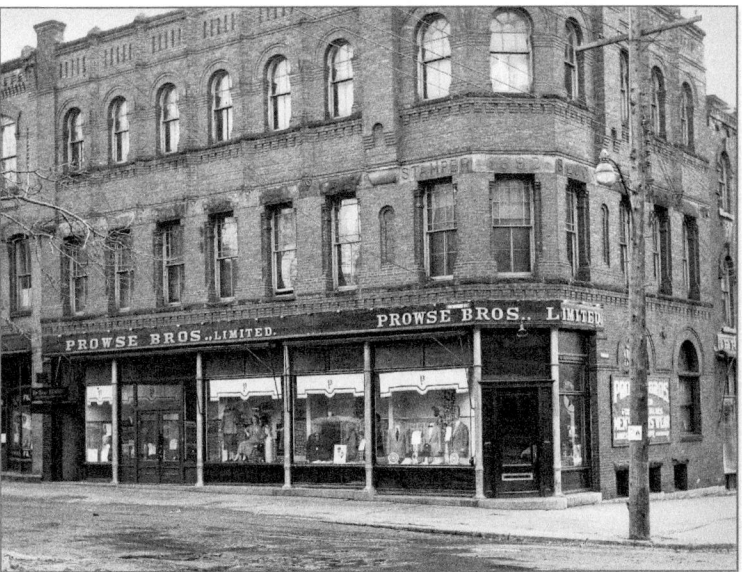

Prowse brothers remained active as a store selling carpet, men's wear, boots and shoes until the 1960's. They sold the Queen Street building to Canadian Tire. ▣

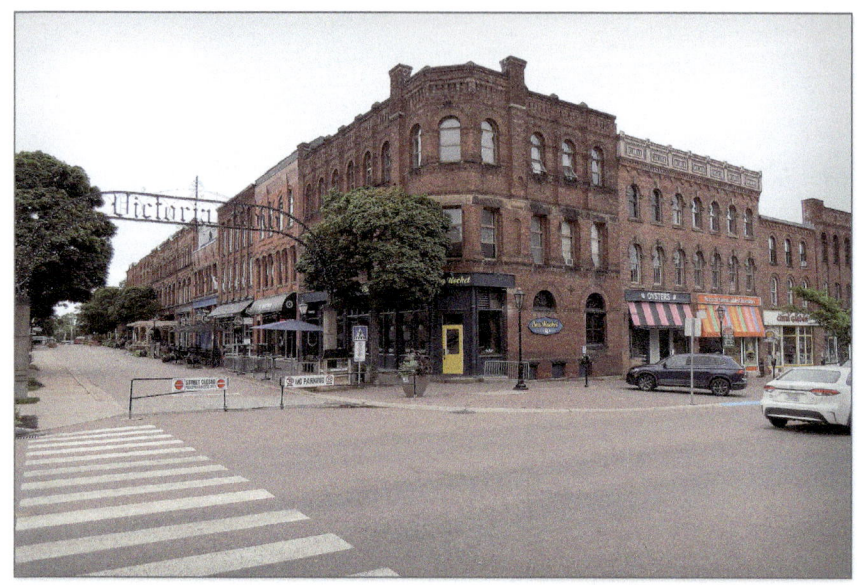

This corner here was recently Anne of Green Gables Chocolate. Following the July 2022 renovations, it was opened as the Sea Rocket Oyster Lounge. Anne of Green Gables Chocolates has moved further south down this block on Queen Street. ▪

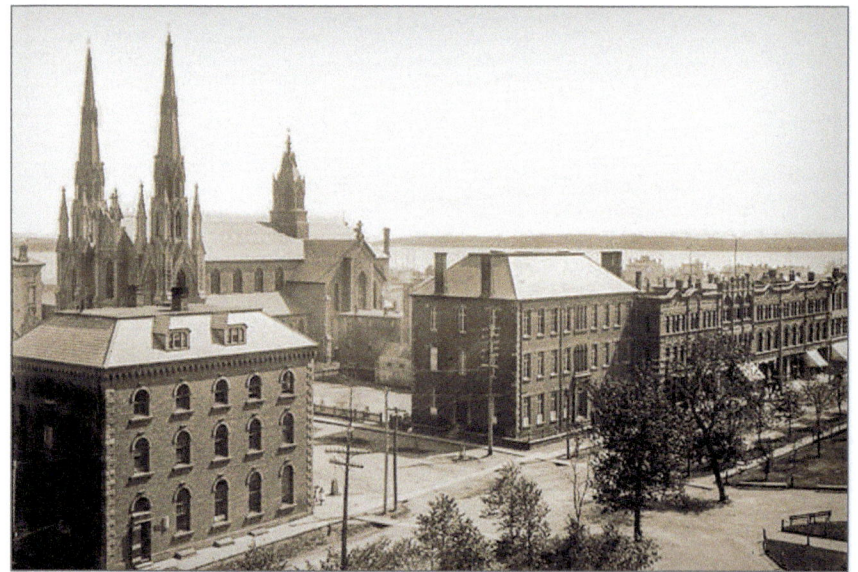

Looking southwest, c.1898, showing the old Bank of Nova Scotia on the left at the southeast corner of Great George and Richmond Streets, with Queen Square School on the southwest corner. In the background is St. Dunstans Cathedral recently completed.

Queen Square School for boys operated from 1878 to 1962. ▪

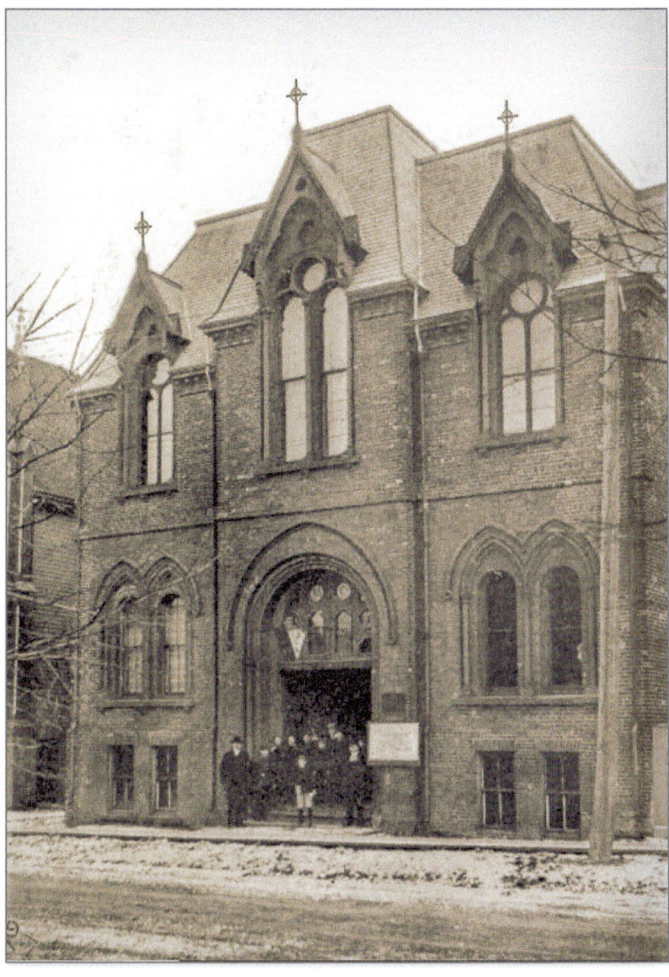

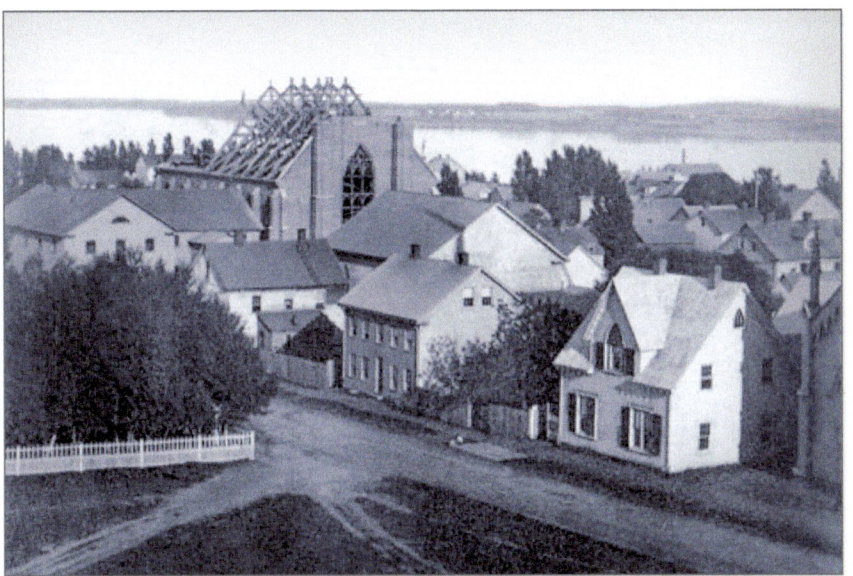

A picture from 1863 shows the Methodist Church (now Trinity United) under construction. The right edge of this photo shows Queen Square Presbyterian Church, which was opened for worship on July 25, 1860. Note in the background there is no Hillsborough Bridge. The bridge was not installed until 1905. ■

East of the former Bank of Nova Scotia on Richmond Street, the YMCA erected a building where the west end of Murphy's Pharmacy Recreation Centre is now. It was reported to be the first building built for the YMCA in North America, where previously they used rented premises. This picture is from 1903. A new YMCA was built at the southeast corner of Prince and Euston Streets, with the corner stone laid on August 19, 1948. That location is now home to the Y-Lofts. ■

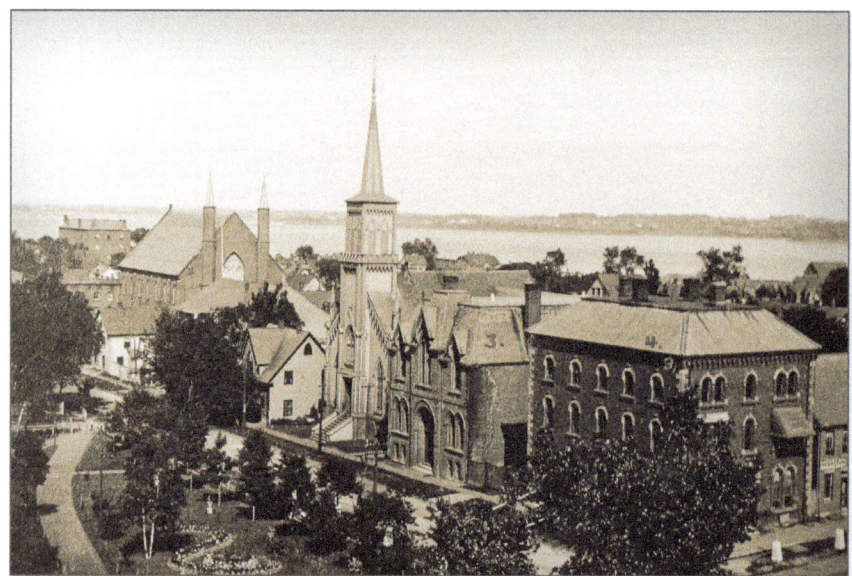

This picture of the south side of Richmond Street from Great George Street to Prince Street. The building on the corner with No. 4 on the roof is the former Bank of Nova Scotia. Next going left is the YMCA building, with Zion Church as No. 2. The church with the two spires is the First Methodist Church (now Trinity United). ▪

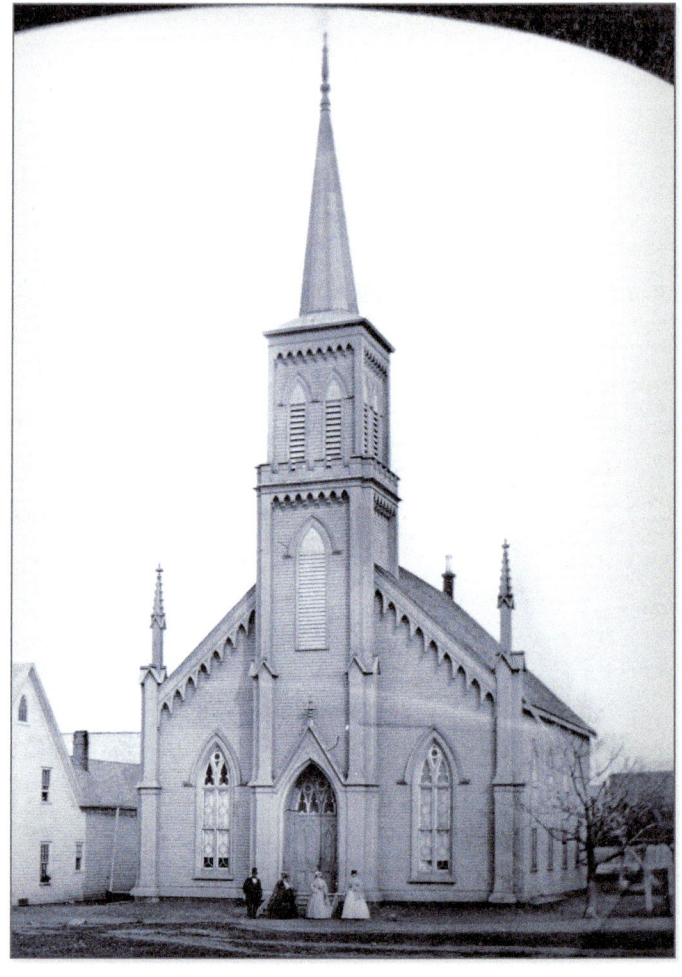

Queen Square Presbyterian Church was opened for worship July 25, 1860. Contractors for the building were David and William Fraser of Pictou, Nova Scotia. The frame of the wooden building was cut and erected in Pictou. It was then dismantled, marked and shipped to Charlottetown. It was re-assembled on the new foundation by Heartz Brothers, master builders of the day. ▪

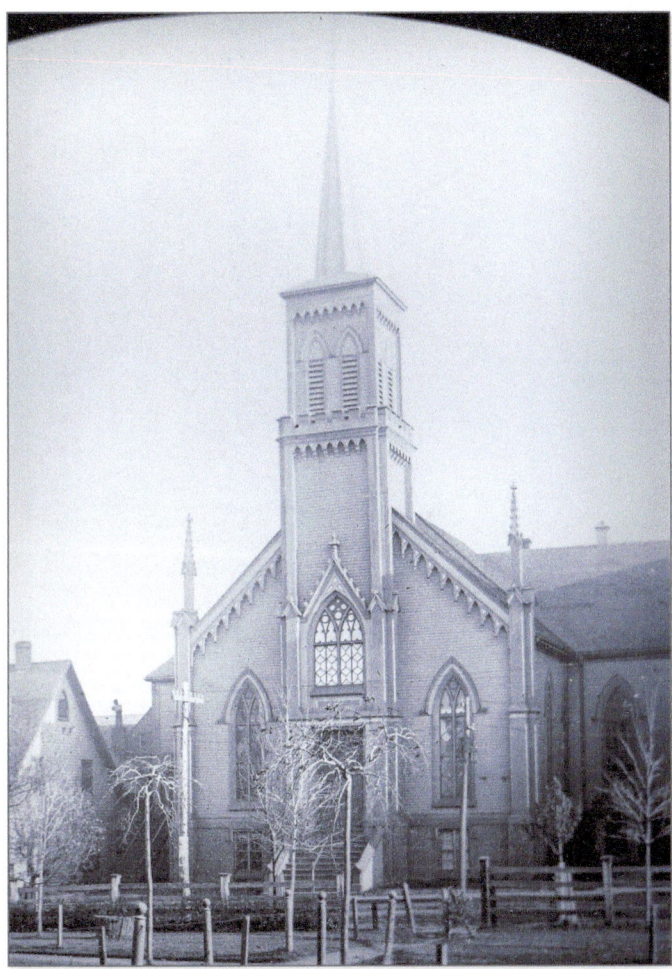

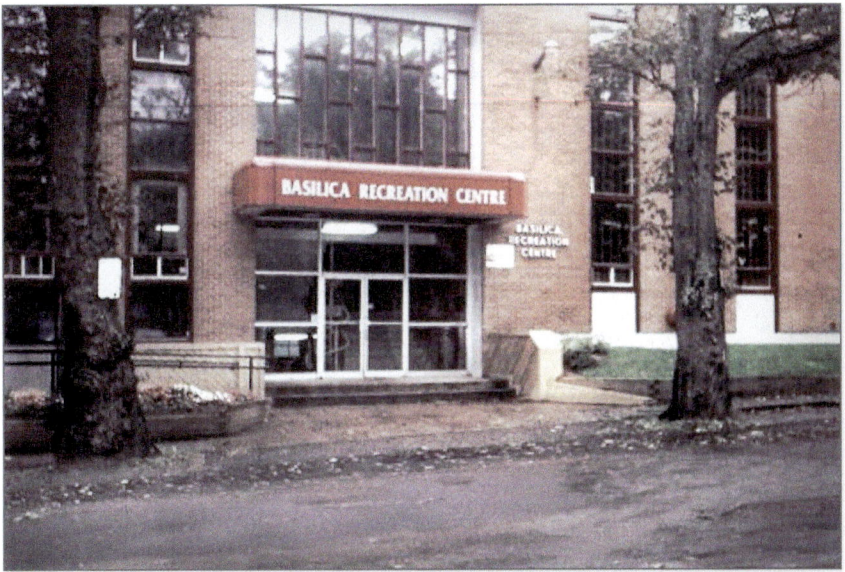

Holy Name Hall was demolished together with the former YMCA building, and a new Basilica Recreation Centre was erected. This building contained bowling alleys, a gymnasium and meeting rooms for various groups. ■

The Church was remodel in 1879, raising the building to provide a basement, as well as adding a wing. With the congregation later moving to the new Zion Presbyterian Church in 1913 at the northwest corner of Prince and Grafton, and a subsequent fire at St. Dunstans Cathedral, the Presbyterians sold their former church to the Roman Catholic Episcopal Corporation for $5,000. This former Presbyterian Church, then was named Holy Name Hall. ■

Prince Street

Prince Street runs from the waterfront through Water Street up to Euston.
It then extends at a slight right angle as Upper Prince Street all the way to Allan Street.

Prince Street could easily be called Church Street, as it contains, Trinity United,
St Paul's Anglican, Zion Presbyterian, Salvation Army and First Baptist.
Charlottetown by some accounts is called the city of churches and trees.
This street is a fine example.

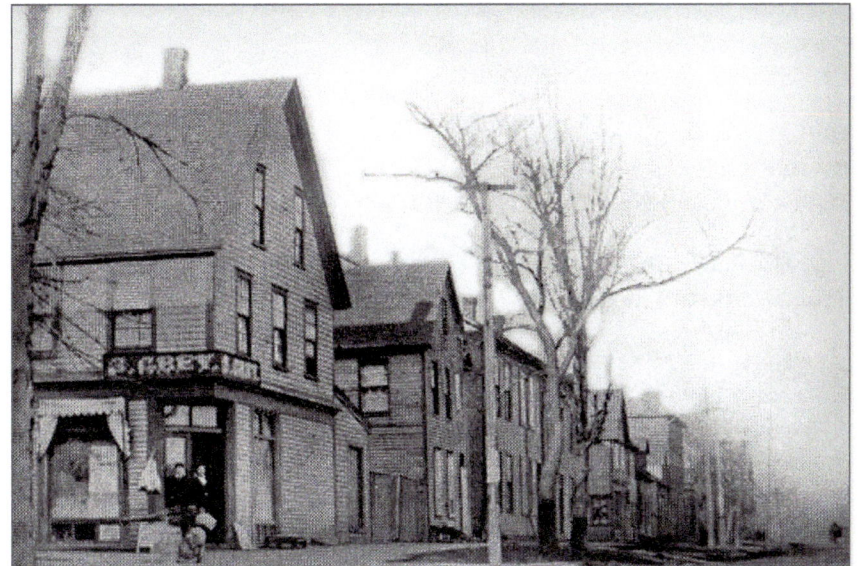

C1900, taken from Water Street looking north up the west side of Prince Street. In 1924 this was: 141 Water Street, P. T. Murphy Grocer. In 1937 it was: 11 Prince Street, Prince Grocery. This could be the origin of the name of the store: Water Prince Corner Store. Cr: Smith-Alley Collection PARO ▪

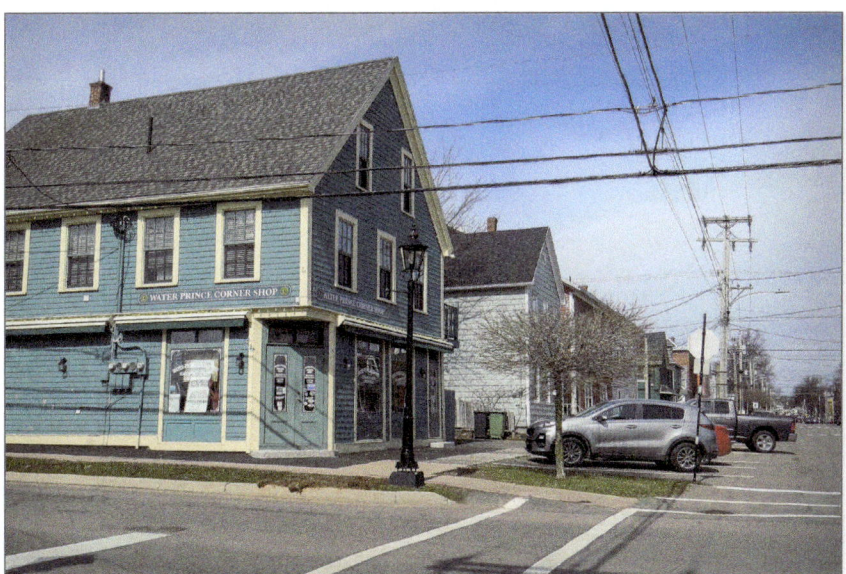

From April 2022, the Water Prince Corner Shop on the corner. Famous for lobster rolls and chowder, they provide outdoor seating in season. ▪

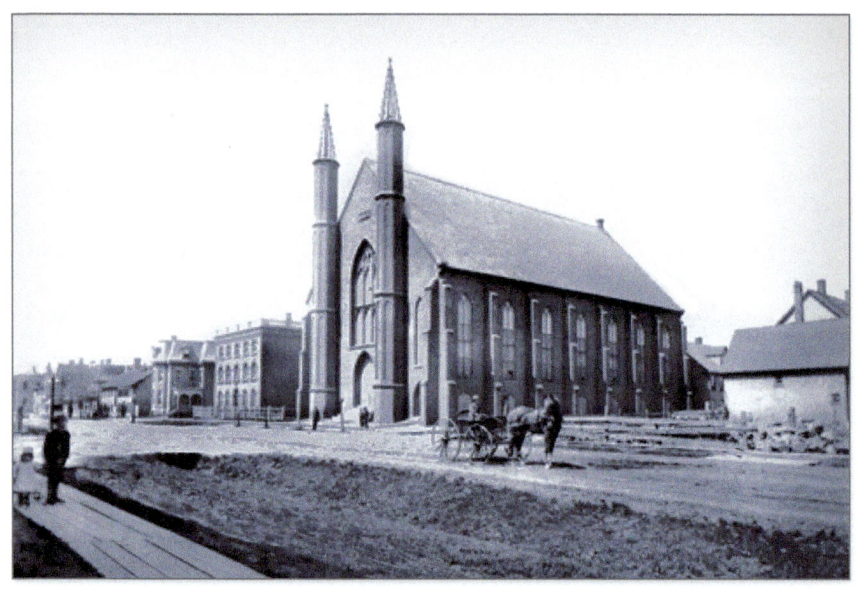

Trinity United was erected in 1863, and dedicated on November 13, 1864, as the Wesleyan Church, replacing an earlier church on this site. The Wesleyans or Methodists formerly had a chapel on the north side of Richmond Street between Queen and Pownal dating from 1816.

This church was built to seat 1,200, at a time when Charlottetown had a total population of 7,000. This is the oldest church building still used as a church in the city. Following the Union question in 1925, this Methodist joined what is now called the United Church of Canada.

This picture is from 1900. Note the wooden sidewalks. The H. H. Houle house with the mansard roof, mentioned on the following page, is shown in this picture. Heartz Memorial Hall was later erected north of the church and was dedicated on July 4, 1911. It was later destroyed by fire on October 28, 1969. ■

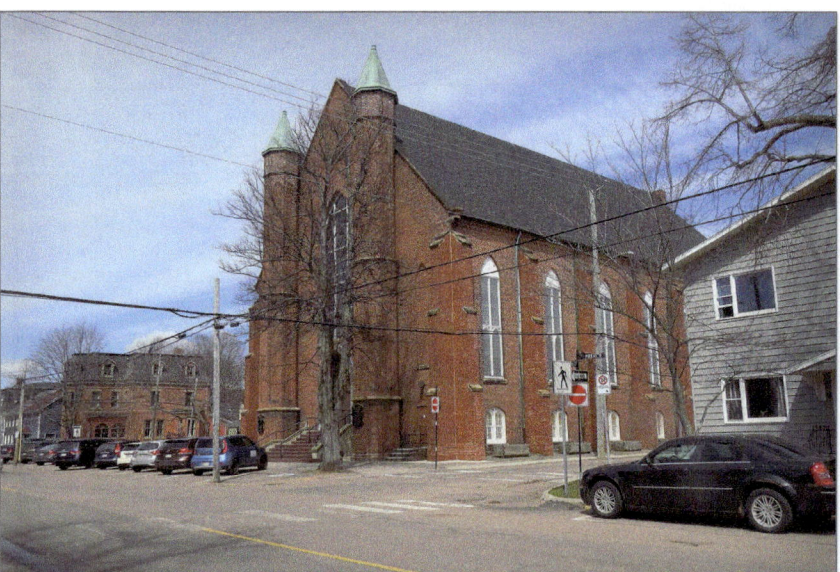

This current picture of Trinity United Church shows the shortened towers together with a recent new roof. The towers were shortened for safety concerns. ■

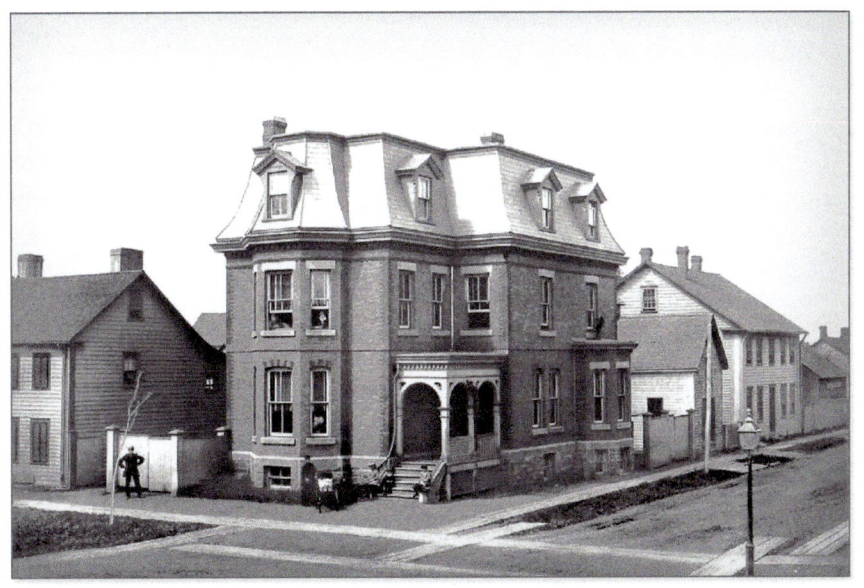

Designed by William Critchlow Harris, at 96 Prince Street on the northeast corner of Richmond, this building was built in 1879 for H. H. Houle, track master of the Prince Edward Island Railway. Dr. Al Saunders had his clinic here in the 70's. It is visible in the earlier picture of the First Methodist Church. In the newer picture, the open porch has been enclosed. As well, the front window on the third floor has been enlarged.

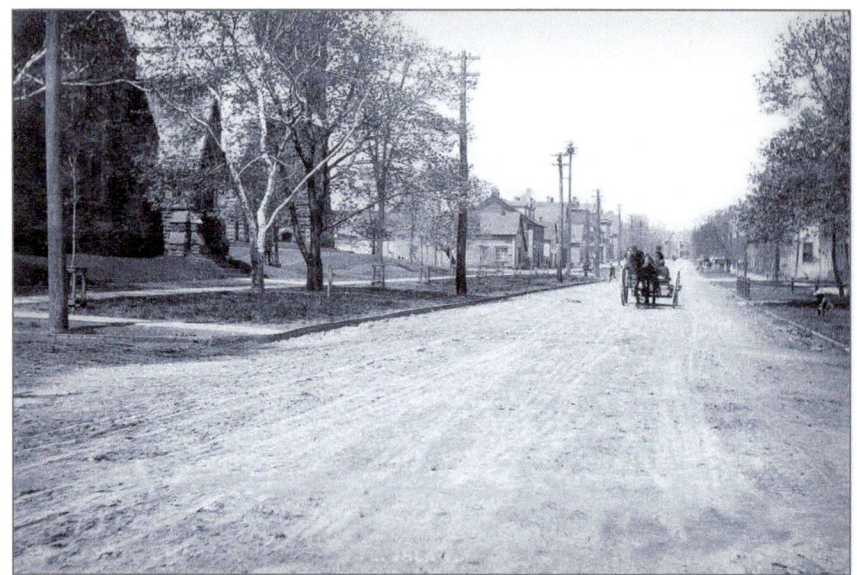

Looking north up Prince Street in 1908, with St. Paul's Anglican Church on the left. St. Paul's, designed by William Critchlow Harris, was opened for worship on May 10, 1896. This is the third church on this site, the first completed in 1802.

The next building on the left side of Prince is on the corner of Grafton Street. This was known as Hobbs Corner after John Hobbes, a cap and hat maker and the only maker of top hats in Charlottetown. This site was purchased in 1906 for the erection of Zion Presbyterian Church. Zion built their new building in 1911-13, replacing their former church on Richmond Street. It was timely in that the move coincided with the destruction by fire of St. Dunstans Cathedral. Zion loaned the Catholics their former church until the new Basilica was completed, an unthinkable accommodation at the time between the two denominations. ■

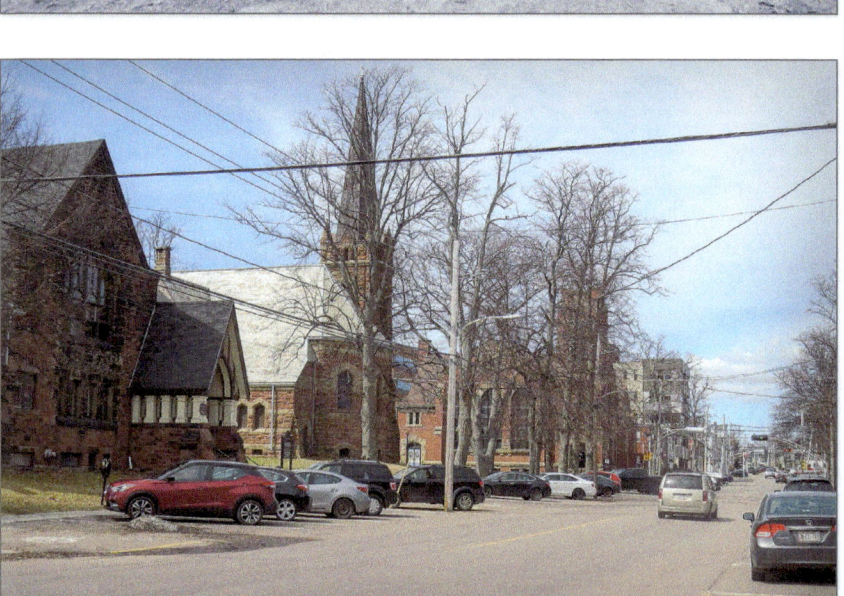

This picture from 2022 shows the same view, with St. Paul's Anglican, Zion Presbyterian and the Maritime Electric prominent along the west side of Prince Street. ■

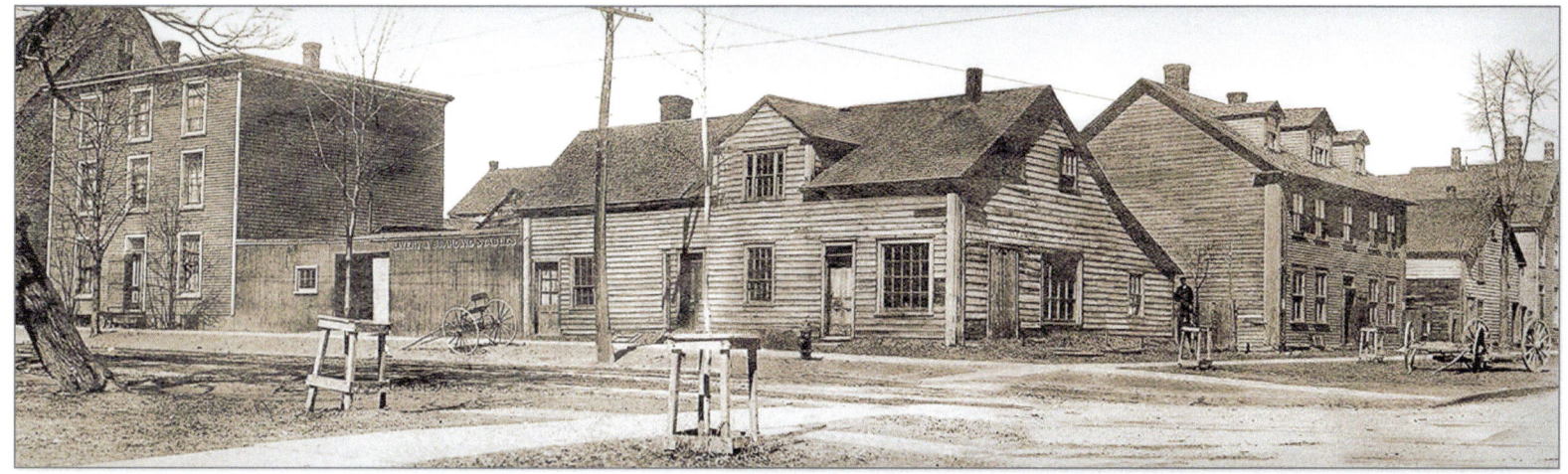

The picture, taken May 5, 1911, of the site of the new Zion Church on the northwest corner of Grafton and Prince Streets. The large two-story house with three dormer windows was moved to 206 Grafton. (see following page) ▪

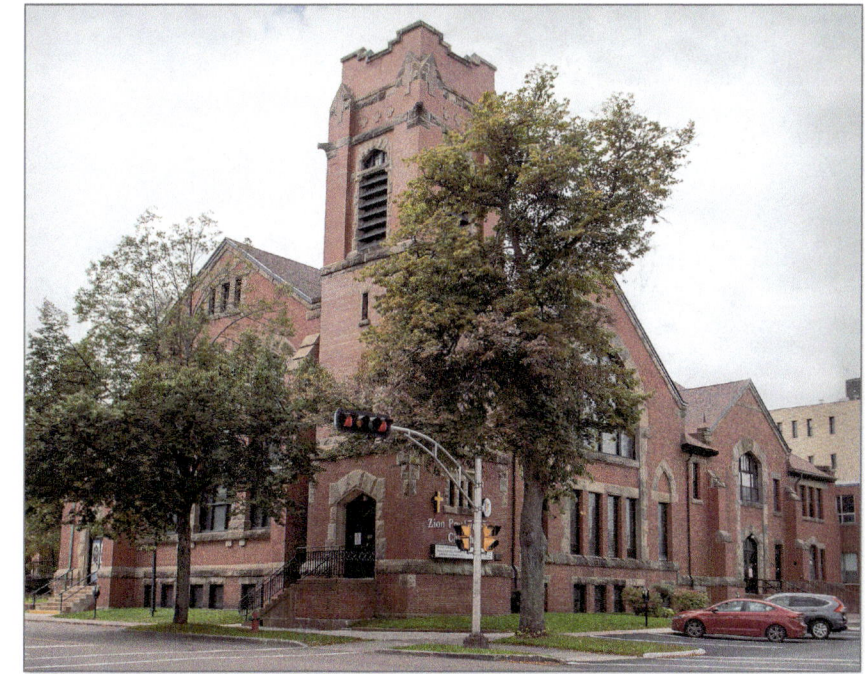

This recent picture is of Zion Presbyterian Church. ▪

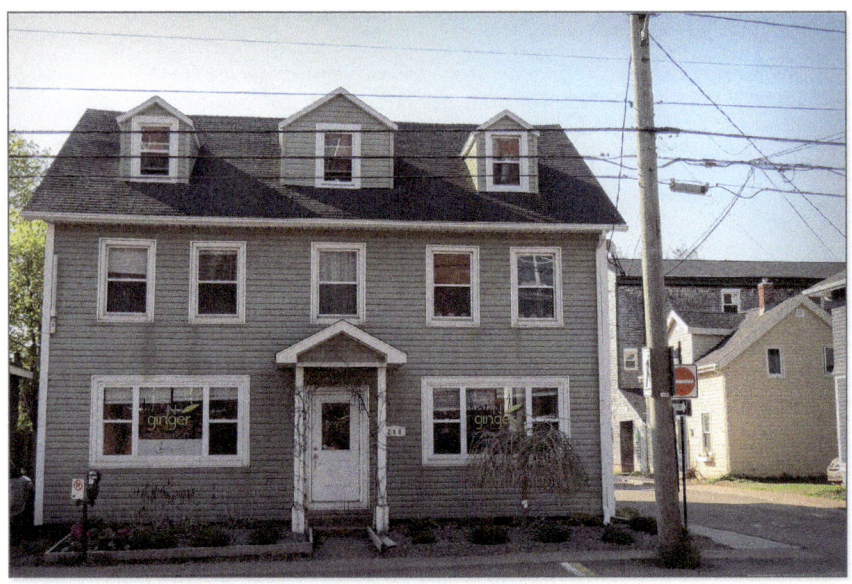

The large building with three dormer windows in the May 5, 1911 picture above, was removed from the site and is now at 206 Grafton Street. ▪

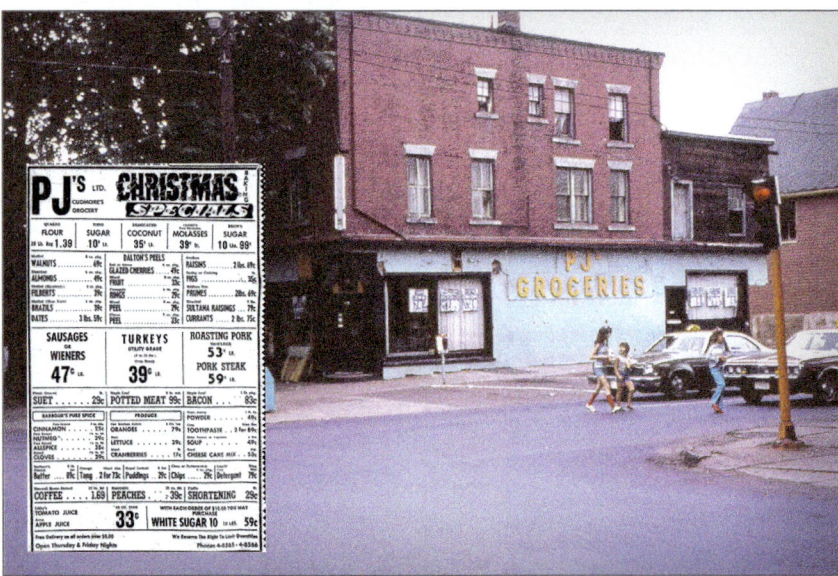

PJ's Grocery Store on the corner of Prince and Kent Streets is from September 1973. P. J. was Peter Jenkins MacDonald. ▪

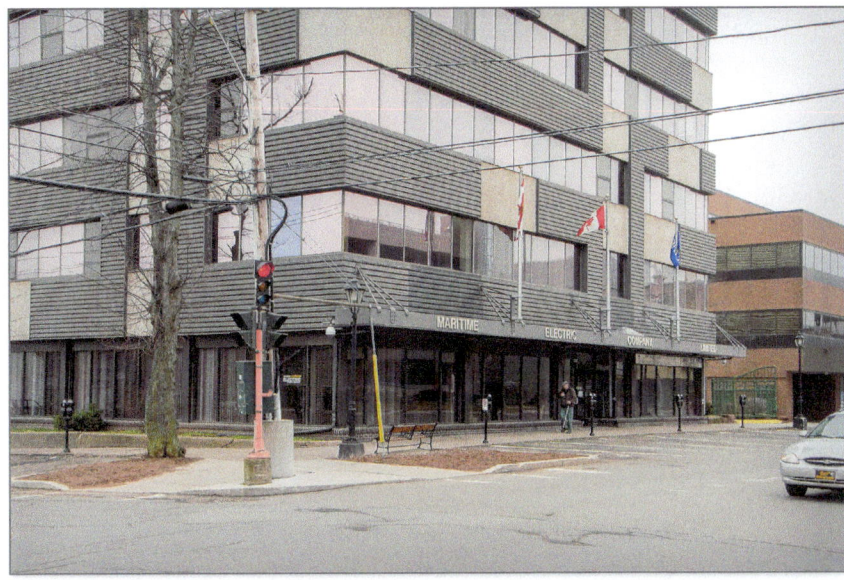

P.J's Grocery was replaced in 1978 by this office building. Maritime Electric bought the completed building in 1989. ▪

This picture, from pre-1911, of the west side of Prince Street from Kent to Grafton. This is the present-day block from Maritime Electric south to Zion Presbyterian Church. The house with the five windows on the second floor and the three gable windows on the roof, together with the building to the left was removed for the construction of Zion Presbyterian Church in 1911. (I did not use the picture for the parade, rather the houses) ▪

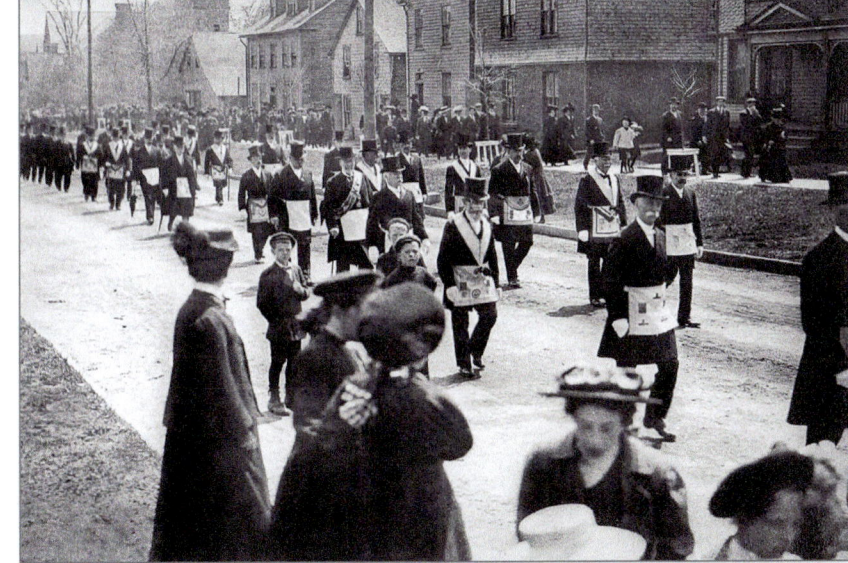

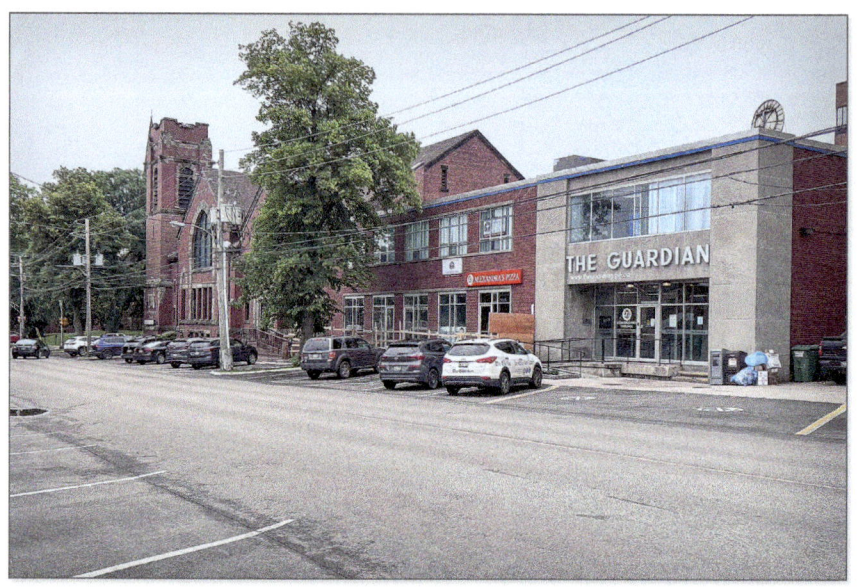

Taken in 2022, this block contains from Right to left: Maritime Electric (just out of view), the Guardian Office and Zion Presbyterian Church. The Guardian office has recently been renovated with multiple separate entrance for small retail outlets, together with a raised walkway/entrance where a flower bed once stood.

The brick building high on the right is the Department of Veteran Affairs. ▪

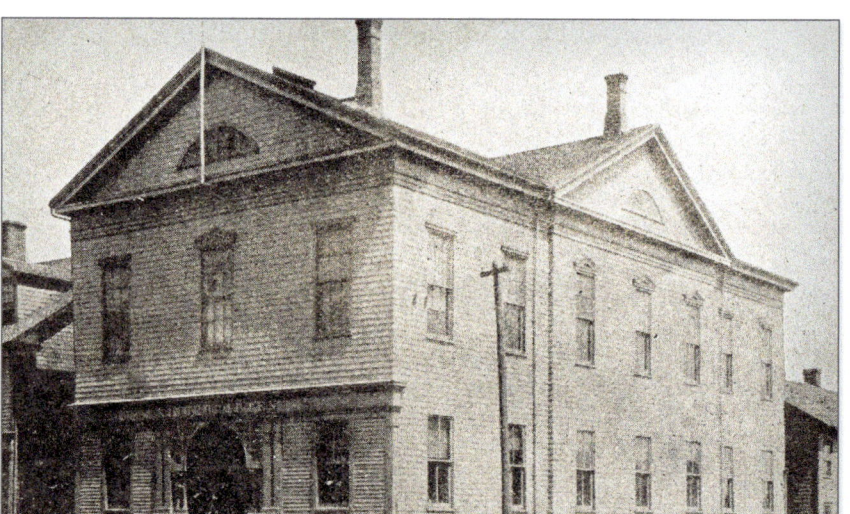

Across Prince Street on the northeast corner of Prince and Grafton in a building originally known as the Athenaeum. It was later the Temperance Hall, and served as the Methodist Sunday School. This picture from 1898 was listed as the Wesleyan Methodist Kindergarten and Primary. The word "Kindergarten" is shown above the arch in the door. Note the young trees just planted and surrounded for support. Compare to the larger trees in the next picture. ▪

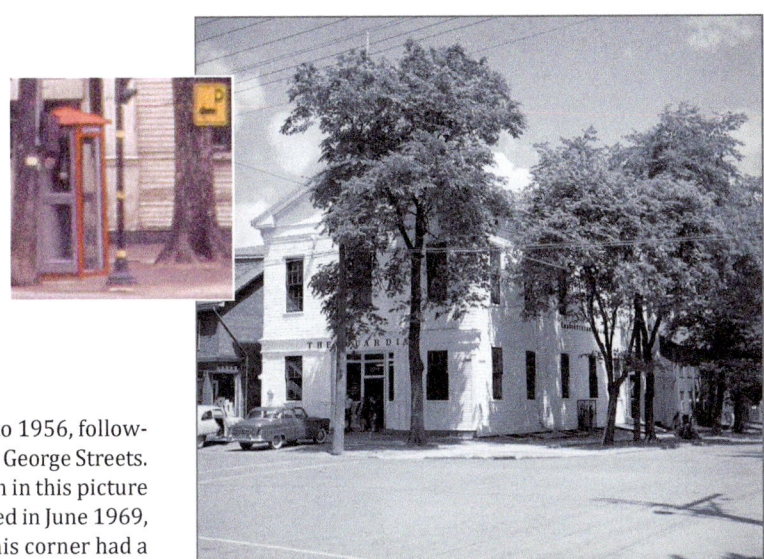

This building was home to the Guardian from 1924 to 1956, following their fire at the northeast corner of Kent and Great George Streets. (see writeup under Great George Street) The location in this picture was later Storey Electric. This building was demolished in June 1969, and is now parking for the Polyclinic. In May 1969 this corner had a phone booth. ■

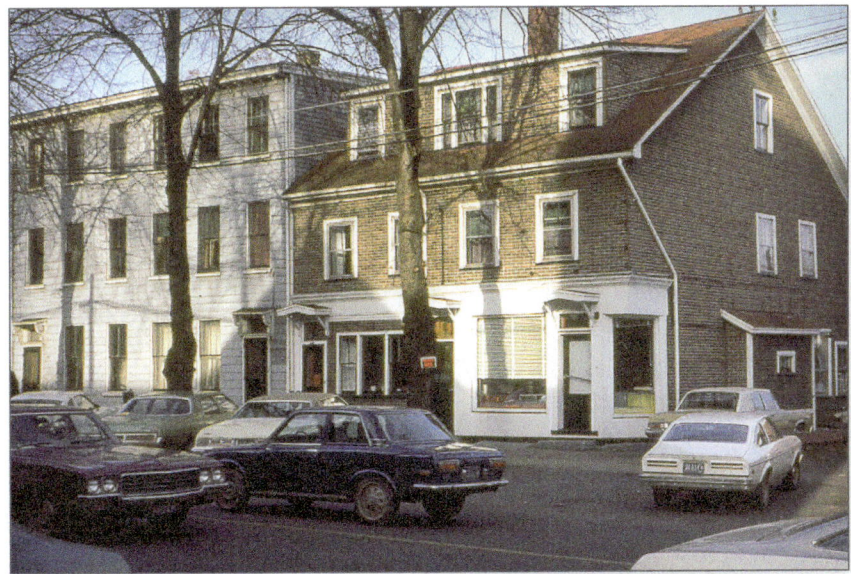

From November 1976, of the east side of Prince Street between Grafton and Kent shows 142 Prince Street, formerly Worth's Drug Store (J. Ernest H. Worth). The grey three-story building on the left was demolished for a parking lot of the new Polyclinic. ■

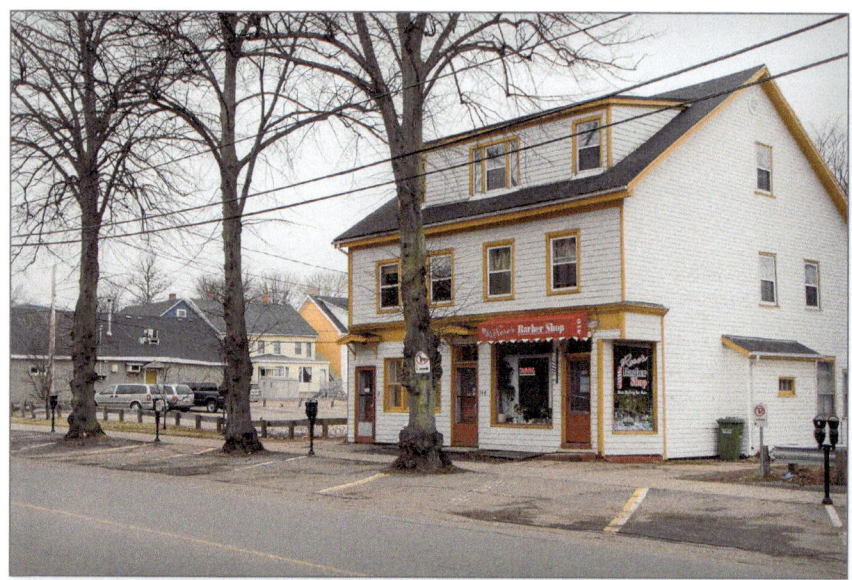

142 Prince Street: This picture taken in 2013 was Rose's Barber Shop. The low building on the far left at 166 Prince Street was the Velvet Underground, later named Jack Cameron's Eatery & Nightclub. ▪

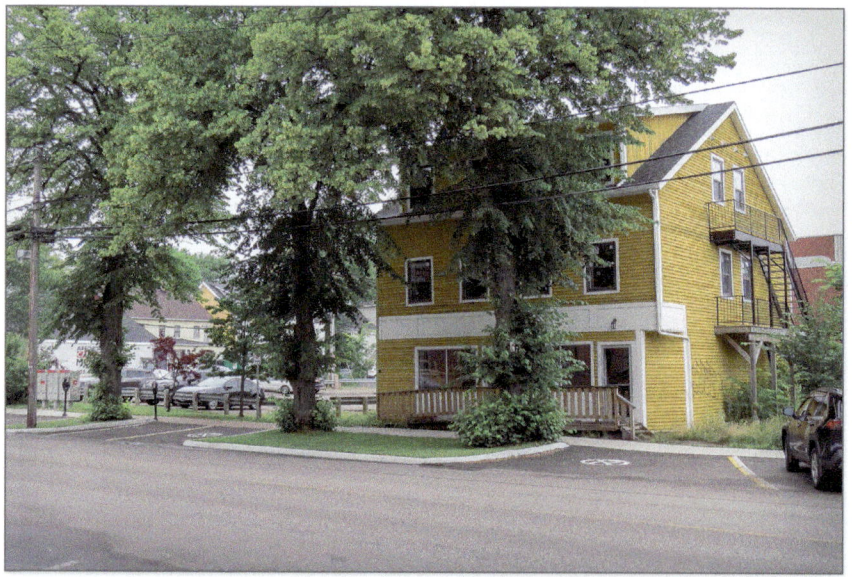

This picture from 2022 shows the building since renovated in 2017 following a fire. Behind this and to the right is the Polyclinic on Grafton Street. ▪

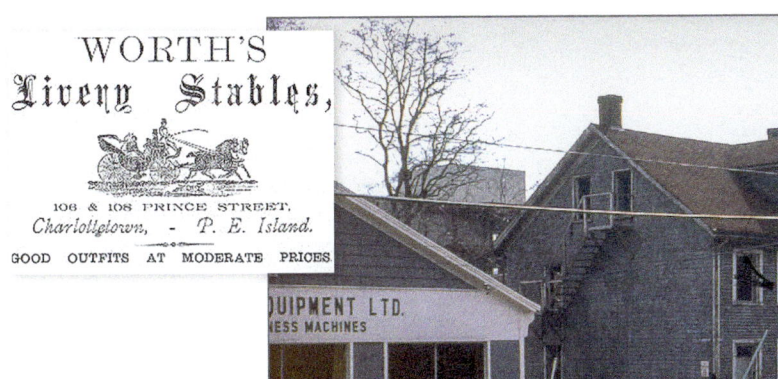

WORTH'S
Livery Stables,

106 & 108 PRINCE STREET,
Charlottetown, - *P. E. Island.*

GOOD OUTFITS AT MODERATE PRICES

Picture taken May 1977 shows:

164 Prince Street, Cudmore Business Equipment. In the late 1800s it was the site of Worth's Livery Stable. In 1922 it was listed as the Charlottetown Garage Company. From the late 1930s this was Duvar's Garage and Service Station. In 1938 the original building was destroyed by fire and replaced by Duvar. In 1937 it was listed as MacKenzie's Filling Station.

The center building had a tenant in this building in 1937, listed as the Protestant Orphanage Office.

154 Prince Street, with the sign "Fresh up with 7-Up" was Hoods Pharmacy. McLeod & Bentley Law Office (W. E. Bentley) was also in this building in 1960. This building together with the three-story buildings on either side were removed to create the parking lot for the Polyclinic. ■

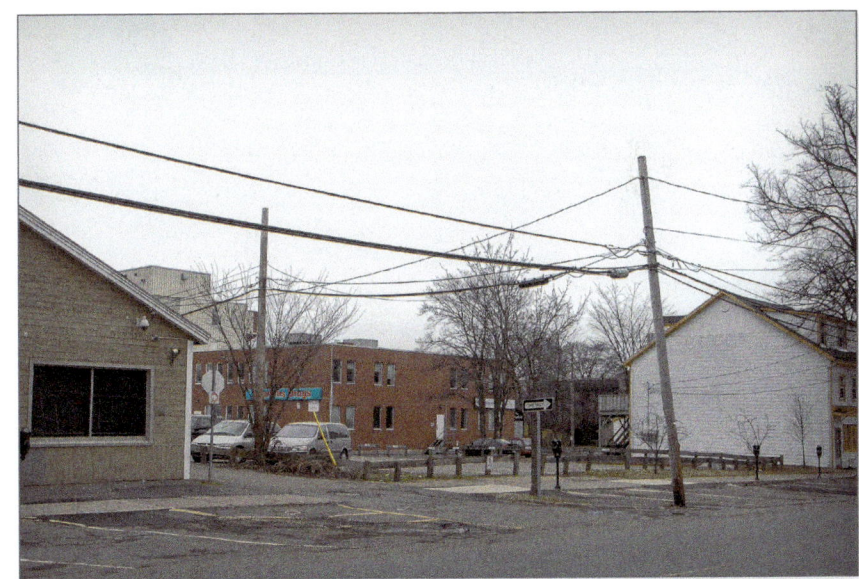

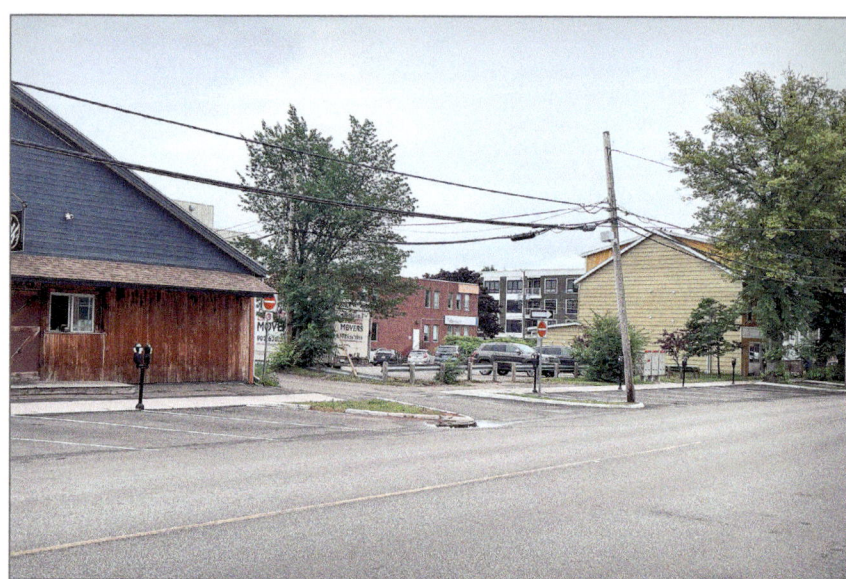

This picture taken July 2022 showing the Polyclinic parking lot in the centre. Plans were recently made and abandoned to build a condominium in this parking lot. ■

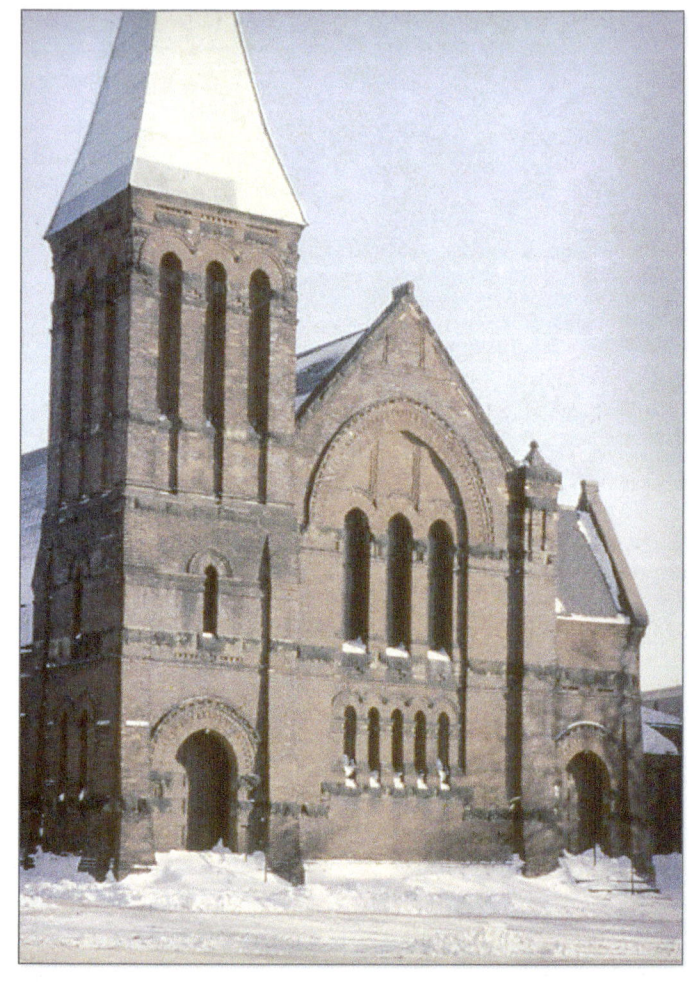

200 Prince Street, on the southeast corner of Fitzroy Street, the Baptist Church, was opened for worship on January 11, 1891. They subsequently constructed a new First Baptist Church at 235 Prince Street, on the northwest corner of the same intersection. ■

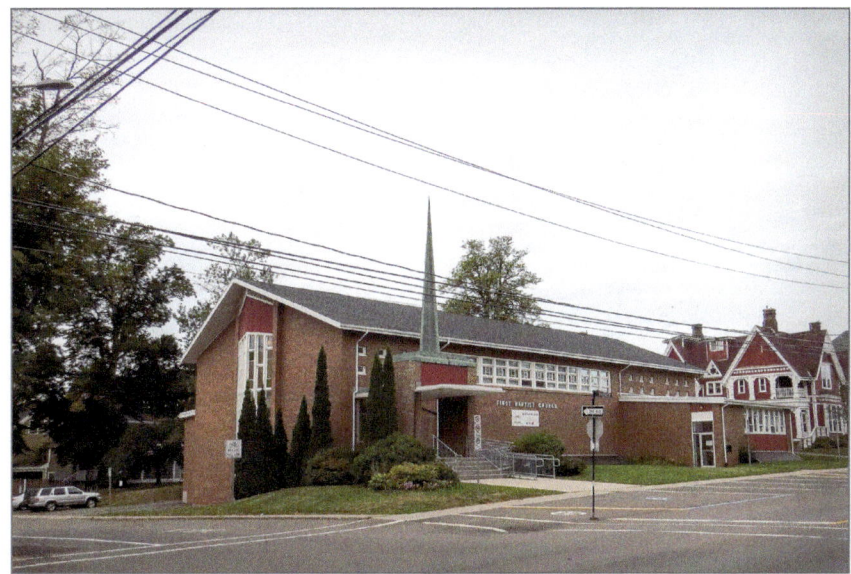

The cornerstone was laid on the new Baptist Church on October 26, 1958, with the church opened for worship on May 17, 1959. ▪

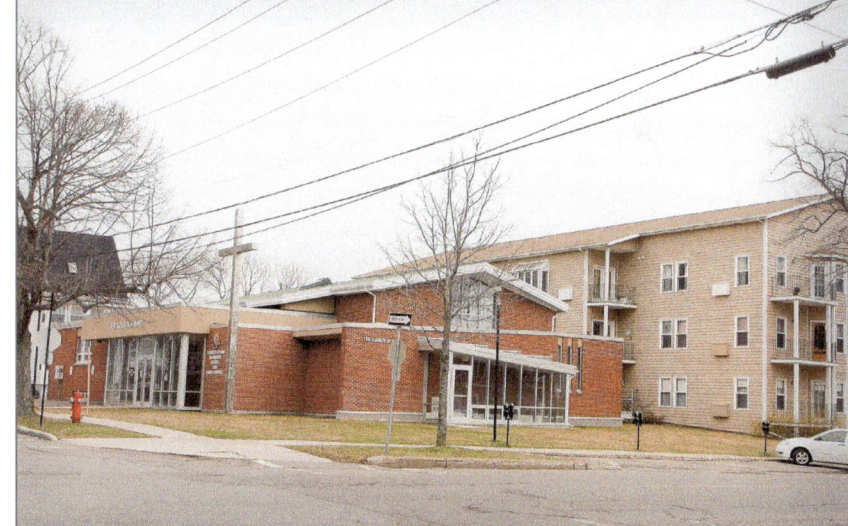

The Salvation Army constructed a new Corps building on the former Baptist Church site, opening in December 1966. The Corps having moved here from 178 Great George Street. The old building on Great George Street was crushed under the weight of snow on January 5, 1971. To the right in this picture is the Prince Street Condominiums. This was formerly the site of the first Polyclinic from 1925 to 1946, before their move to Fitzroy, behind the Salvation Army building. ▪

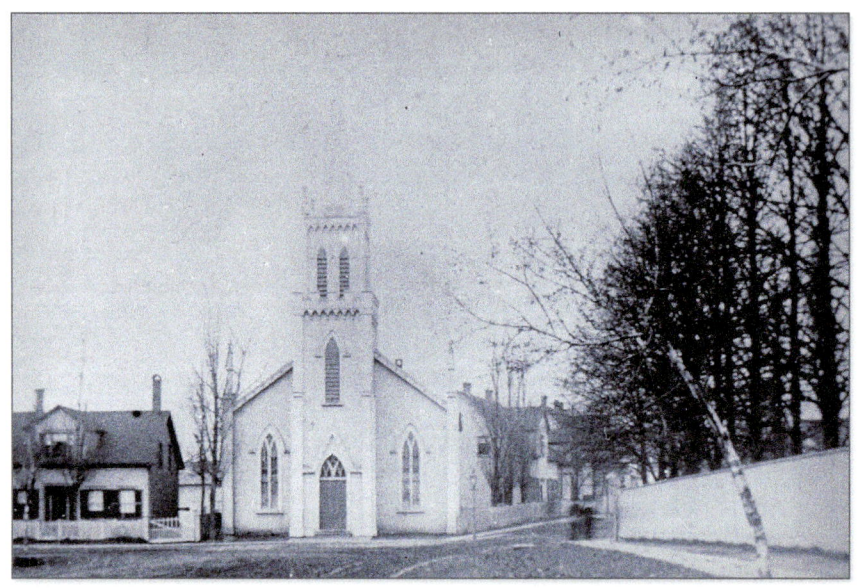

The Free Church Presbyterian on the northwest corner of Euston and Upper Prince Street was built in 1855. This congregation joined with Zion Presbyterian and the now abandoned church was sold to the Salvation Army. They moved the building to the southeast corner of FItzroy and Great George Streets, present day Atlantic Technology Centre. The site on Euston and Upper Prince was listed in 1895 as "Lemuel Hooper operated a shop and dwelling at 82 Euston." George Hughes founder of Hughes Drug Store later built a house on this site, which was later occupied by his son Gordon. ▪

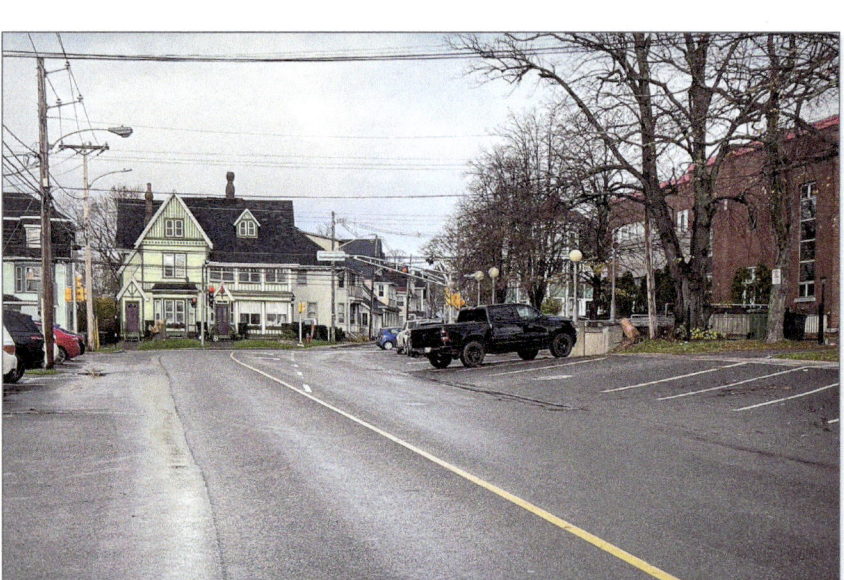

Looking north in 2022, to the end of Prince Street. The Former YMCA, now Y-Lofts is on the right. ▪

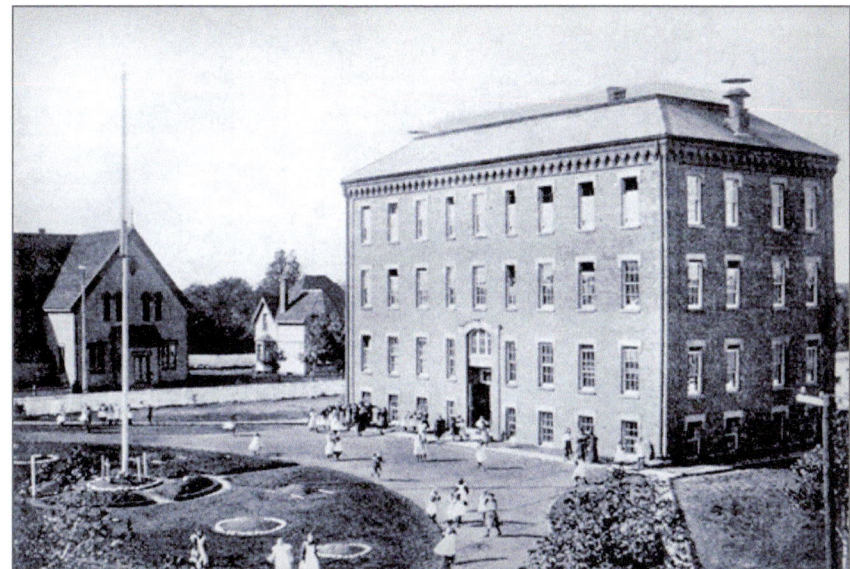

Shown here in 1899, the Wesleyan Academy. This picture shows as well the Wesleyan Church/Upper Prince Street Methodist Church across the street on the left. ▪

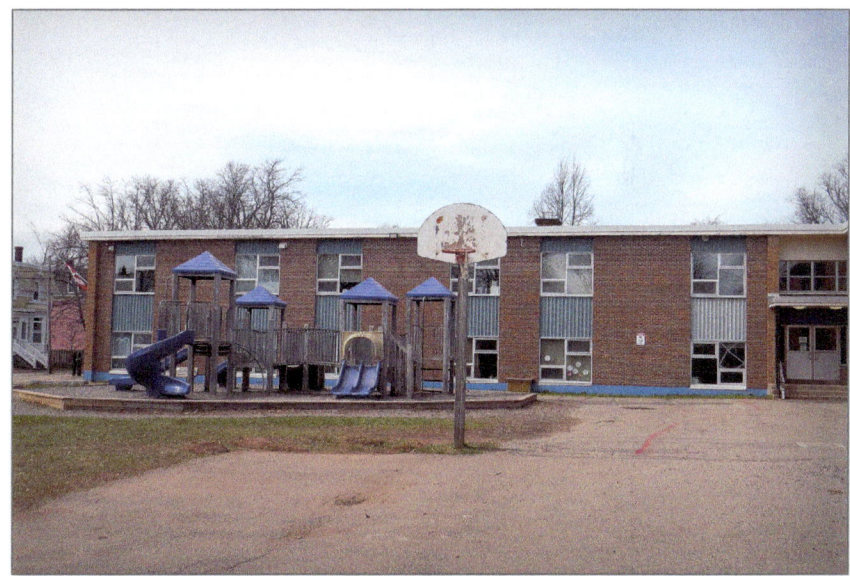

The former school was replaced by the present Prince Street School on the site. The cornerstone was laid on September 4, 1962 by Lt. Col. L. T. Lowther, principal of the school. ▪

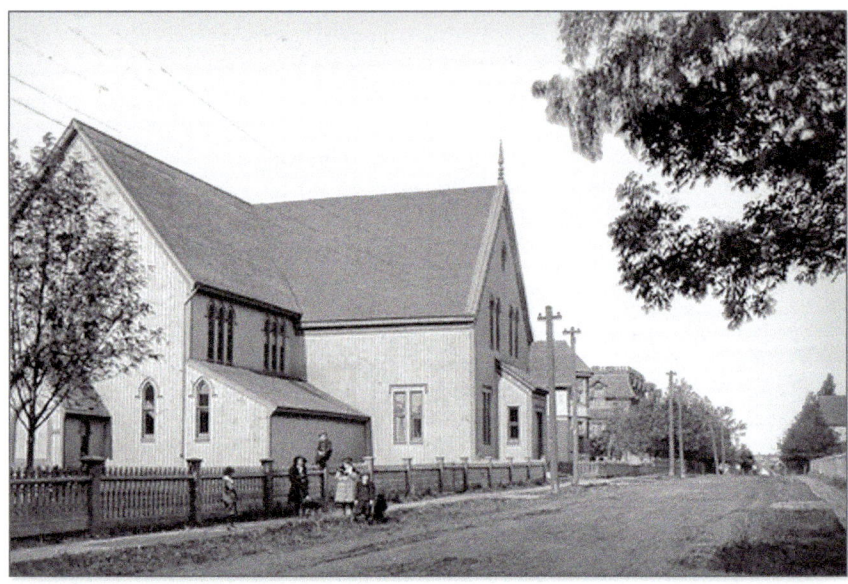

This photo from 1897 shows The Wesleyan Church/Upper Prince Street Methodist Church. It was erected in 1887 and opened for worship on October 14. This building, later known as Grace Church, remained a church until 1918. ■

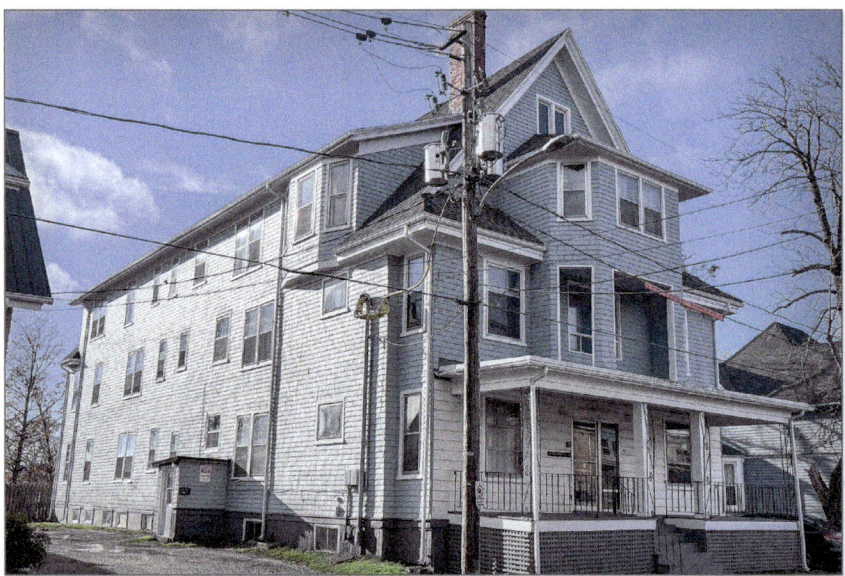

The church was later converted to the Ritz apartment on 55 Upper Prince Street. ■

Great George Street

Great George Street, runs from the harbour north through the heart of the City,
to Euston Street. It is intersected by Queens Square. Queens Square in bounded by Queen,
Grafton, Prince and Richmond Streets.

Some confusion can be expected when referencing older addresses. In 1970,
Upper Great George Street from the War Memorial to Euston, and then Elm Avenue and
the Malpeque Road were all renamed University Avenue. Recently, Great George Street
reclaimed its name to the portion from Grafton to Euston.

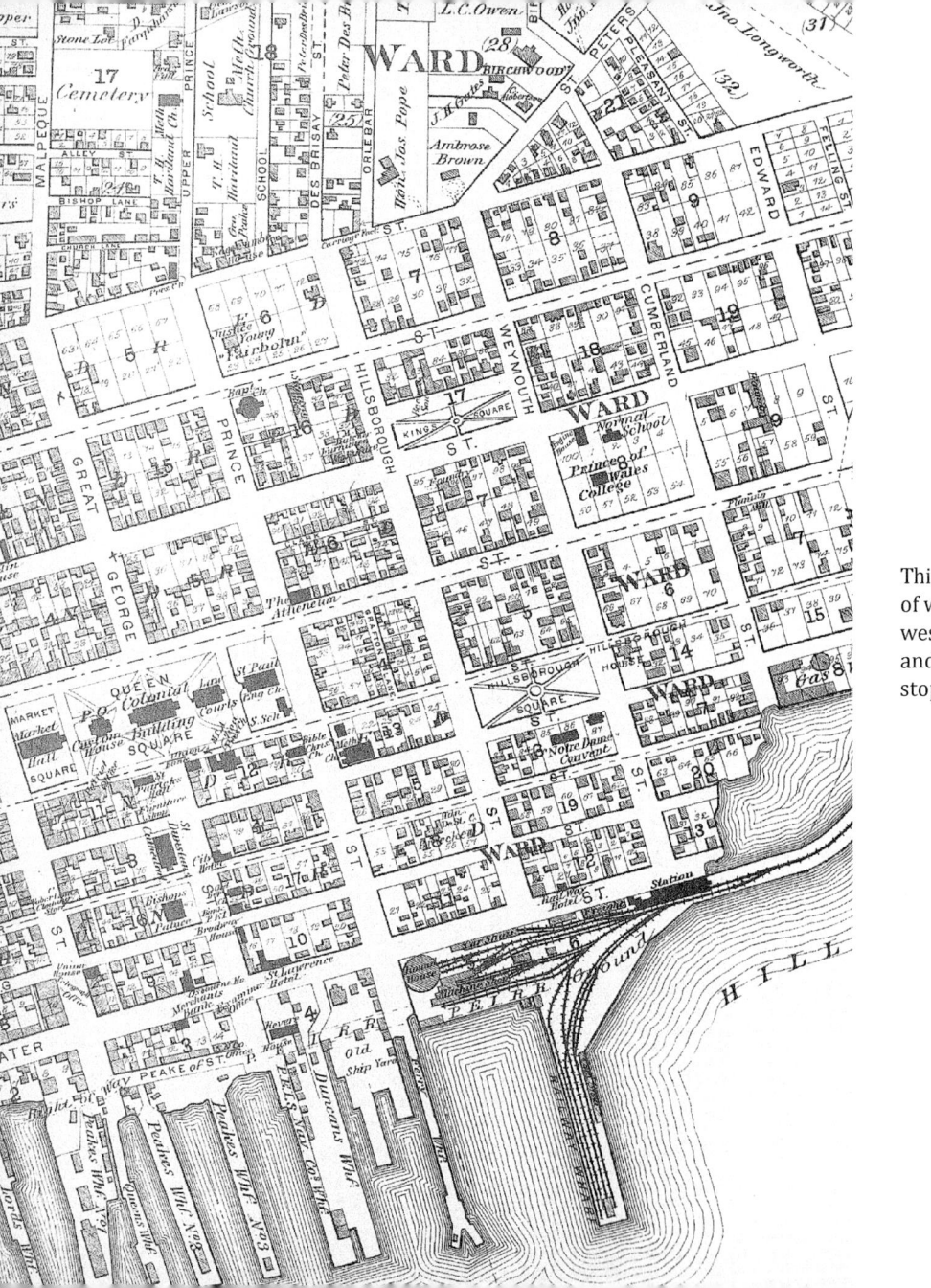

This map is from the 1880 Meachum & Co. Atlas. It shows the number of wharfs from Hillsborough Street to Pownal. Peake Street running west to east below Water Street was late named Lower Water Street and the rail line was extended along this area to Pownal Street, stopping behind Atlantic Wholesalers Limited. ■

Lower Water Street had lumber dealers like MacDonald - Rowe Woodworking Co. Ltd pictured here in April 1977. S. Albert MacDonald and William Rowe started this business in 1911. Previous to this is was Robert Palmer & Co. Sash and Door Factory listed at 36 Lower Water Street. The train track ran between these two buildings on the right. ▪

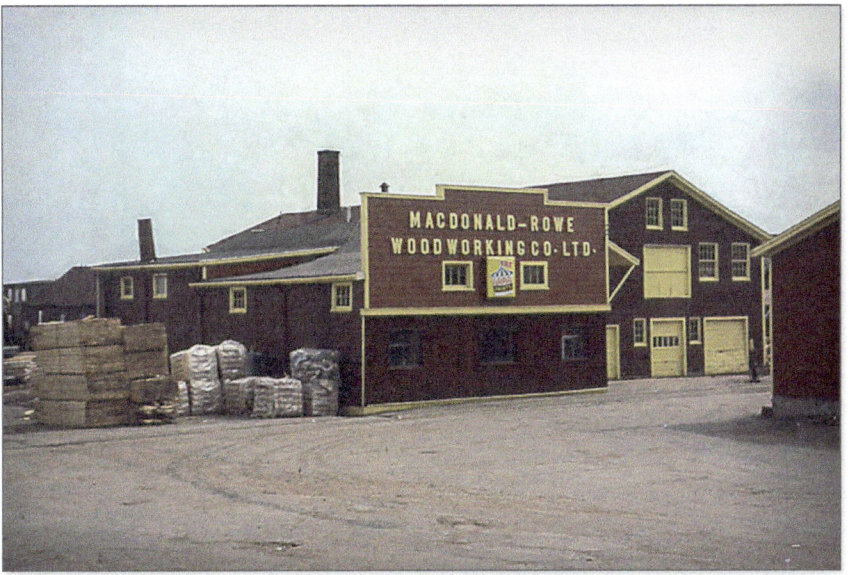

Bottom left, from August 1980 shows MacDonald - Rowe warehouse on Lower Great George Street.

This location present day it is the Island Beach Co. (bottom right). ▪

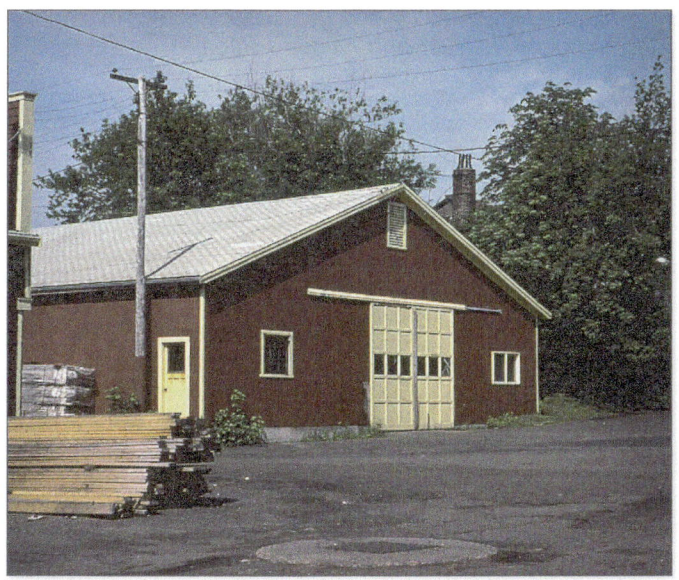

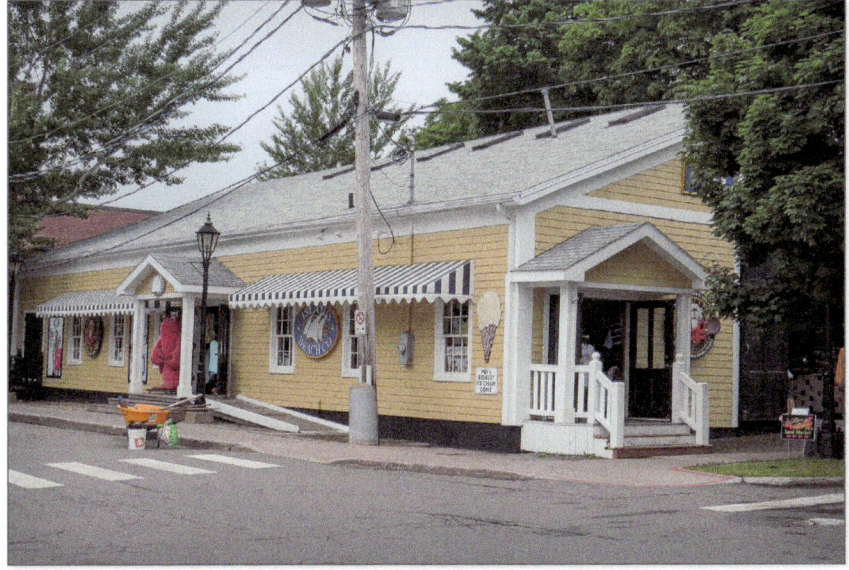

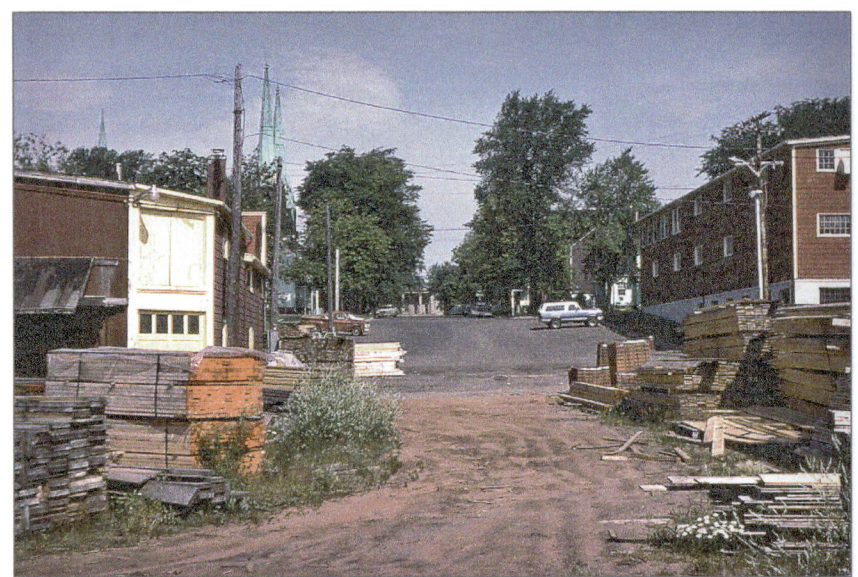

Looking north up Great George Street, August 1980. The spires of the Basilica stand out as well as Province House at the end of the pavement under the trees.

The building at the right is Associated Shippers, wholesalers in potatoes, with MacDonald - Rowe Woodworkers at the left.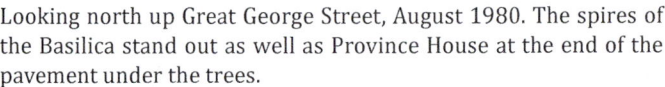

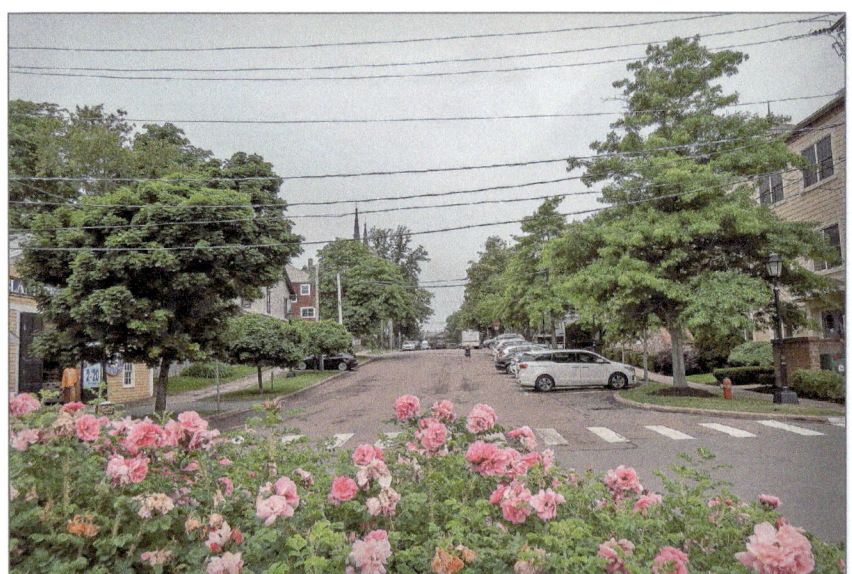

20 Great George Street: The July 2022 picture with the Gray Group building on the right. Until 2012, it was the law offices of Cox & Palmer, who located to the top floor of the former Dominion Building at 97 Queen Street. This building underwent extensive exterior renovations in 2023.

This picture from April 1977 shows Great George Street south of Water Street. At 6 Great George Street was Bruce Stewart & Co. Limited as well as Charlottetown Marine Industrial Limited. At the left edge of this picture is, today, the Gray Group building. At the right you catch a glimpse of the Texaco Tank farm with black tanker train car in the yard. Note the railway crossing sign, as the train ran along lower Water Street to Pownal Street.

Today this area is the Confederation Landing Park.

Bruce Stewart with Andrew McNair started Bruce Stewart & Co. in 1892. At its height they employed more than 50 men. The business closed in 1980. ▪

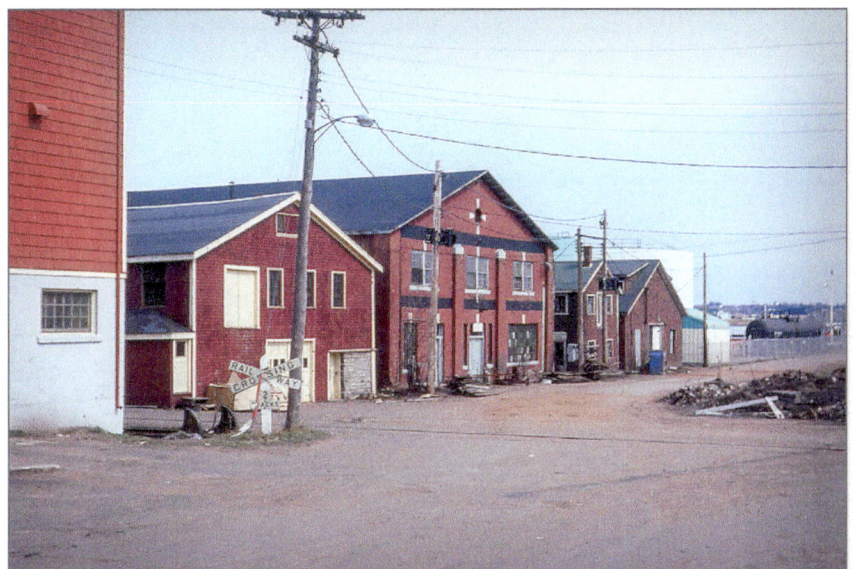

Looking southeast on the waterfront. The double roof building in the foreground is Peake's Quay at the foot of Great George Street. The Texaco storage tanks are being removed to make way for the Confederation Landing Park. The large warehouse on the pier is where cruise ships dock today and are welcomed to Charlottetown. ▪

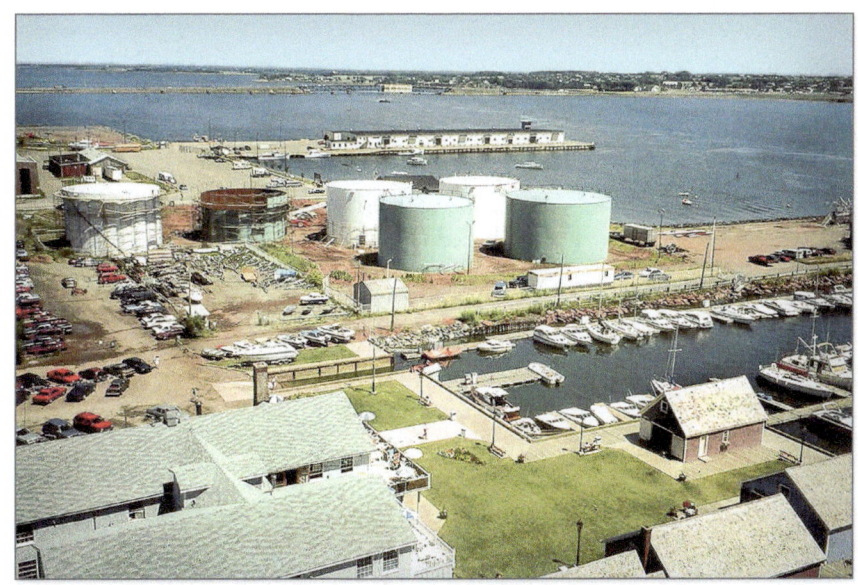

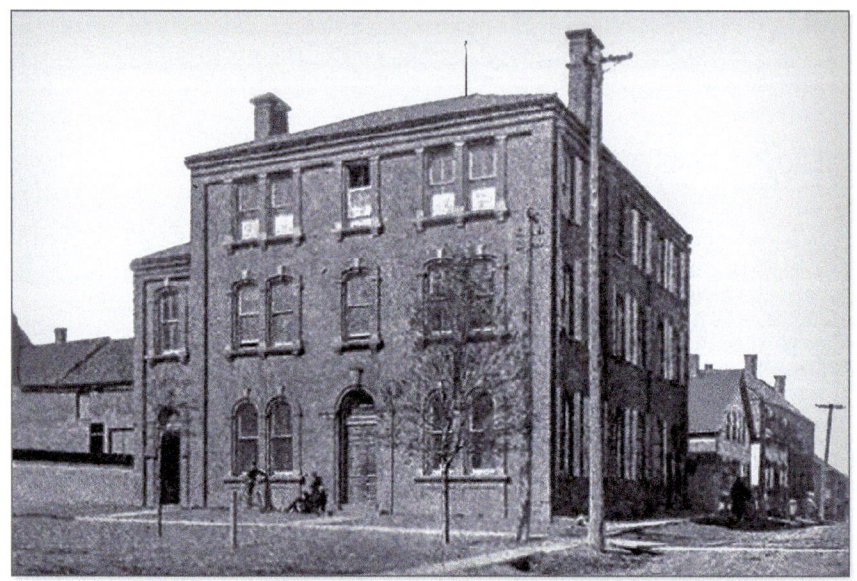

40 Great George Street at King Street: The Customs House.

The Bank of Prince Edward Island operated first on Grafton Street in 1856, moving to the James Peake Building (now Merchantman Pub) at the foot of Queen Street from 1858-1868. In July 1868 the bank moved in to their new premises at 40 Great George Street. Following Insolvency in 1882 the bank was acquired by the Bank of Nova Scotia. The building later housed the Merchants Bank of Prince Edward Island until it later was absorbed into the Canadian Bank of Commerce, now CIBC. This building was at one time a Post Office and later a Customs House.

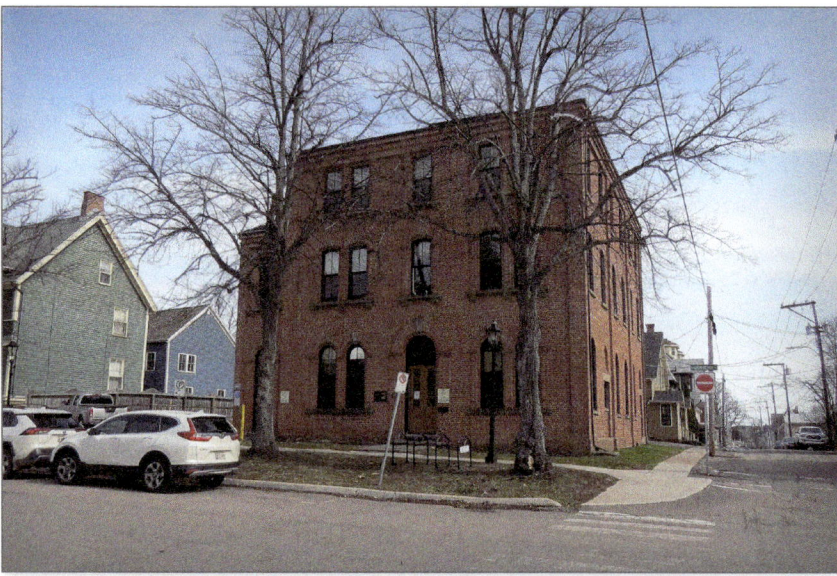

Lately at various times it held offices of Holland College and the Crown Prosecutor. Note the change in the size of the tree in front.

Started in 1872, the Episcopal Residence was first occupied in 1875 by Bishop Peter McIntyre. However, it was nine years later that the interior was done. In 1913, with the fire that destroyed St Dunstans Cathedral, it was felt opportune to add a section to the Bishops Residence, as the men and equipment were on site. The second of four Catholic churches on the site is shown in this picture. ■

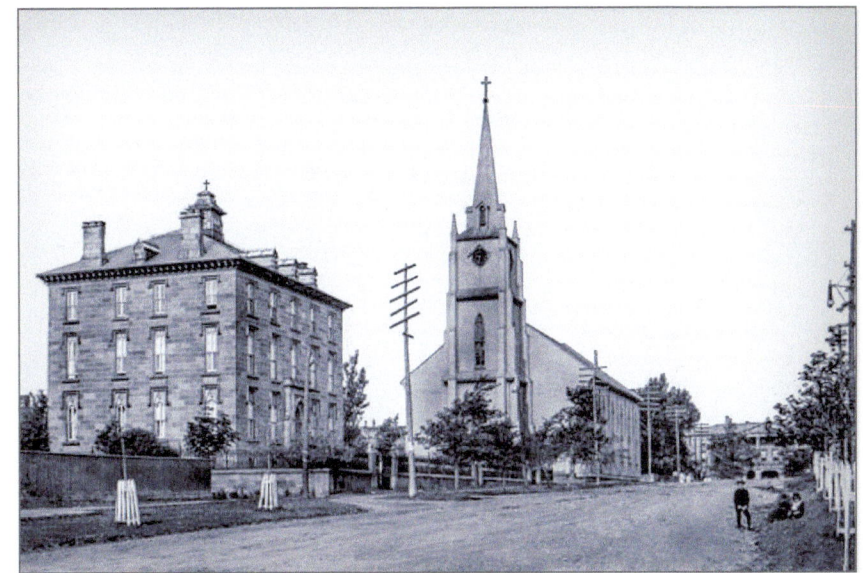

From August 2022 showing the new 1913 section on the west of the Episcopal Residence. The kitchen and staff dining were moved to this new wing from the basement. In 1920 balconies were added on the south side by Bishop Louis O'Leary. This building remained the Bishops Residence until 1964 when a new residence was built at 350 North River Road (now called Catholic Centre). The building on Great George Street was subsequently sold to St Dunstans University Board of Governors. This building was since renovated as apartments and meeting space. St Dunstans Basilica is shown to the right.

In all, there were four Catholic churches on the Great George Street block between Sydney and Richmond Streets, with the first built in 1815. A larger Wooden Church constructed on the site in 1843 was later moved in 1897 to make way for the stone Cathedral. Unfortunately, sixteen years later, the Cathedral was a total loss in a fire on March 8, 1913. The new St. Dunstans Basilica was started right away, opening in 1916 with its spires enhancing the City skyline. ■

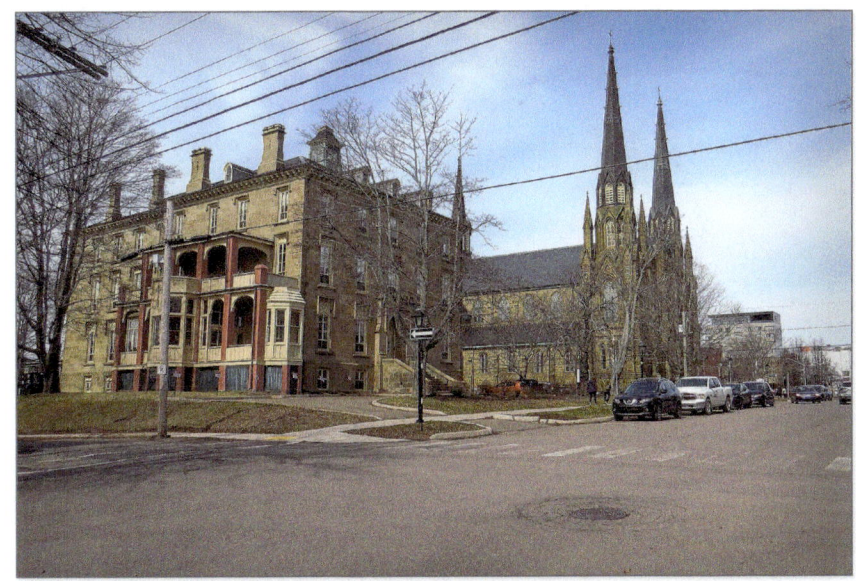

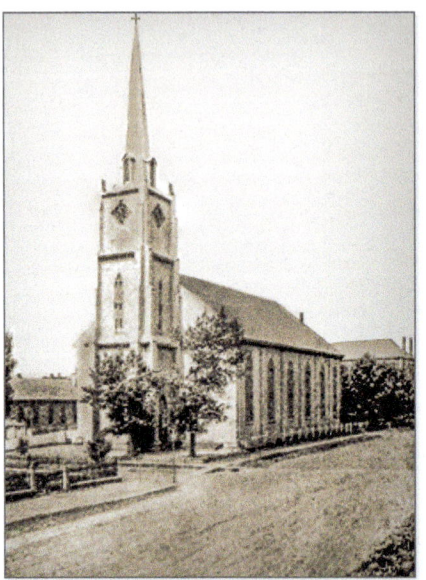

This photo from c.1870 shows the second church on the site. This church was moved on rollers to be placed across Great George Street. It was used for services until the new Cathedral was ready for worship. It was later used as a school until Queen Square School at the southwest corner of Richmond and Great George was completed. The building was then demolished. ▪

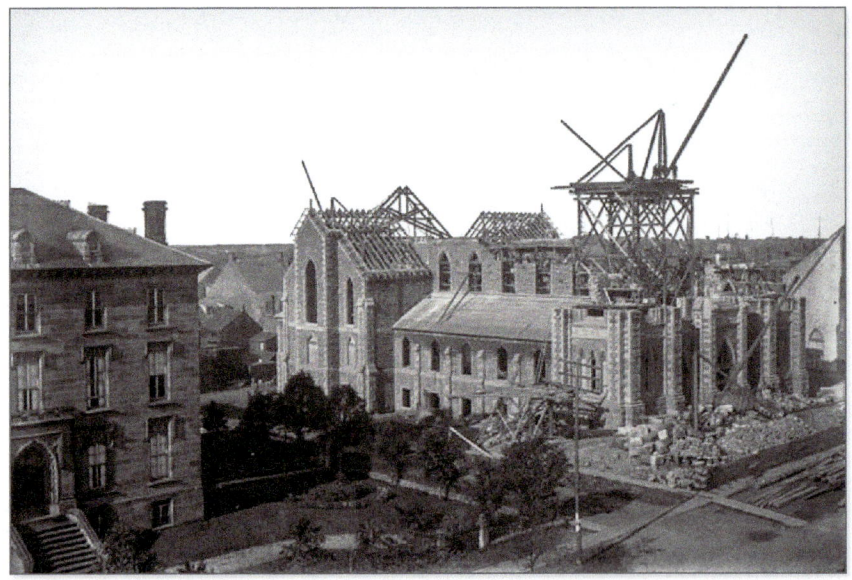

From October 1, 1897 showing the St Dunstans Cathedral under construction. ▪

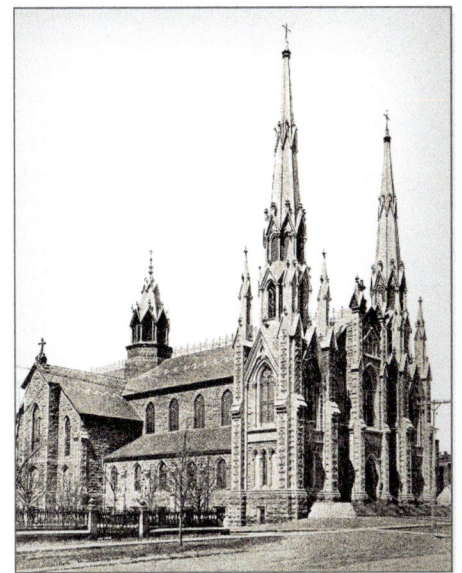

The completed Cathedral with picture taken in the early 1900's. This church was completely destroyed by fire on March 8, 1913. Work set about to construct a new church, using blocks salvaged from the Cathedral and lined with brick inside to strengthen the structure. ▪

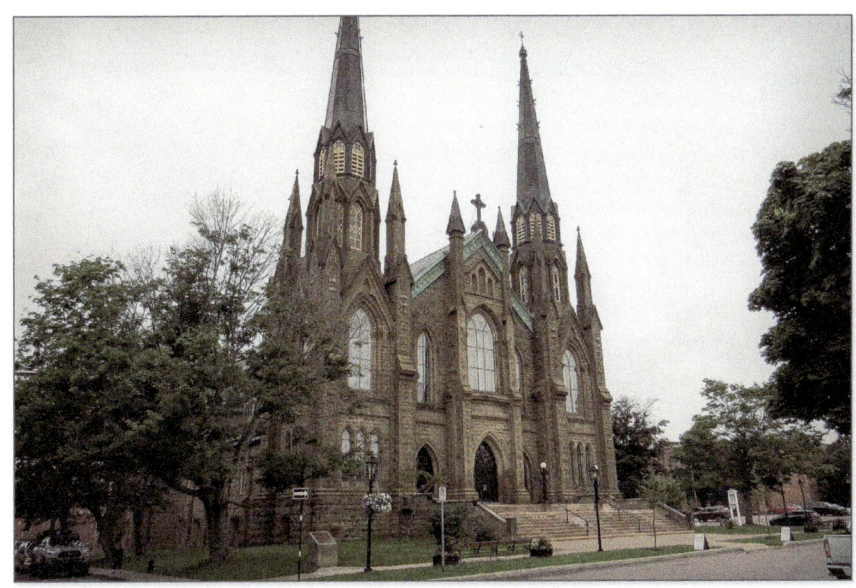

St. Dunstans Cathedral was completed in 1916 following the devastating fire of March 8, 1913. The Cathedral was designated St. Dunstans Basilica in 1929. The church is named after St. Dunstan the Anglo-Saxon saint from Glastonbury, England. This building was designated a National Historic Site of Canada in 1990.

The bells were recently refurbished and placed again in the towers after being stored for a long time. ▪

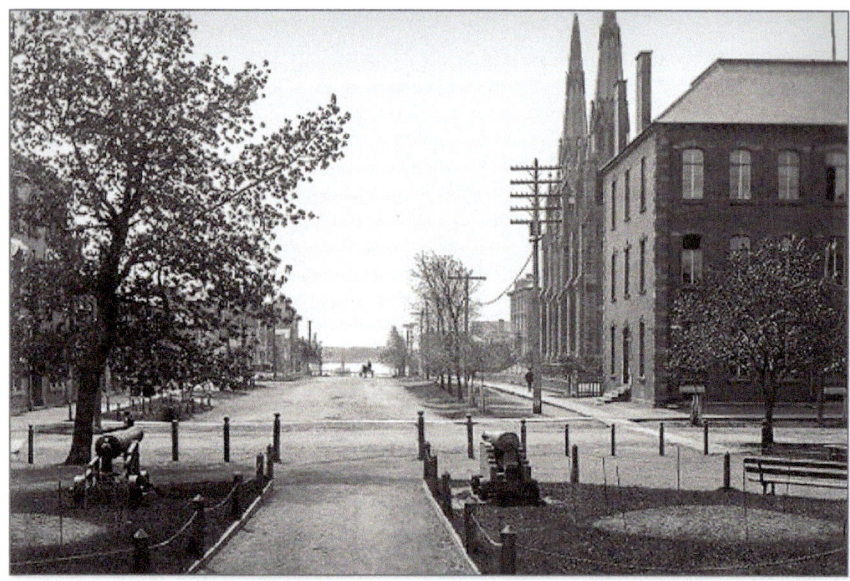

Looking south on Great George Street from Province House down to the harbour. This picture c.1900 has Queen Square School on the right at the southwest corner of Great George and Richmond. St. Dunstans Cathedral towers are shown.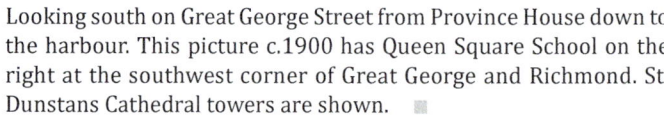

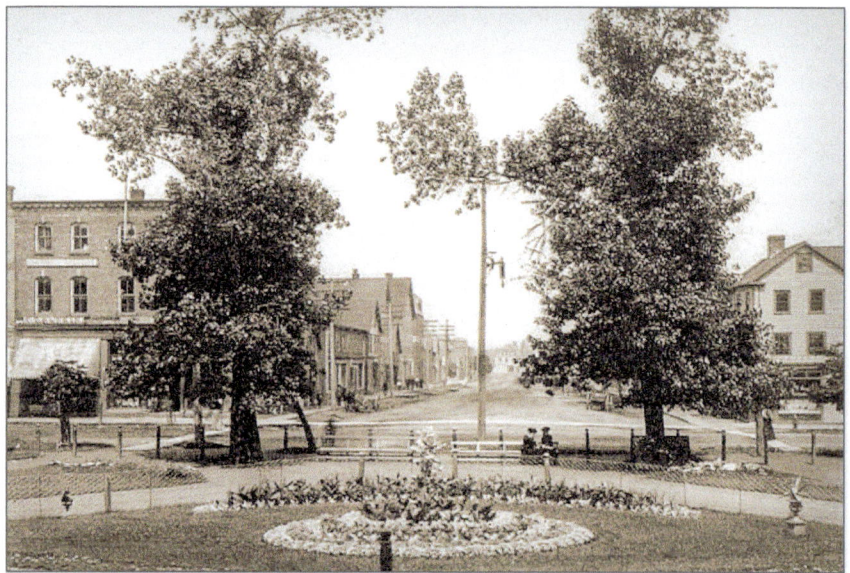

Looking north up Great George Street from Province House to Euston Street. The garden is on the north of Province House. In this picture c.1900, you will note there is no war memorial. Wooden sidewalks are shown by the buildings and across the streets. ▪

This photo taken from inside Province House in 1960 shows the War Memorial, with the Capital Theatre on the right and Bank of Nova Scotia on the left. At the end of Great George Street is Cudmore's Grocery on Euston Street.

The veterans memorial consisting of three seven foot four inch soldiers marching over uneven ground in single file, was designed by George William Hill of Montreal. This memorial, originally placed in 1923, recognized the dead from World War I and later, World War II and the Korean War were added. The bronze statues are placed on eleven tons of granite, with a total cost of the project at $16,000.

Note: a cenotaph usually lists the names of the dead whereas a war memorial lists the wars, and recognises those buried elsewhere. ▪

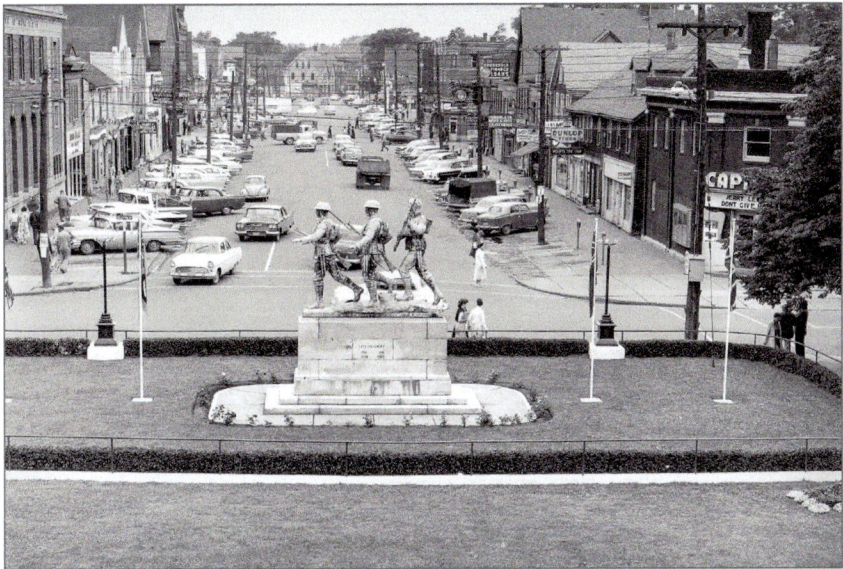

From 1964, the picture shows the east side of Great George street from Grafton to Kent and beyond. The yellow sign is for Dows Men's Wear, now located across the street. ▪

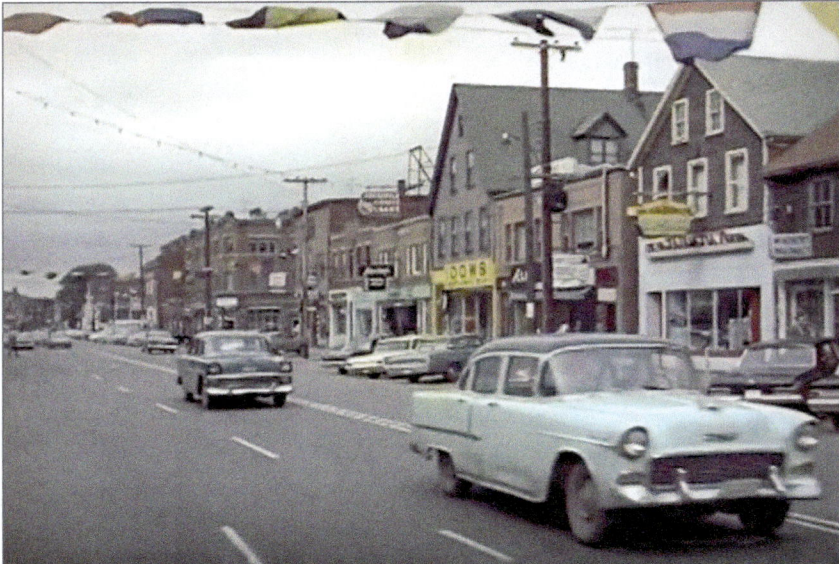

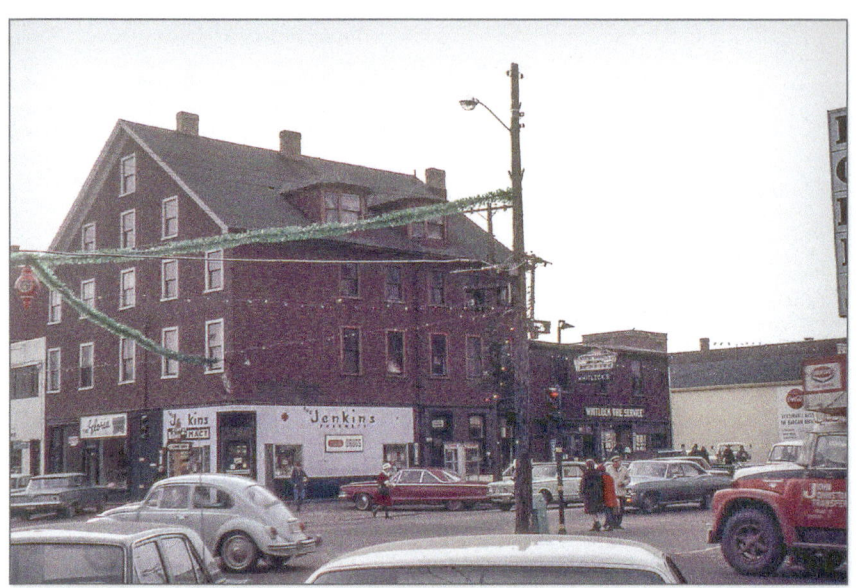

The intersection of Great George and Kent Streets had the following building at this corner over time:

Southwest corner: 159 Great George Street was Jenkins Pharmacy from 1939. Ralph Jenkins operated a pharmacy here until 1970. Partial sign at the far right is for Lords Supervalue Pharmacy.

155 Great George Street was Gloria Ladies Wear, which relocated here after the fire on Grafton Street in August 1955.

Beside the Jenkins Pharmacy to the right at 138 Kent Street was Whitlock Tire Service (J. Edgar Whitlock). They used to change tires between the sidewalk and the street. Right of Whitlock Tire was the parking lot and back entrance to R. T. Holmans.

Note the phone booth by the red car. ■

The new two-story building was constructed at 151 Great George Street, and now contains offices. ■

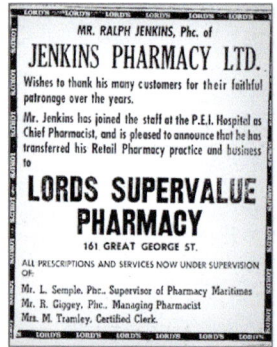

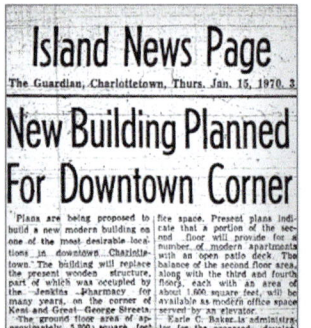

Island News Page

The Guardian, Charlottetown, Thurs. Jan. 15, 1970. 3

New Building Planned For Downtown Corner

In 1970, Ralph Jenkins became chief pharmacist at the P. E. I. Hospital and he transferred his business to Lord's Supervalue Pharmacy across Kent Street. ■

Following the closing of Jenkins Pharmacy, it was announced on January 15, 1970 that a new four-story building would be constructed on the site. ■

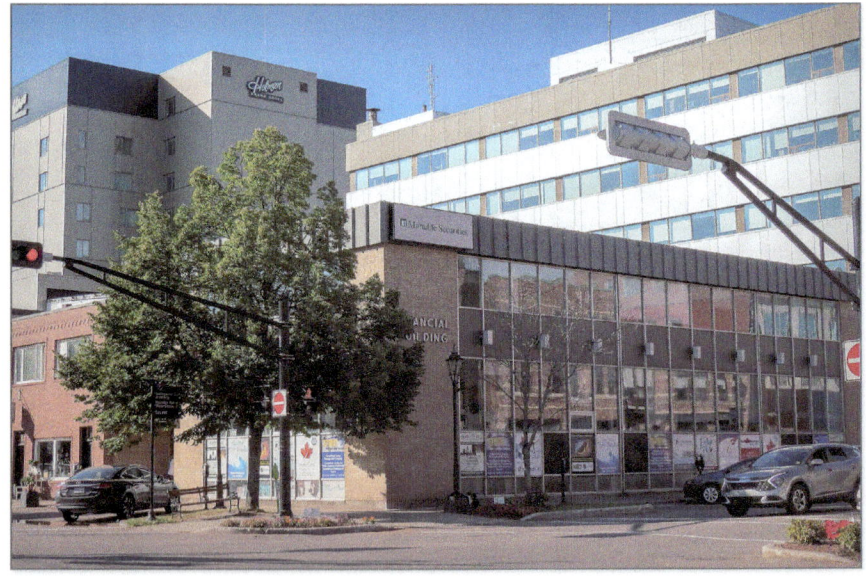

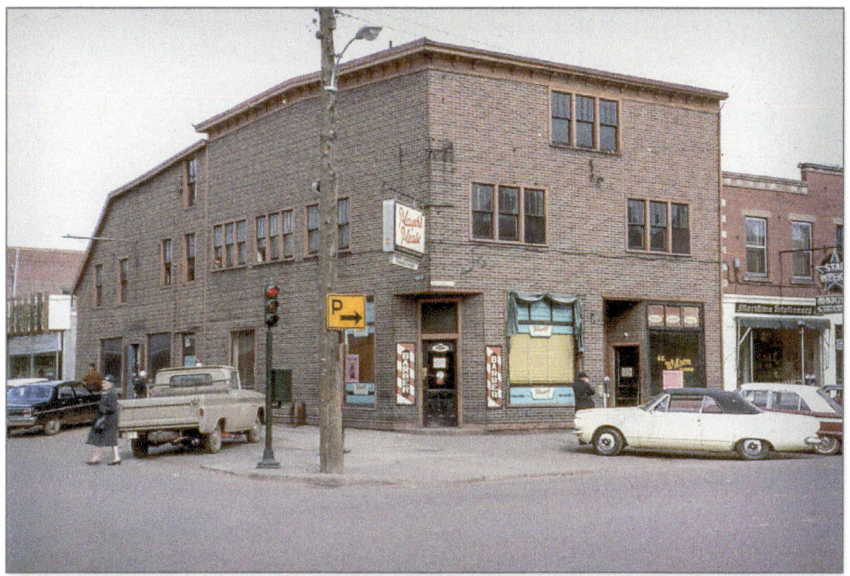

Southeast corner: 158 Great George Street, Fred Lambrose Tobacconist was located here in 1965. The building was demolished and replaced by a new brick building by Dan Tweel. To the left of Lambrose's was the Simpson-Sear catalogue order office at 156 Kent Street. To the right is Maritime Stationers at 154 Great George Street. Note the overhanging sign "Star Weekly". The Star Weekly was published from 1910 to 1973. ■

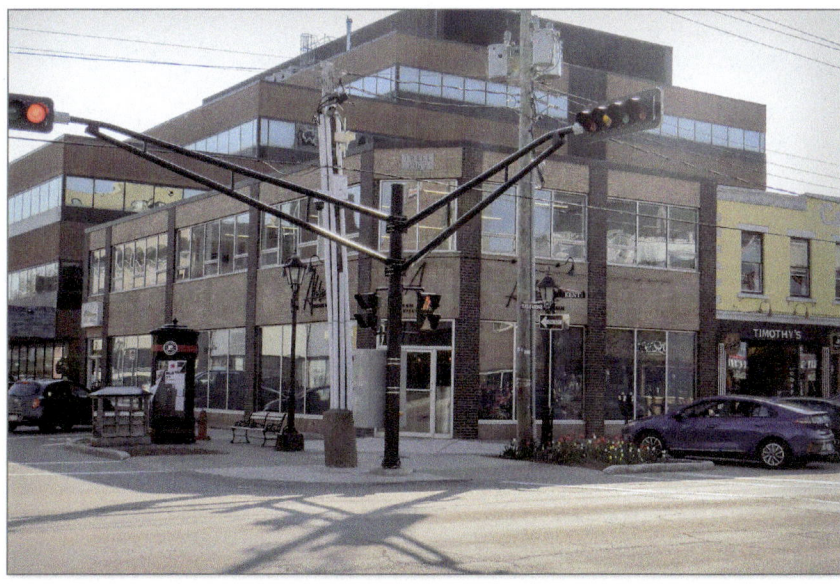

Tweel was famous for placing a date engraved in stone on the face at the top of his buildings (this one 1965). In 2013, Citi Financial was located in the ground floor with corner door. Recently in 2022 it is an art gallery and gift shop. DVA is prominent in the background, running through the block from Grafton to Kent Street.

Note the change in size of the traffic lights at this corner. ■

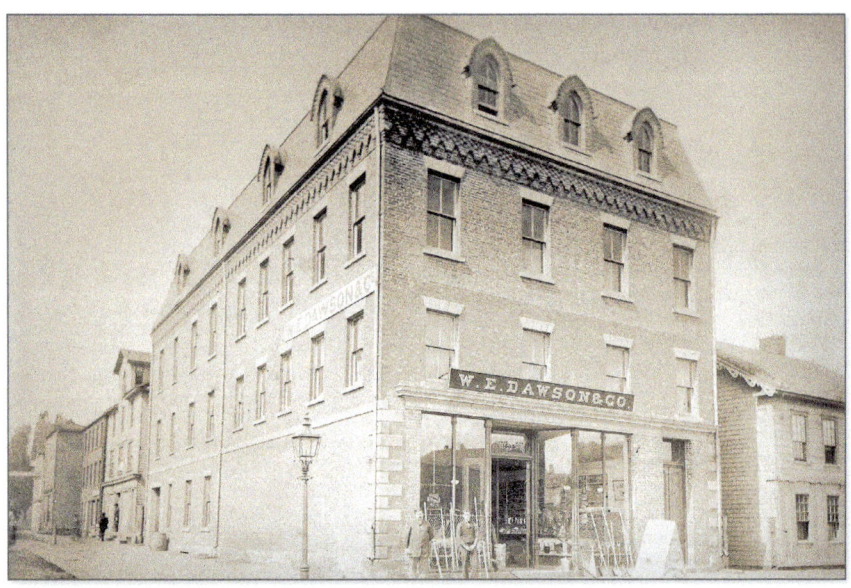

Northwest corner: 161 Great George Street. Originally W. E. Dawson Hardware operated here from 1861 to 1901. William Eddison Dawson (b. 1829 - d. 1902) was twice mayor of Charlottetown from 1878 to 1882 and from 1893 to 1897. Stanley Shaw and Peardon, Hardware, then operated out of this building from 1903 to 1952. ■

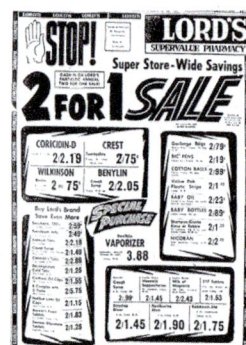

The building in June 1966 was vacant, having been New Way Furniture and Lord's Supervalue Pharmacy. The ad for Lord's Supervalue Pharmacy is from the Guardian, January 1970. ■

This building at 161 Great George Street was home to Sam the Record Man shown in this picture from 1983. ▶

The metal siding was removed in 2014 by the current owner, Chris Tweel, and restored to its original beauty from over 150 years ago. McInnes Cooper law offices now occupy a portion of this building. ▼

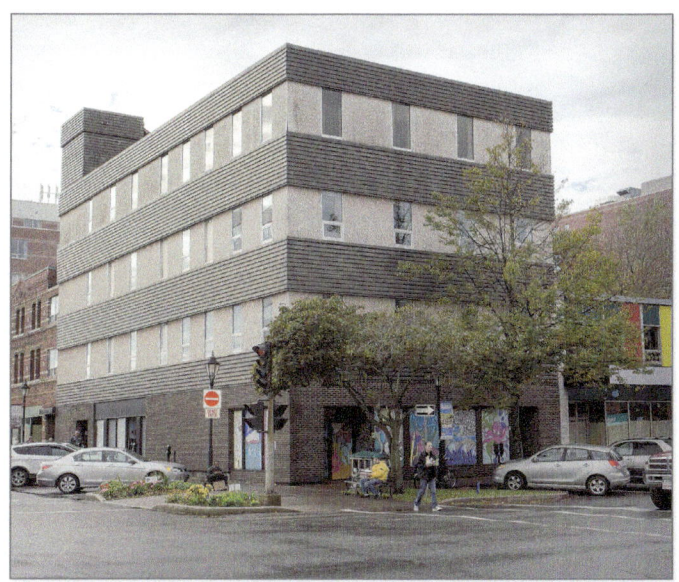

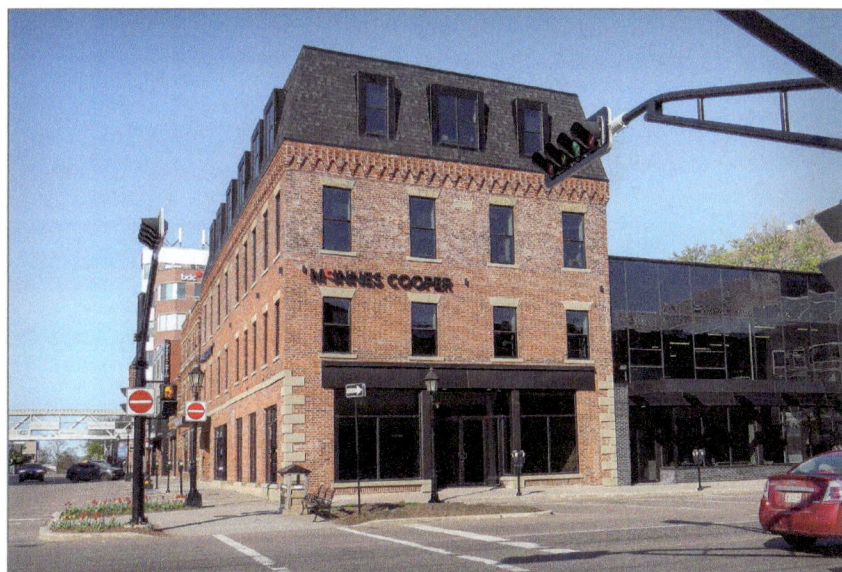

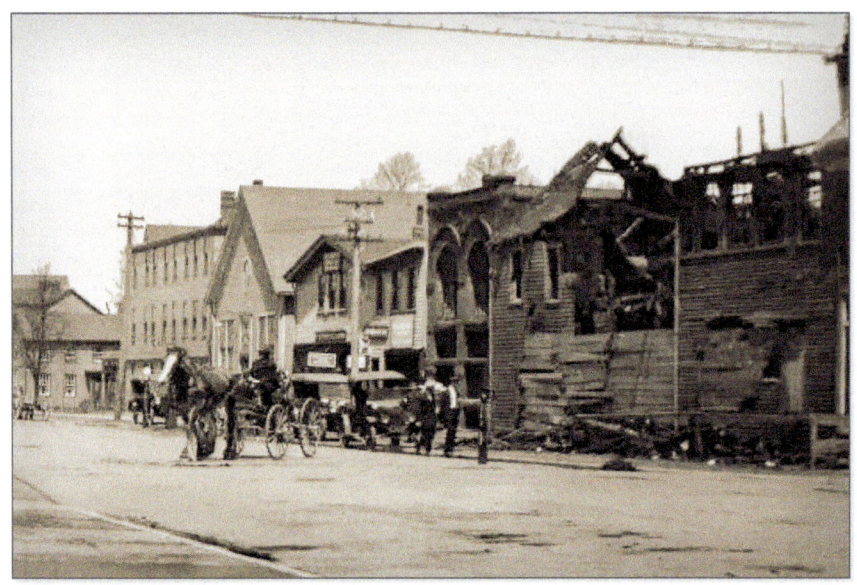

Northeast corner: 160 Great George Street containing the Guardian office was burned in a total loss on April 28, 1923. The Guardian relocated to the Athenaeum building on the northeast corner of Prince and Grafton. Also lost in the fire was the uptown branch of the Anglo-American Telegraph Company.

The high-pitched roof building above the horse and wagon is the former Salvation Army Corp. This building was here from 1890 to 1971. ▪

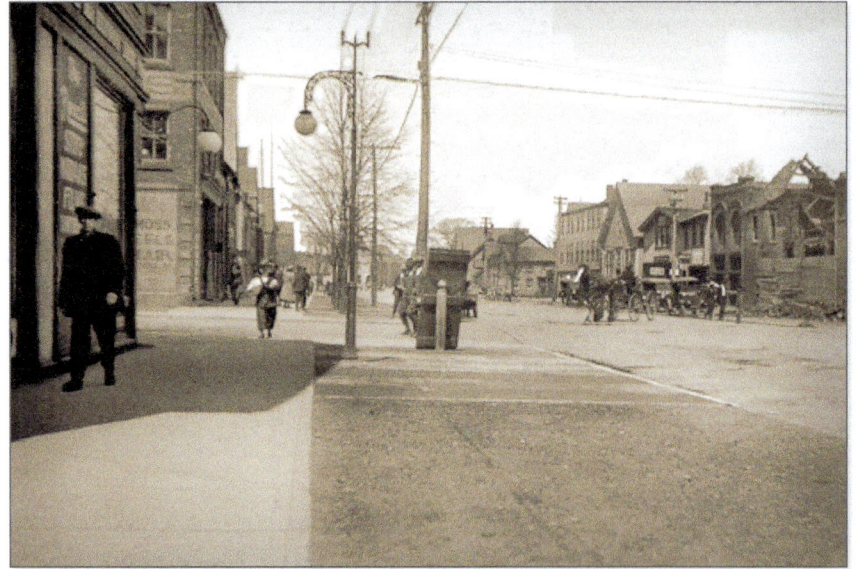

Shown here, following the fire in 1923, looking north. This first intersection on the left is where Kent Street crosses Great George, with the brick building on the left being Stanley, Shaw and Peardon. Across the street the remnants of the fire with a completely different block of building than what is there now. Ford Model T's and horse and carriages shared the road at that time. Cr: City of Charlottetown Archives: Francis P. Hennessey and Stella M. Mullen Collection. ▪

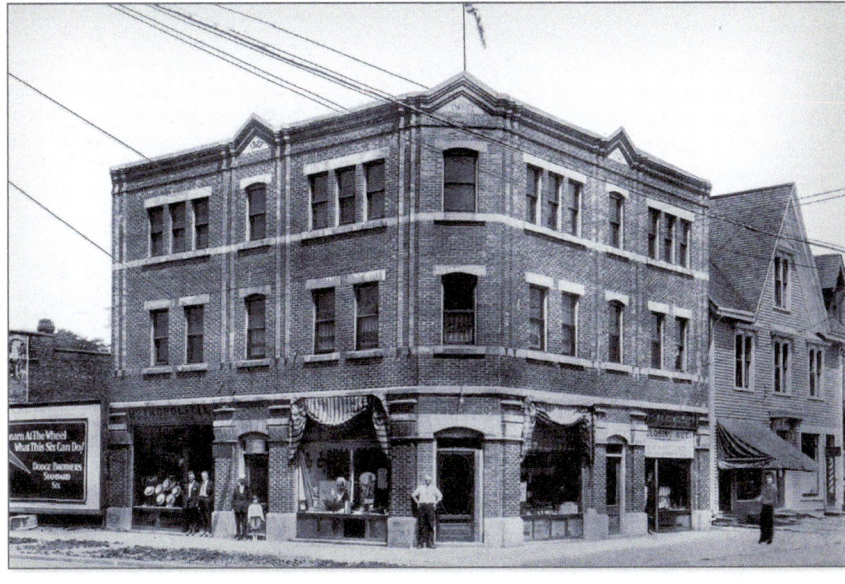

Following the fire this corner lot was bought by Nemir Tweel. He built a brick, three story building in 1927. (this picture from 1930). Many may remember the long-time corner tenant as Tweel's Gift Shop. ▪

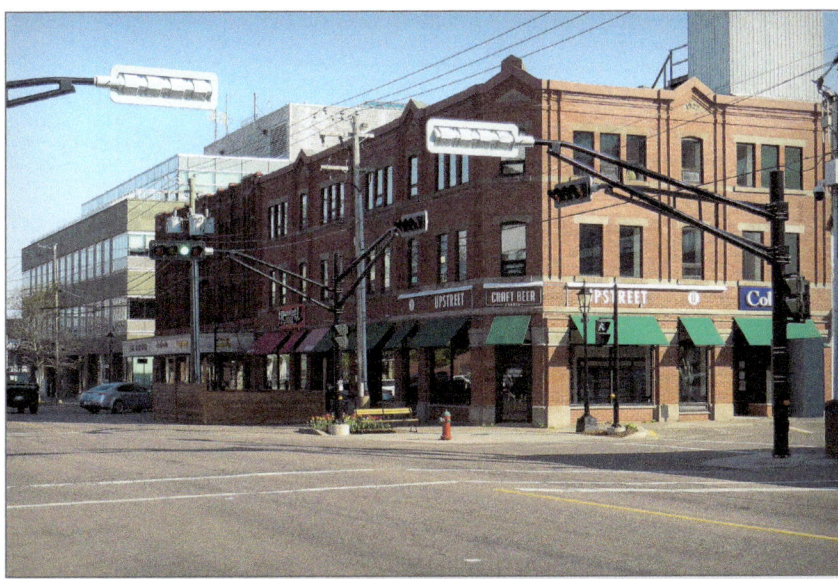

This corner was recently a Starbucks, but it is now the home of Upstreet Craft Beer. ▪

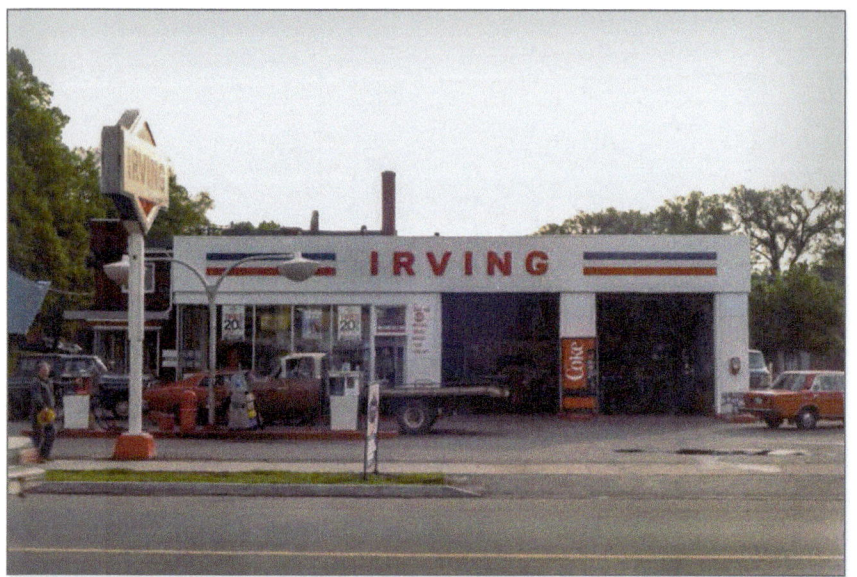

The southeast corner of Great George and Fitzroy was home to the Salvation Army building in 1886. They had bought the Free Church building located at the head of Prince Street (on Euston) and moved it to this new location. The building was renovated and lighted with electricity. On October 3, 1890, the Salvation Army laid a cornerstone for a new building on this site. In December 1966 the Salvation Army moved to their present location at 158 Fitzroy on the southeast corner of Prince Street. The now abandoned church was crushed under the weight of snow on January 5, 1971.

Following this, the site on Great George Street was a service Station and subsequently demolished to make was for the Atlantic Technology Centre.

This Irving Service Station was on the corner of Fitzroy and Great George in 1983. It was common in those days to have a service bay or two, as most mechanics could fix anything on a car, from installing and balancing tires to minor engine repairs. ▪

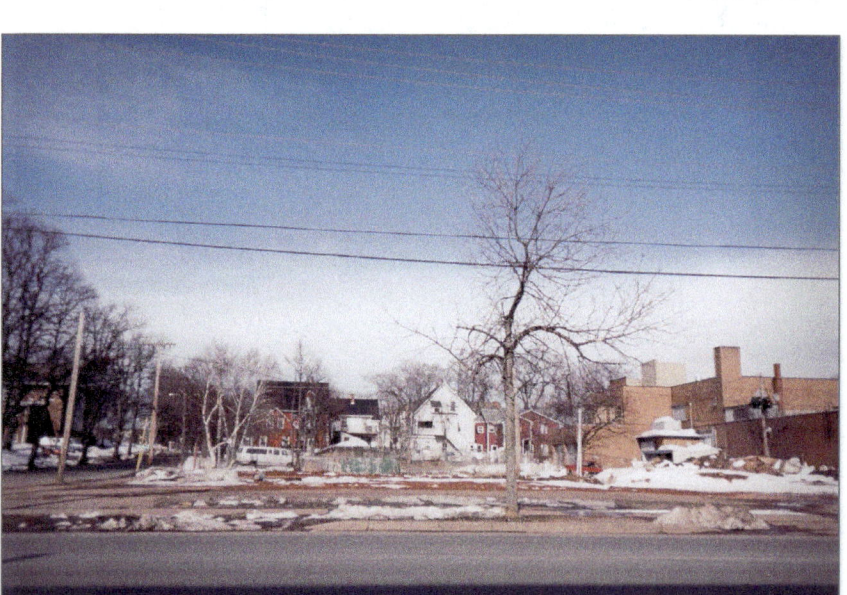

Following demolition of the service station, and in this photo, you may recognize the large brick building on the upper right as the back of Eaton's Department Store on Kent Street. Eaton's was removed for construction of the Fitzroy Parkade, built in 2001. While running right through the block, the Parkade opened unto Fitzroy Street. It was designed to accommodate 508 vehicles. A small section was added to the Kent Street side in 2020.

The brick building at the left, through the trees, is First Baptist Church on Prince Street. ▪

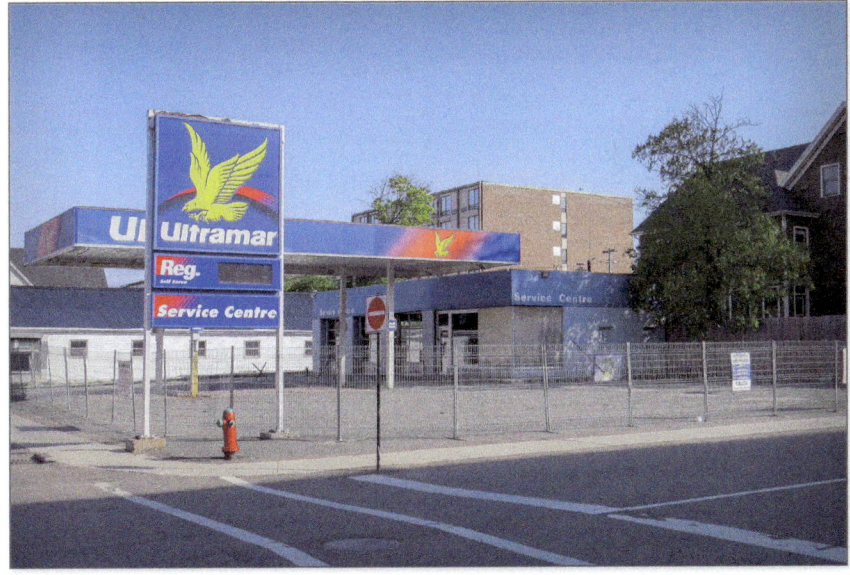

176 Great George Street is now the site of the Atlantic Technology Centre. The centre was officially opened on September 8, 2002. The Provincial Archives and Records Office (PARO) is now located in the lower level of this building. ▧

The northeast corner of Great George and Fitzroy holds one of the last two service stations below Euston Street in Charlottetown. (the other at the southwest corner of Euston and Weymouth Streets) This one closed recently for retail sales. The building was demolished in September 2023. Recently used for parking, it was fenced for security purposes. ▧

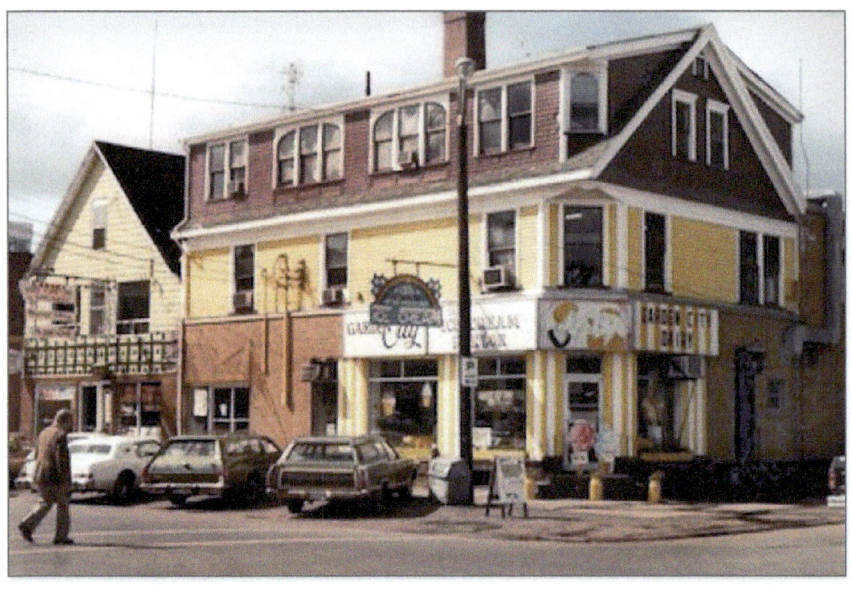

Garden City Dairy, at 189 Great George Street originally advertised at the Pure Milk Company in 1927, served ice cream at the front counter. It was located on the southwest corner of Great George and Fitzroy.

An ad in the Guardian of 1927 said "The City is supplying us with Pure Water. The Garden City Dairy has the Pure Milk". ■

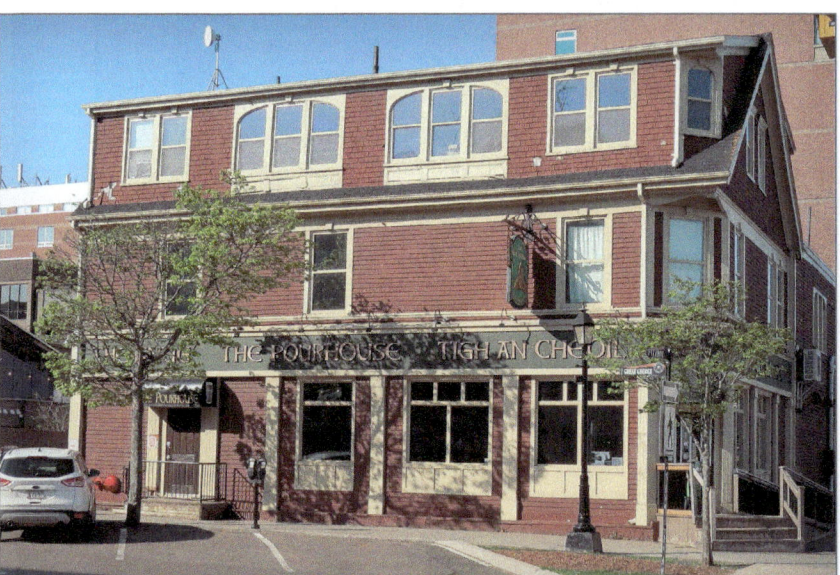

This corner location is now The PourHouse, offering pub style dining and live music. The brick building right is the Financial Tower on Fitzroy Street. The brick building background left is BDC Place, facing Kent Street, part of the Confederation Court Mall complex. ■

This picture of this site looking south from Euston Street shows the vacant lot where Bobby Taylor's Esso Service Station was located on the corner of Great George. The blue building was offices of Coldwell Banker Parker Realty. Other businesses on this block were The Flower Cart, Island Petroleum, Island Coastal Services Ltd. and Proud & Moreside Blacksmith & Welding.

The high brick building center right is BDC Place, part of the Confederation Court complex. ■

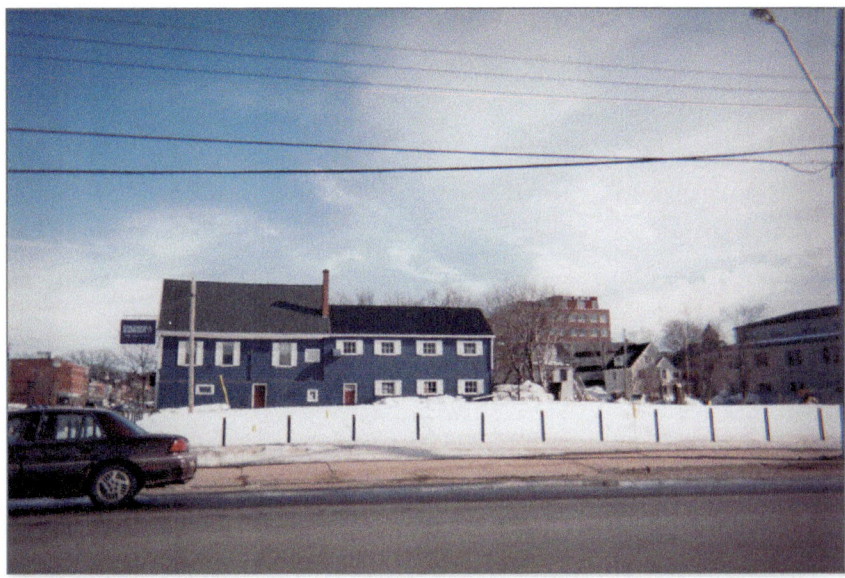

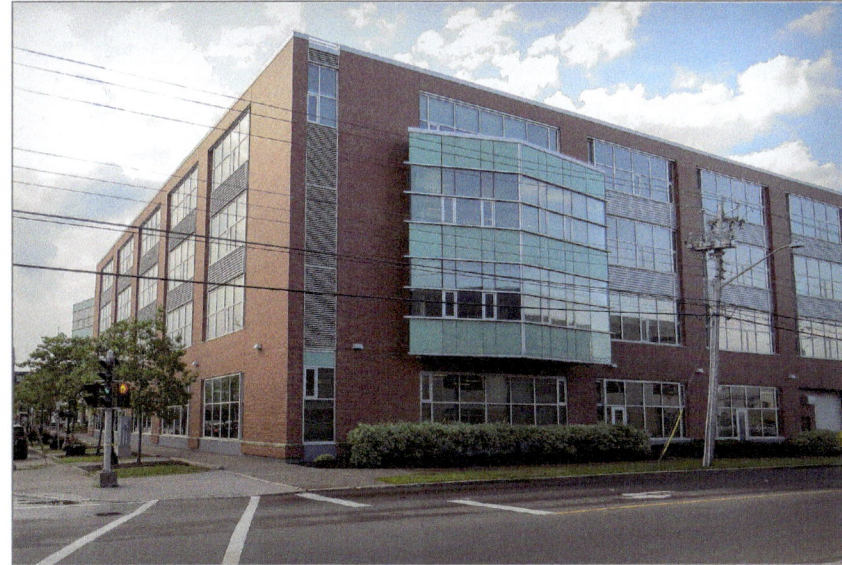

The Jean Canfield Building was constructed in 2003 on the west side of Great George between Fitzroy and Euston Streets. It holds federal government office including DVA and Employment Insurance. ■

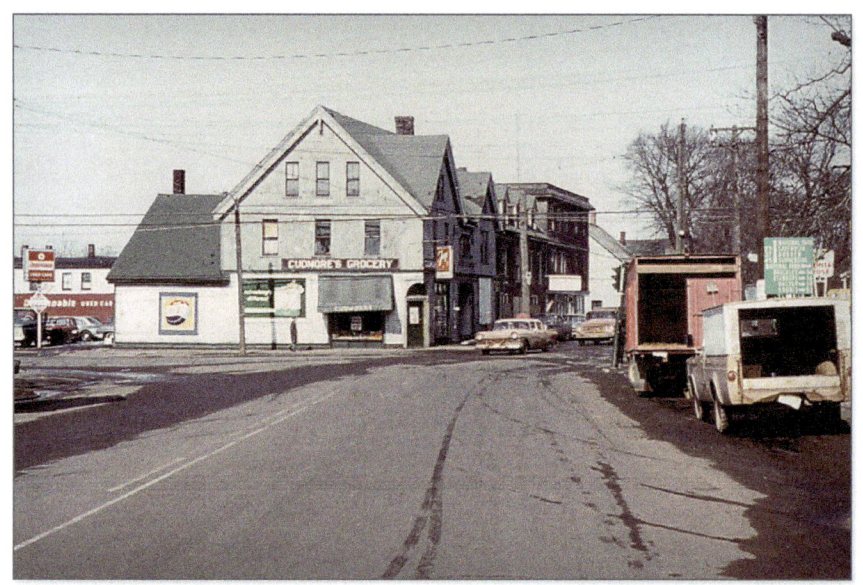

Looking north on Great George Street from Fitzroy Street in this 1966 photo, is Cudmore's Grocery (W. J. Cudmore). Previously it was L. C. Worthy, Grocer and Baker. (sometimes knows as Worthy's Corner). In 1899 it was W. Pickard Co. grocers.

The green sign far right has an arrow pointing up Elm Avenue (now called University Avenue) stating: 25 - Cavendish; 37 - Borden; 45 - Summerside. National Park (arrow pointing right): Brackley - 14; Stanhope - 16; Dalvay - 18 and Souris - 52. (all distances in miles)

Just right of this sign is the White Rose sign on the northeast corner of Euston and Elm Avenue. This was Walter MacDonald's Service Station. This site was later the Sea Treat Restaurant, changed to Prince Edward Restaurant in 2013. It was recently Asia Republic, and since listed for sale. ▪

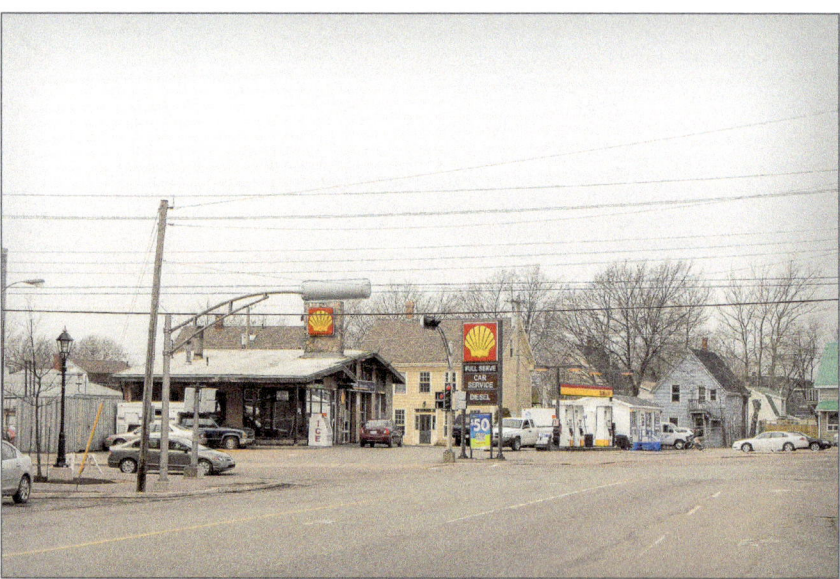

Cudmore's Grocery location was later a Shell Service Station, shown in this picture from 2013. This station was demolished on September 26, 2014. ▪

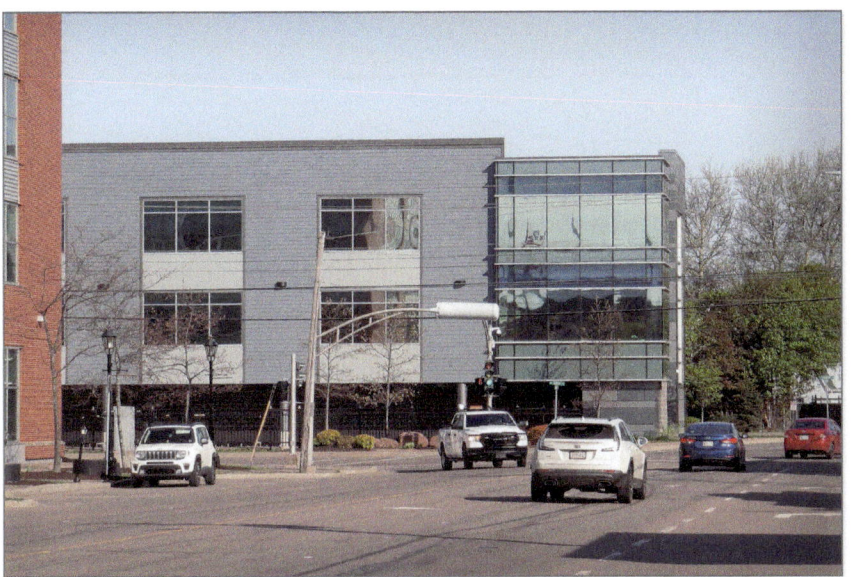

This corner location is a new extension to the Invesco Building on Euston Street. This extension was added in 2014.

Water Street

Water Street starts at Haviland Street in the West and extends through to the Hillsborough Bridge intersection of Grafton Street. Originally Water Street stopped just after Weymouth Street, by the train station. (see map at start of book)

This photo of the far west end of Water Street, taken in 1893. The structure at the far right was built in 1890 as a three-tenement building. It was designed by renowned architect William Chitchlow Harris. *

This building is call Dundas Terrace after the former Dundas Esplanade. (see map in book introduction)

Moving left/east along Water Street is 8-10 Water Street. This house was constructed in 1860s by Benjamin Davies, father of Sir Louis Henry Davies. (see below)

20 Water Street: William Bourke built this house in 1871. Prominent features on this house is the mansard roof with dormer windows.

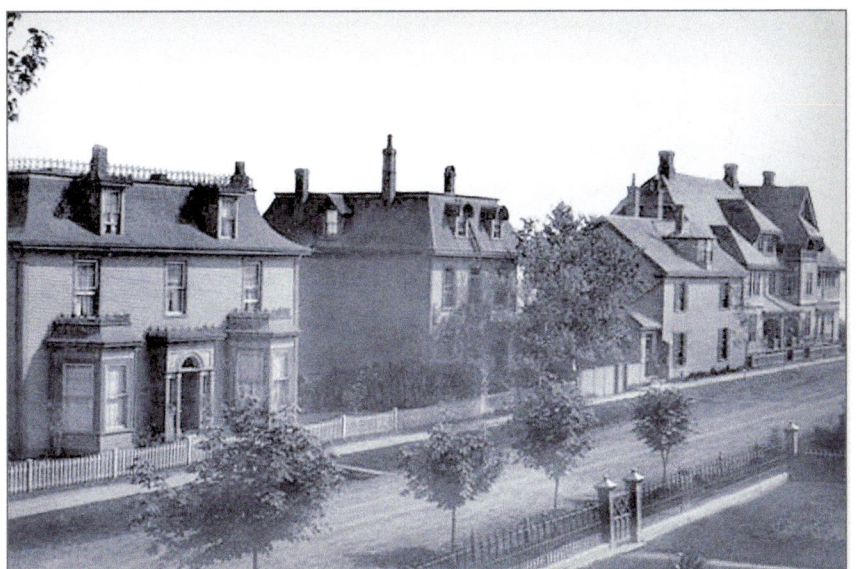

The current picture, taken April 2022, shows the same block of Water Street, with the new Sail Apartments building, on the left at the southwest corner of Water and Pownal, completed in 2020.

To the right of this new building is a white house at 24 Water Street. It was built in 1883 as a warehouse, and converted to an apartment in 1925. The roof treatment and small balcony highlight the efforts to showcase this renovation.

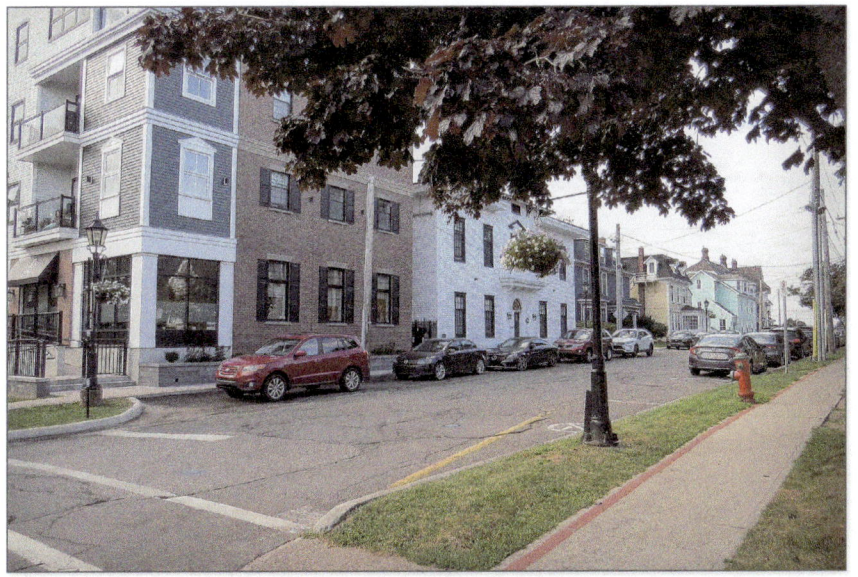

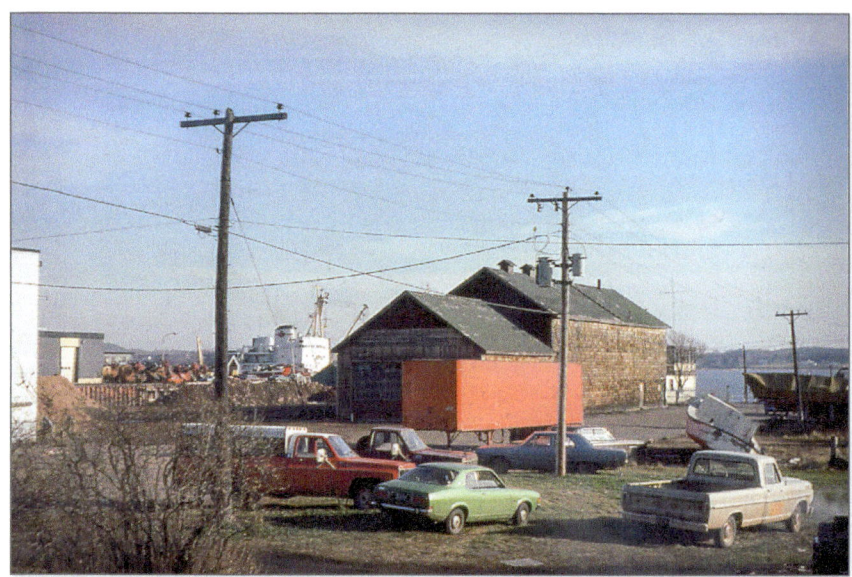

Taken November 1976 looking southeast on Lower Pownal Street.

The edge of the white building on the left is Atlantic Wholesalers Eastern Ltd. Note the railway spurs at the end of the building, where the train tracks on Lower Water Street ended.

In the centre is the government garage, with the white building behind and to the right being the Charlottetown Yacht Club. The club was established in 1922, with the building dating from 1938.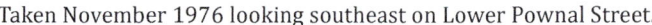

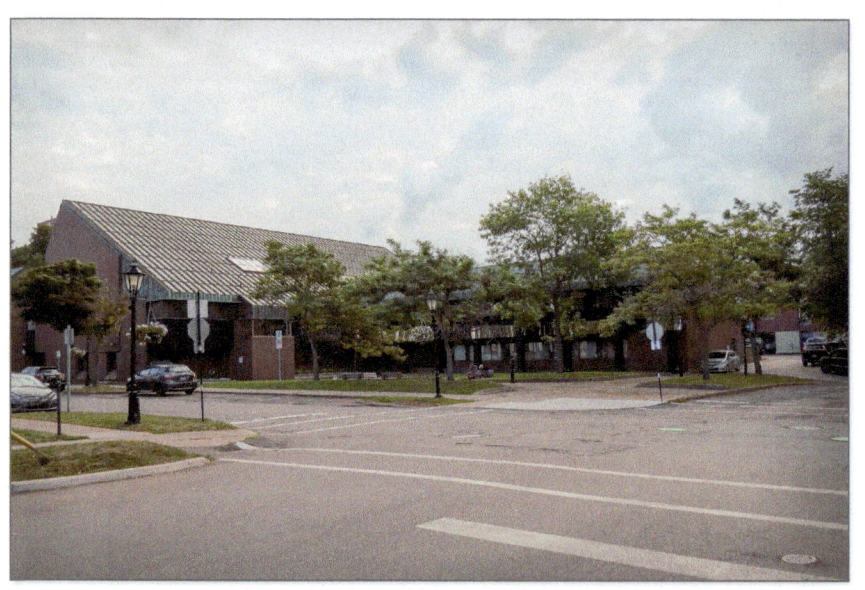

The Sir Louis Henry Davies Law Courts building is on the southeast corner of Water and Pownal Streets. Sir Louis Henry Davies (1845 - 1924) was the third premier of Prince Edward Island from 1876 to 1879. He was knighted by Queen Victoria in 1897. Sir Louis Davies was appointed to the Supreme Court of Canada in 1901, the only Island appointee, and was Chief Justice from 1918 to 1924.

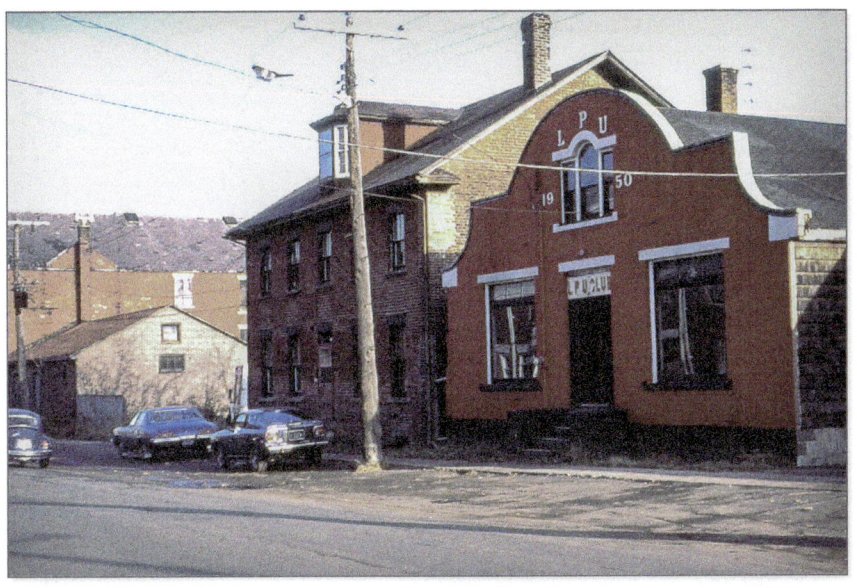

The LPU Hall (Labourers Protective Union) at 48 Water Street togetherer with Atlantic Wholesalers at the southeast corner of Water and Pownal were removed to make way for the Law Courts building.

The building to the left, with rounded dormer windows, is still there today. ▤

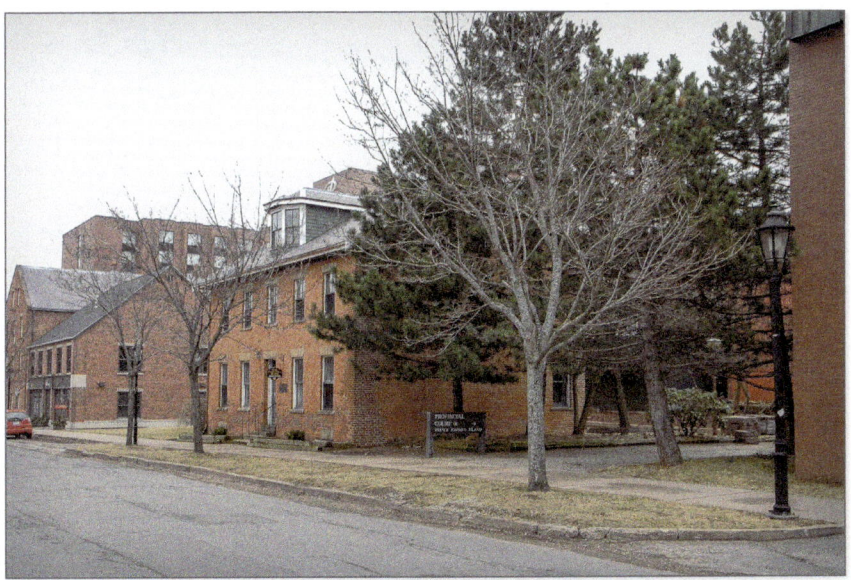

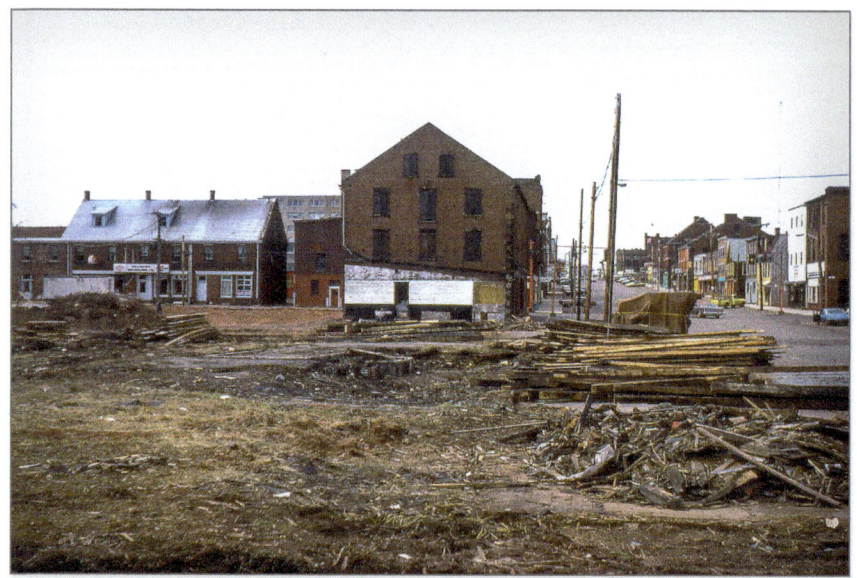

This interesting picture, from April 1977, is looking north up Queen Street from Lower Queen (across from the entrance to present day Delta). The south facing wall of the former Carvel Brothers building, now Merchantman Fresh Seafood & Oyster Bar is all that remains of this block. The white roof building with the two dormer windows, constructed in 1861, is Seaman's Beverage at 57 Water Street. Rundell Seaman was the local bottlers for Pepsi Cola, operating here from 1939 to 1988, before moving the West Royalty Industrial Park. This building was later the law offices of MacNutt and Dumont.

This picture is also in the Queen Street section of this book because of it's relevance on both streets. ▪

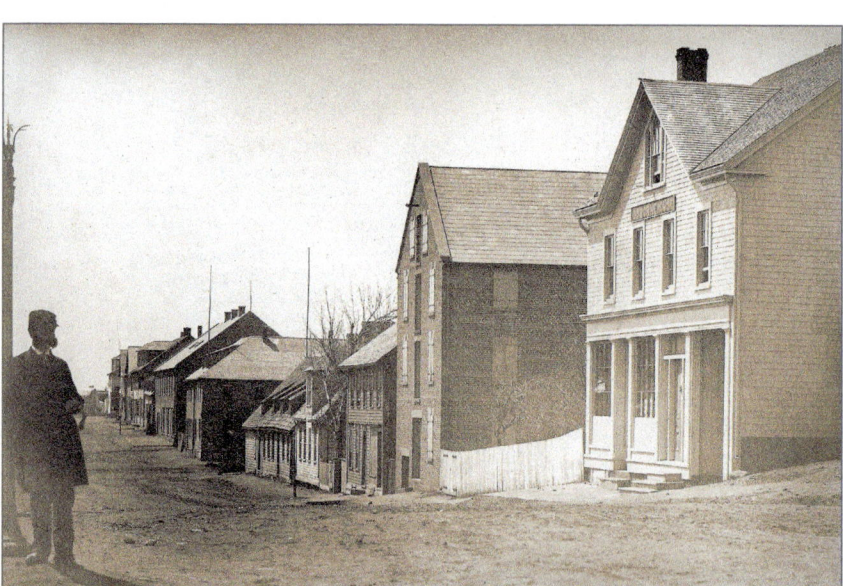

Looking west on Water Street from Great George Street, this picture was taken in 1866 before the Great Fire of July 15, 1866. On the right is Osbourne House, with the 3 1/2 story brick bonded warehouse built c.1860 next. These two building were the only remaining buildings on the north side of Water between Great George and Queen after the fire. ▪

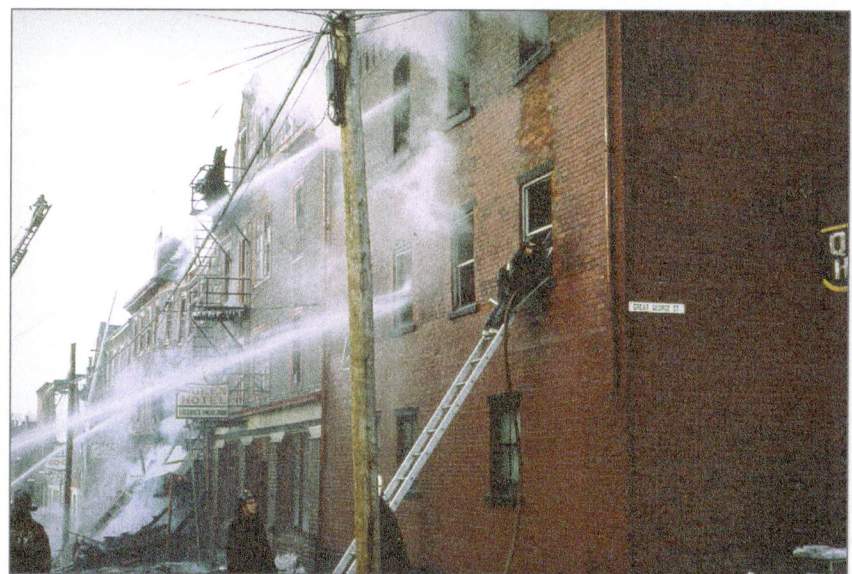

Looking east from in front of the bounded warehouse showing the Queen Hotel, with the edge of the Victoria Hotel across Great George Street on the right. ◼

89-103 Water Street: On January 13, 1965, the Queen Hotel on the corner of Water and Great George Streets was destroyed by fire. The Patriot newspaper of the day reported: "All 7 guests and lone staff escaped." ◼

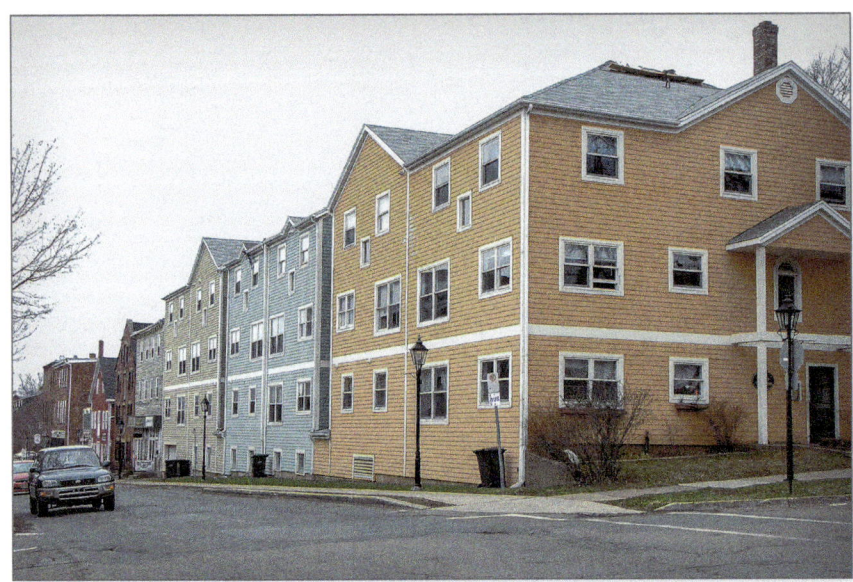

The Gateway Co-operative, at 21 Great George Street It was Charlottetown's largest housing co-op at the time of construction with 28 units, and underground parking. Picture from 2013.

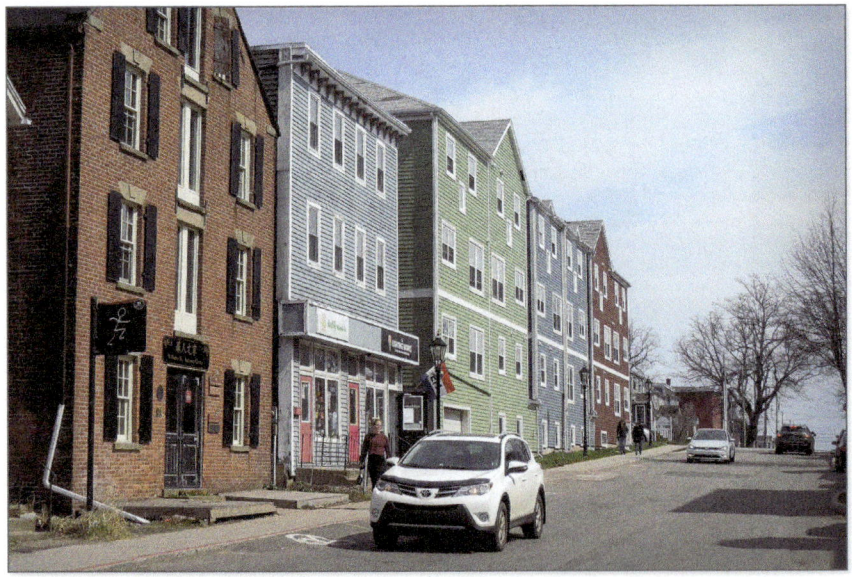

Looking east on Water Street in 2022, the c.1860 bonded warehouse is now offices, with the Gateway Co-operative sporting new colors.

Water Street was the point of entry for Charlottetown in the early years. The boats and then the trains arrived in the city along the waterfront. There were many hotels located in this area to cater to this traffic. Hotels on or near Water Street were the Revere House at lower Great George Street which operated from 1870 to 1890, the Queen Hotel at 89 - 103 Water Street that was destroyed in a fire on January 13, 1965, and Osborne House at 61 - 63 Water Street are examples. The largest of these the Victoria Hotel was advertised in 1843 as: "Having attached Stables and Coach House."

The Hotel Davies, pictured here, was located on the north side of Water Street between Great George and Prince. It was opened on December 15, 1887. ▪

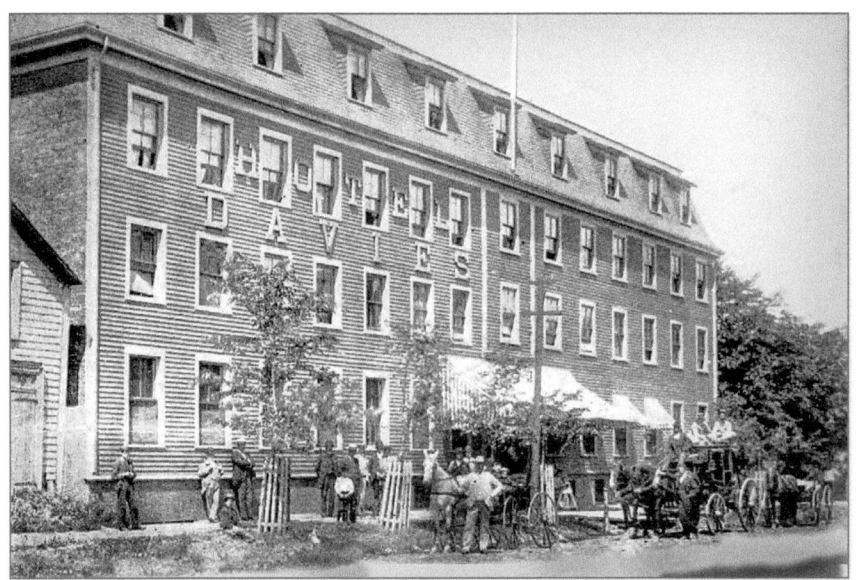

The Victoria Hotel was constructed on the northeast corner of Water and Great George and was joined and took over the Hotel Davies seen in this picture from 1908. It was advertised as having 120 rooms, 66 with private baths. Their large dining room was well received.

The Victoria Hotel was lost in a fire on January 12, 1929. Almost immediately work began on the new $200,000 C. N. R. Hotel at the northeast corner of Kent and Pownal Streets. This hotel was opened on April 15, 1931. The curved ceiling of the C.N.R. Hotel lobby was designed to look like a train concourse. This is now known as the Rodd Charlottetown Hotel.

The building that was demolished for this new hotel on Kent Street, was originally constructed as a house by Lieutenant Governor Robert Hodgson while he was in that position from 1874 - 1879. It was later bought by the Roman Catholic Episcopal Corporation in 1923, and occupied by the Knights of Columbus. ▪

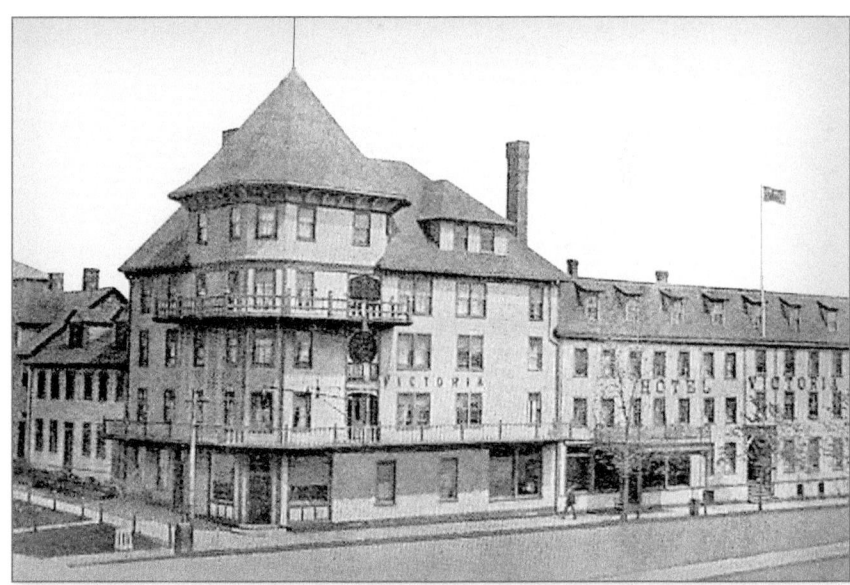

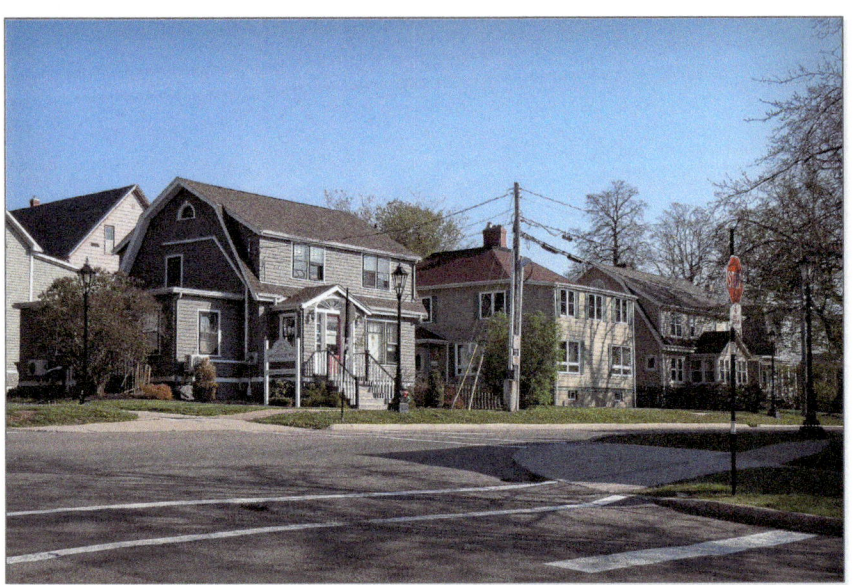

◄ 119 Water Street: This picture from 2022 shows Hospice PEI on the corner of Water and Great George. It was formerly Revolution Media, with residential properties down the block to the east. ■

▼ A building on this corner dates from 1859. The Water Prince Corner Shop at 139 Prince Street is now a tourist and local destination for fine seafood. But in 1900 it was quite a different look, operating as one of the many corner grocery stores in the city. These pictures also in the Prince Street section of this book. c.1900 picture: Smith-Alley Collection PARO. ■

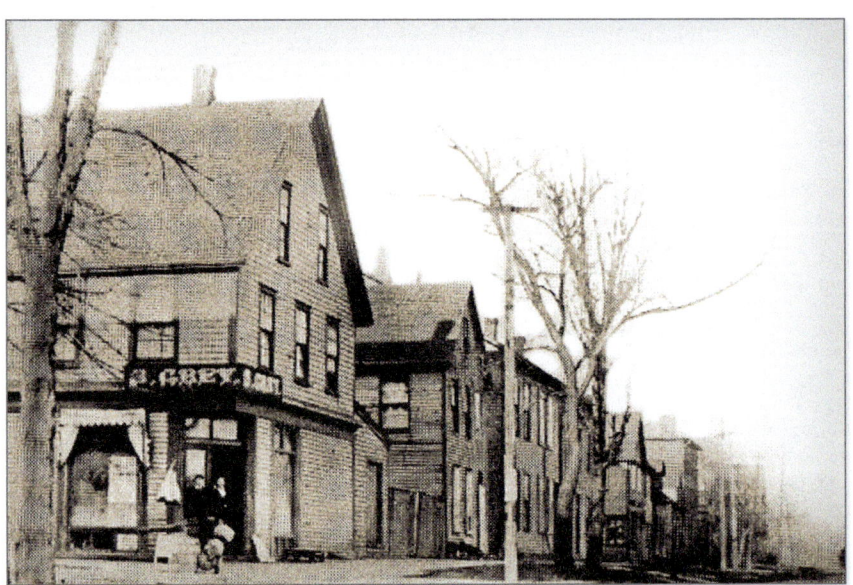

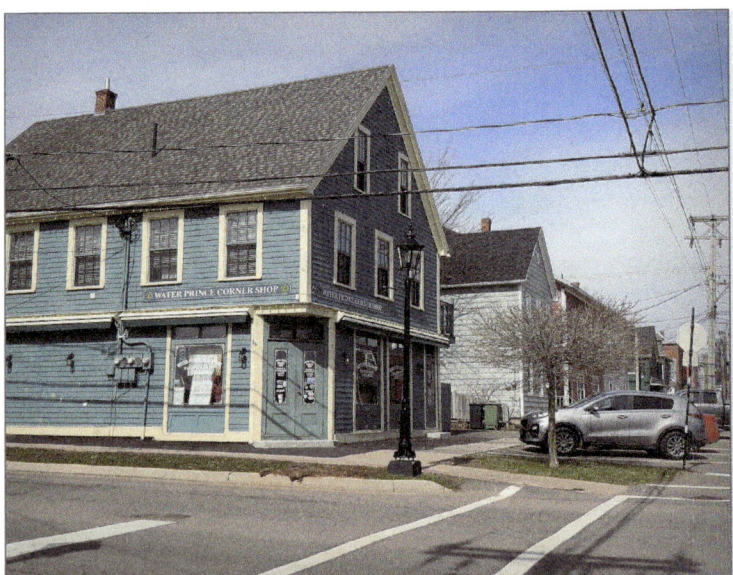

This picture from 1932, shows the roundhouse (train repair building) on the northeast corner of Prince and Water Street. Trinity United Church is shown in the center upper portion of this picture. At the far left upper middle and moving right we can identify: Cabot Building, Province House and the Cole Building. Below the Coles Building with the peaked roof is the former Zion Presbyterian Church, then names Holy Name Hall, following its sale to the Roman Catholic Episcopal Corporation in 1913. This hall was later removed for construction of the Basilica Recreation Centre.

The building immediately below and seemingly attached to the round house is still there today. It is the Visitor Information Centre. Cr: Charlottetown Fire Department. ▶

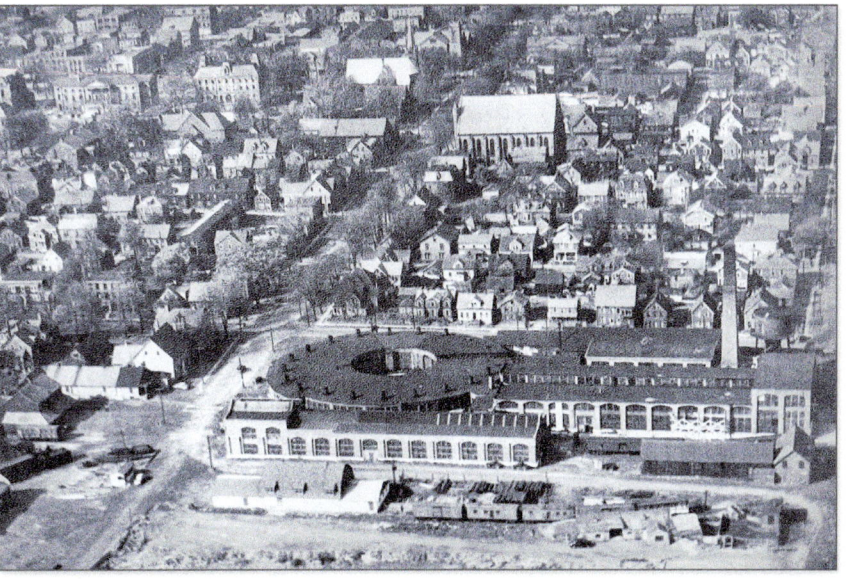

The train repair yard and buildings took up quite a section of the Charlottetown water front east of lower Prince Street. With the Island in debt by constructing the railway across the province, they joined confederation in 1873, with the Federal Government taking over the railway and the debt.

The Brass House, built in 1876 was originally offices of the mechanical branch of the railway. It is now home to Receiver Coffee, at 178 Water Street, which opened on July 2, 2017. ▼

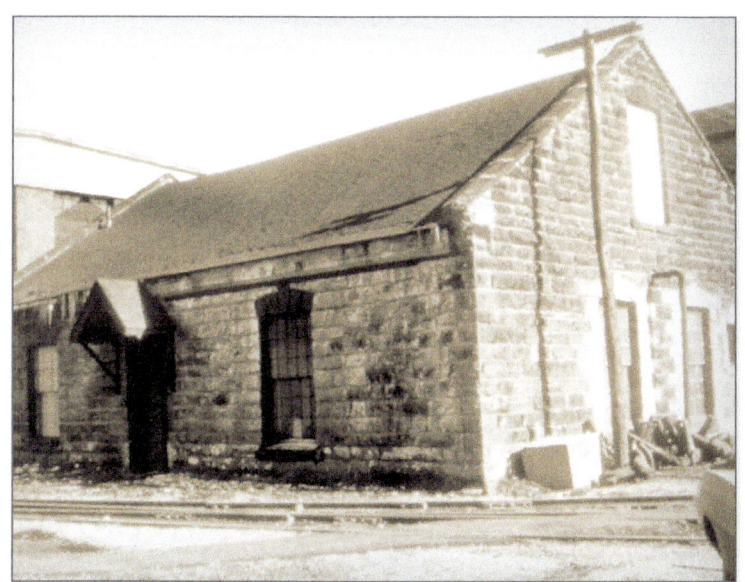

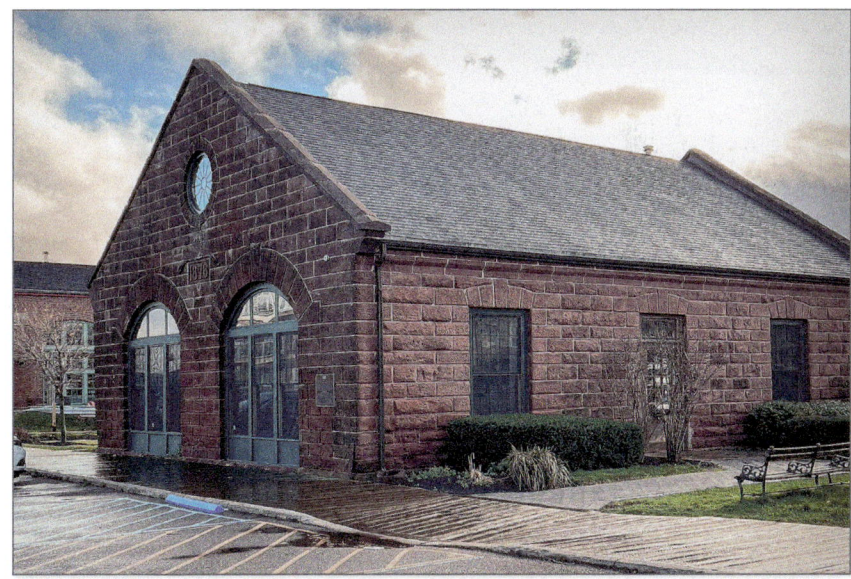

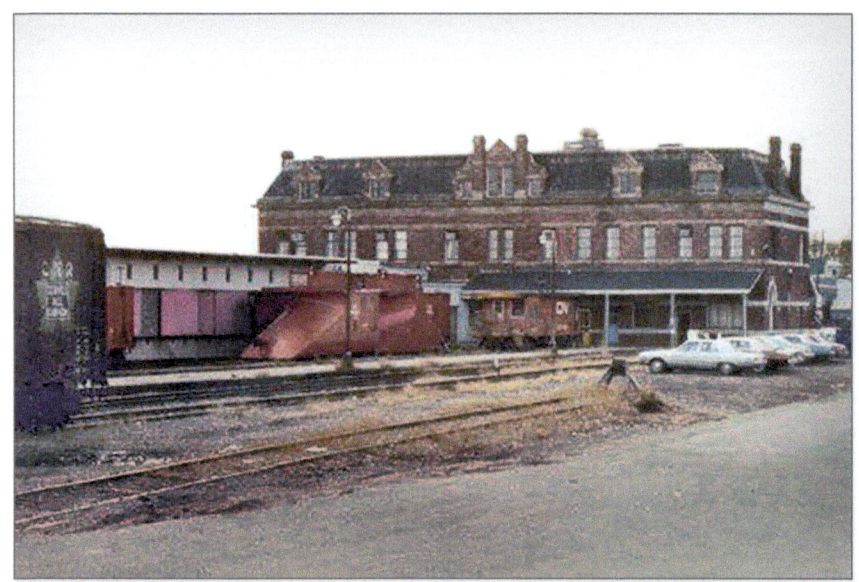

Water Street at the corner of Weymouth Street was the Train Station. To passengers going to and from Charlottetown this was the main connection. They would depart by train for the mainland, crossing the ferry and connecting at Moncton to parts beyond.

This picture from 1970's shows the trains at the back of the station, some as track snow plows. This picture was taken from King Street looking west.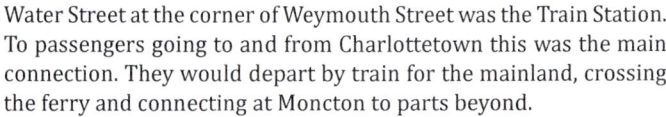

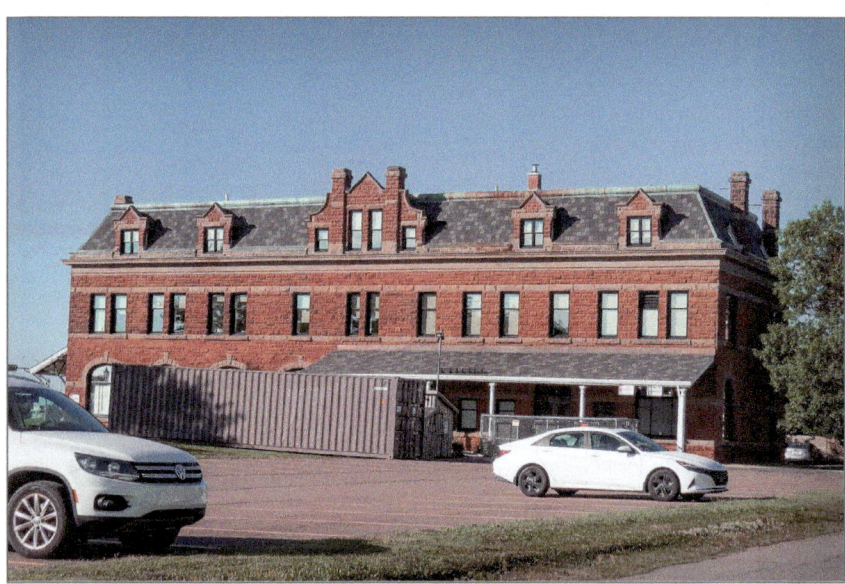

Looking west, in 2022 showing the back of the current occupant, the Workers Compensation Building on Weymouth Street.

Willian Critchlow Harris

(Jun 30, 1854 - Jul 16, 1913)

was born near Liverpool England, moved with his parents to Prince Edward Island in 1856.

He received his early education at Prince of Wales College, and apprenticed with architect David Stirling in Halifax. He returned to Charlottetown in 1877. He designed, among many others:

- (X mentioned in this book)
- St. Mary's church in Indian River,
- Beaconsfield at Kent and West Streets
- Central Christian Church on Kent Street
- South Shore United in Tryon
- Georgetown Courthouse
- St. Patrick's Roman Catholic Church Grand River
- X 96 Prince Street
- X Charlottetown Market Bldg.
- X St. Paul's Anglican Charlottetown
- X DesBrisay Bldg. - Hughes Dug Store - Cows
- All Souls' Chapel which has 18 paintings by his brother, renowned artist Robert Harris

HOW TO GET TO

Charlottetown

IN THE EARLY DAYS

Before the Hillsborough Bridge,
before Airplanes, before the automobiles

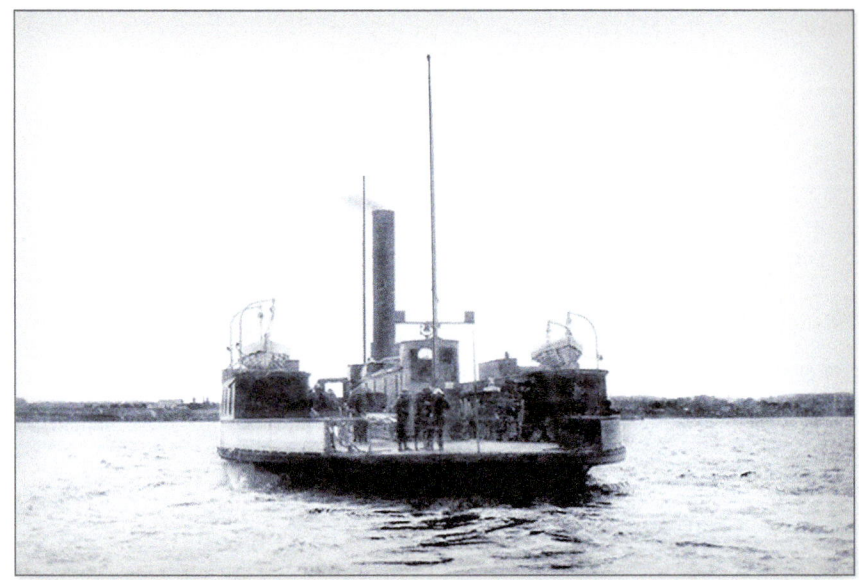

You could go by ferry from Charlottetown to Rocky Point. This picture in from 1908. Many went over for the day for picnics, some just for the ride and others to cottages. In the 1870's the ferry sailed from 7:00 am and every hour from Connolly's new wharf at the foot of Haviland Street. In future years it docked at Prince Street Wharf or Buntain Bell Wharf at Queen Street. Over the years the ferry S. S. Elfin (1900's), S. S. Hillsboro (1920's), S. S. Fairview (1930's -1960's) and the S. S. Southport provided crossing. When the West River causeway was constructed, there was no further need for the ferry. Note: the Steamer Elvin burned to the waterline in 1906. ■

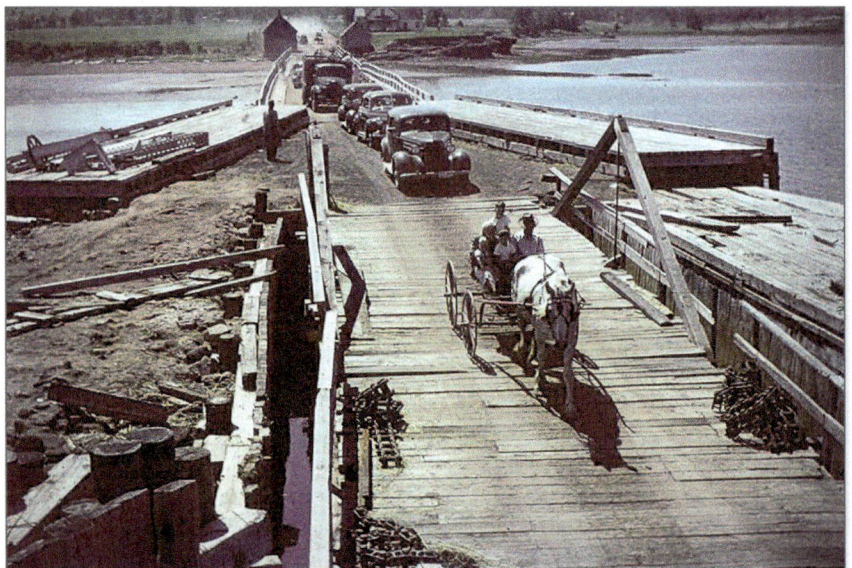

This picture c1940 shows a typical traffic line loading one of the ferries that operated around the island. Ferry service was running from places like: Georgetown to Lower Montague, New Port to Georgetown Royalty, Ferry Road in Cornwall to Charlottetown, and Charlottetown to Mt Stewart (before the bridge in 1905). The latter was used for transporting produce to Charlottetown for market. ■

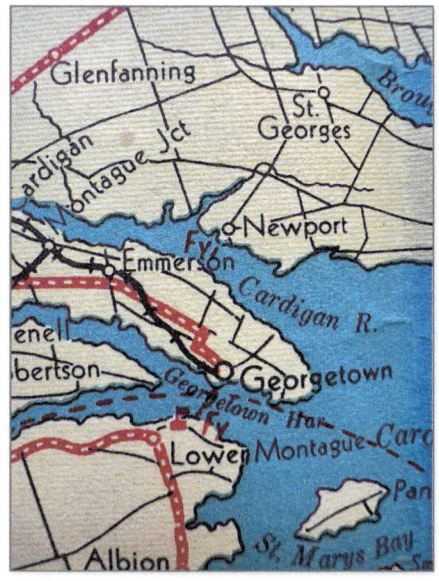

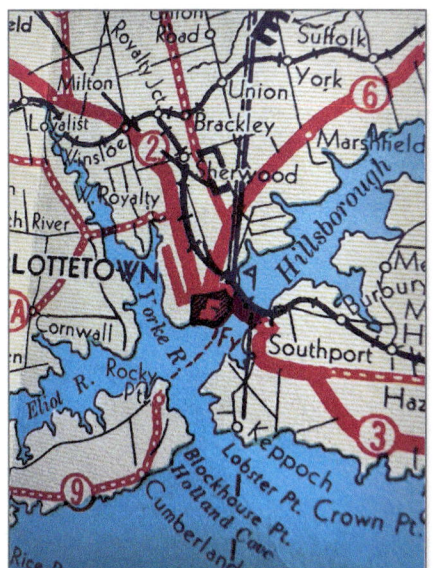

This map of Prince Edward Island from the 1960's shows the ferry routes as FY. ∎

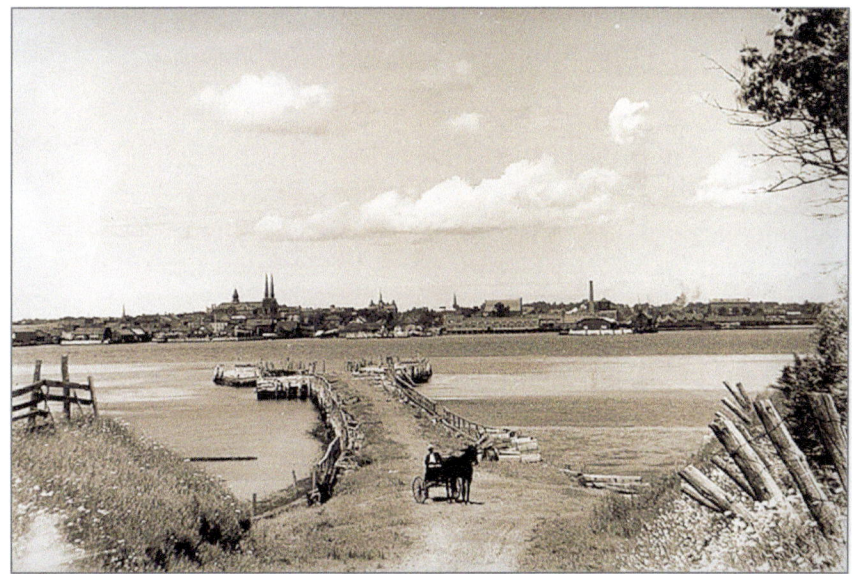

Before the Hillsborough Bridge was constructed in 1905, a ferry took passengers to Stratford arriving at a wharf at what is now the end of Bayside Drive. The ferries over time were the same ones that operated on the Rocky Point run. ∎

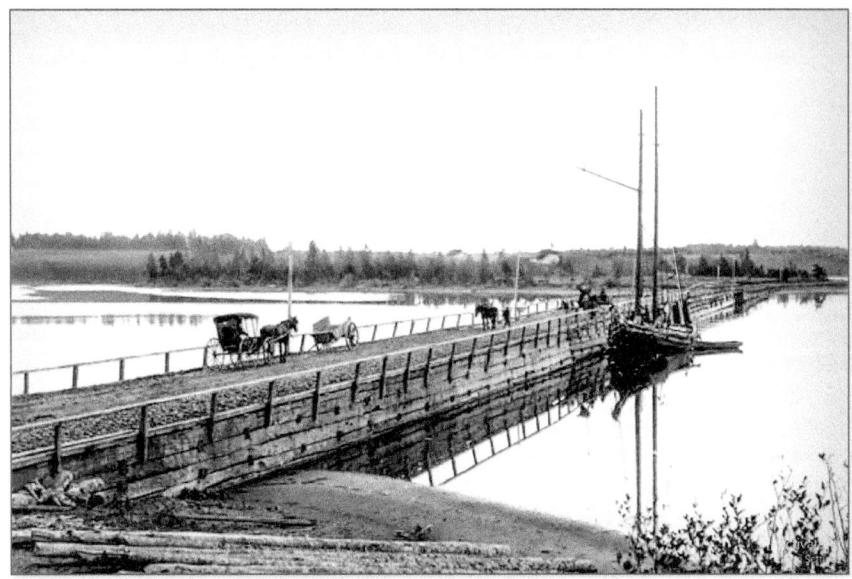

If you were to leave Charlottetown to go to what is now Cornwall, you cross the North River causeway. Pictured here from 1893 the earliest picture of this transportation route.

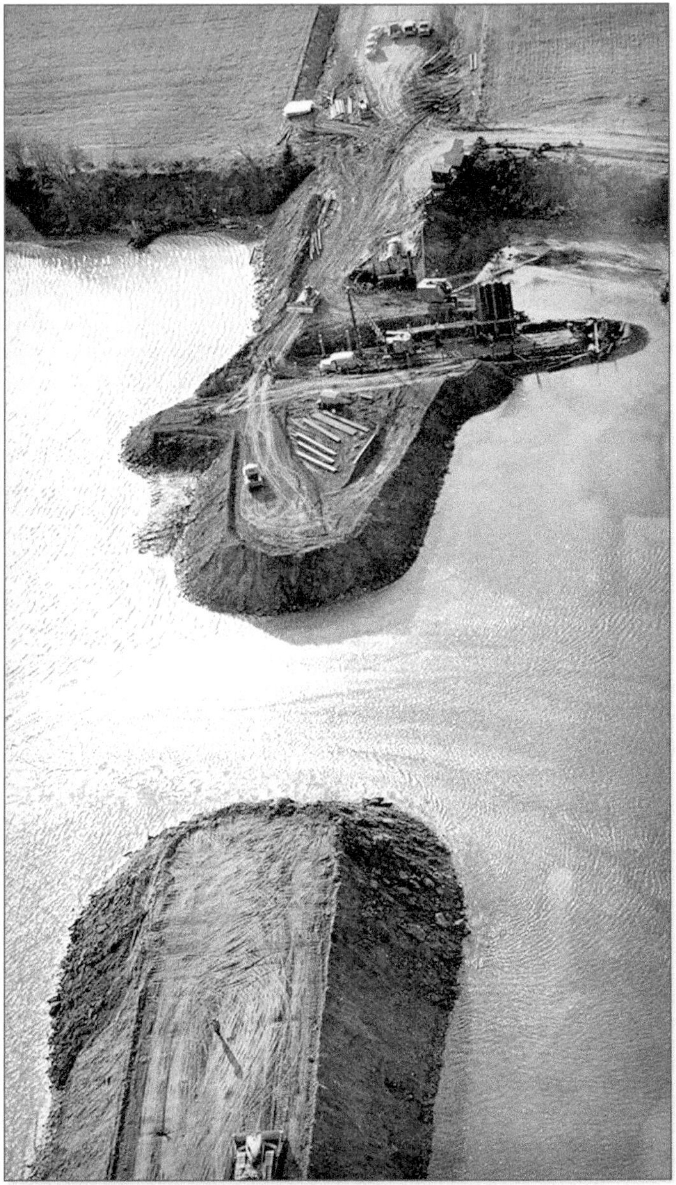

In 1955 a new causeway was constructed.

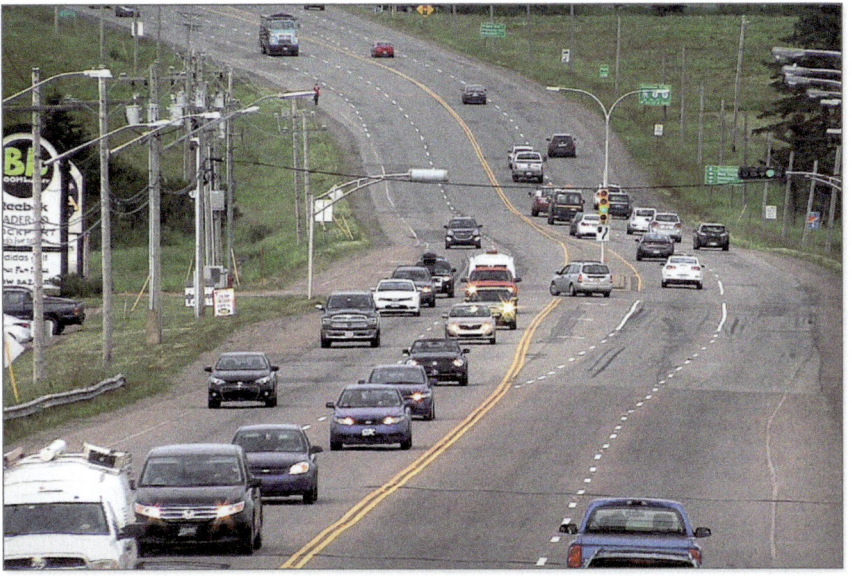

Many upgrades were done over the years until we have the new causeway with the roundabout at Poplar Island. This allows easy access off Capitol Drive to the Boardwalk shops on Milky Way Drive.

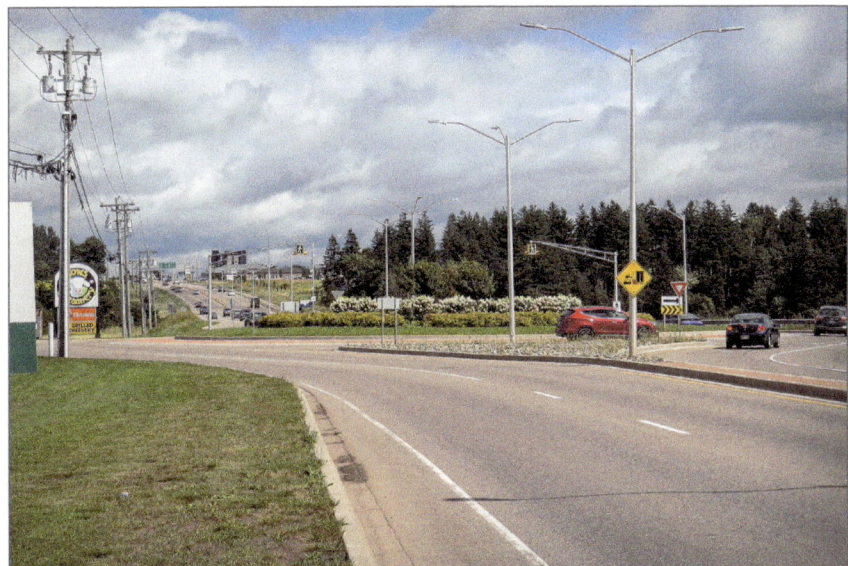

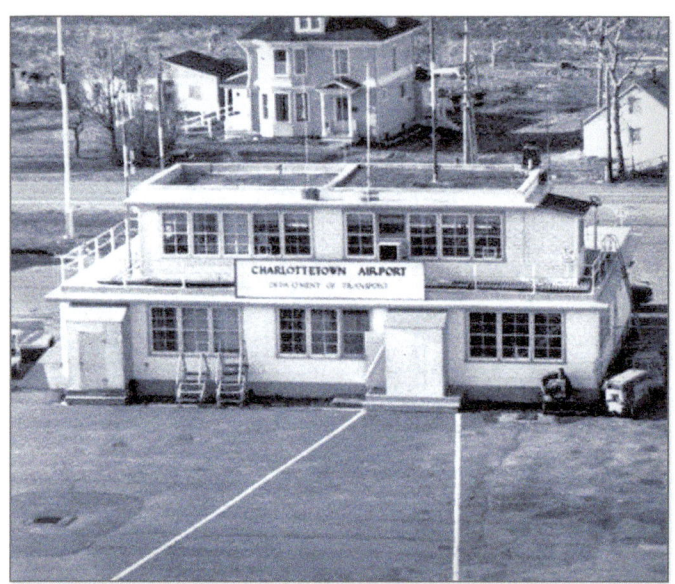

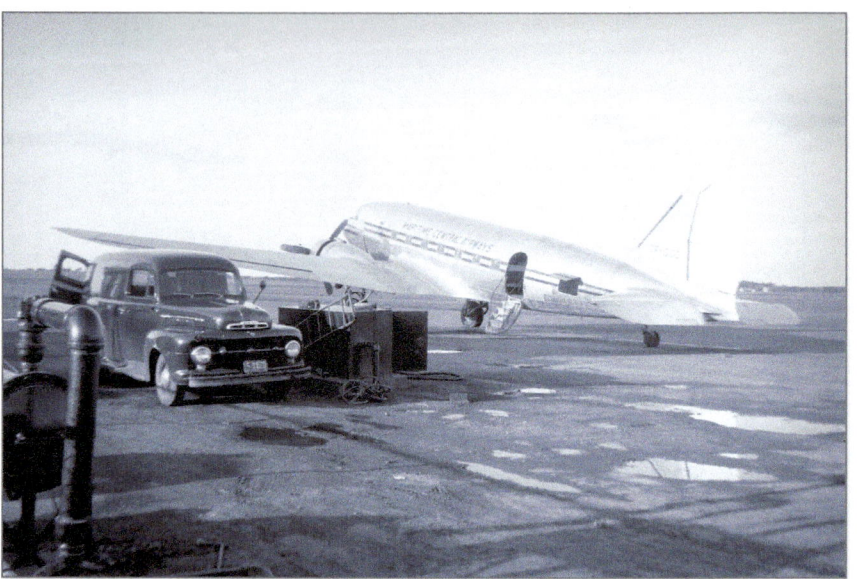

▲ If you were travelling by air to Charlottetown, you went to the terminal, pictured here in 1968. Maritime Central Airways was the earlier carrier to and from the Island. ▪

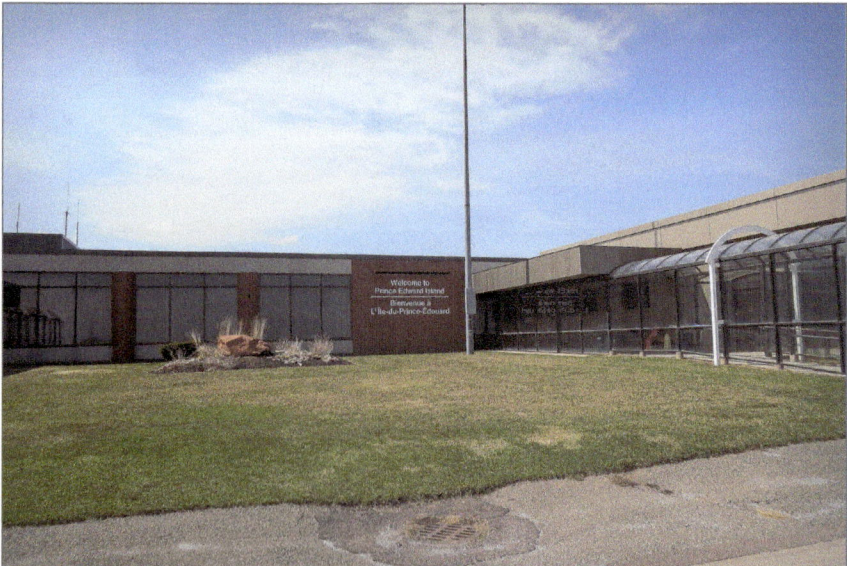

A much more modern building awaits you now. ▪

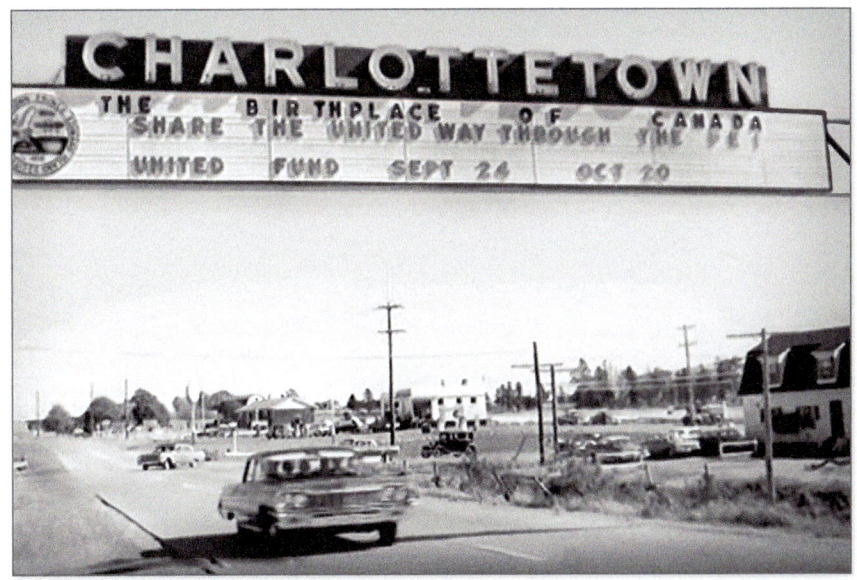

The corner of North River Road/Lower Malpeque Road and Capitol Drive, called Queens Arms, looked different in 1964. This picture, looking east on Capital Drive. This large overhead sign advertised the Birthplace of Canada being the centennial year from the time the Fathers of Confederation met in Charlottetown. There was no traffic lights at this intersection. The Bright Spot was a convenience store at the southwest corner with the barn roof.

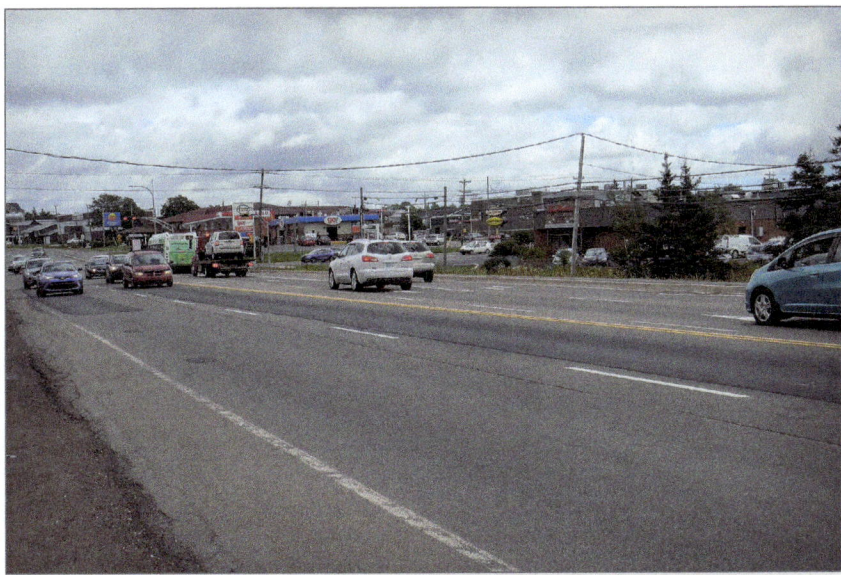

Tim Hortons now occupies the Bright Spot site. The modern service station, with McDonalds and the Comfort Inn are now shown here. Traffic lights are now required because of the large increase of vehicles.

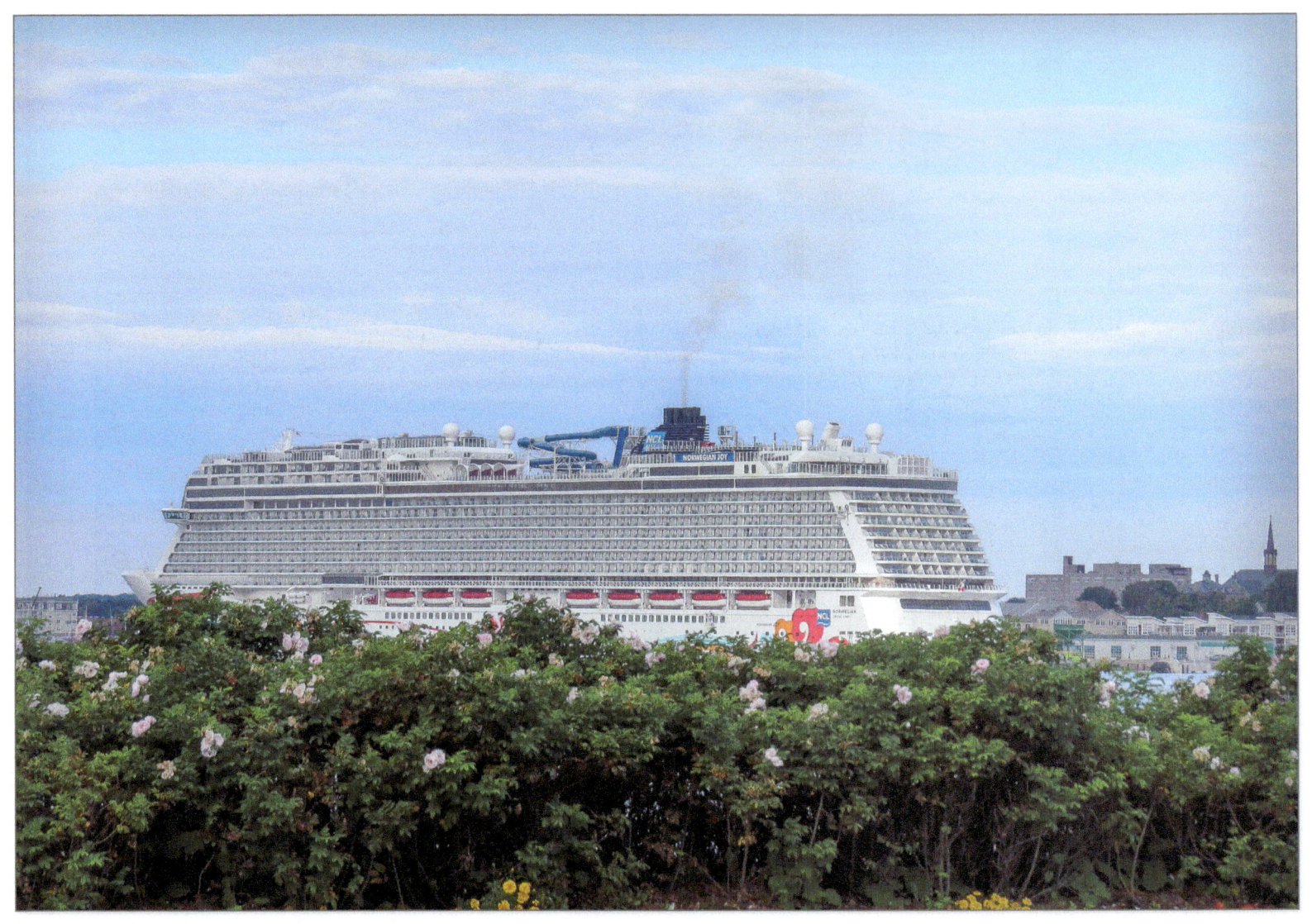

A more modern way to come to the Island is by cruise ship. Charlottetown is a popular port of call for many cruise ships now. ■

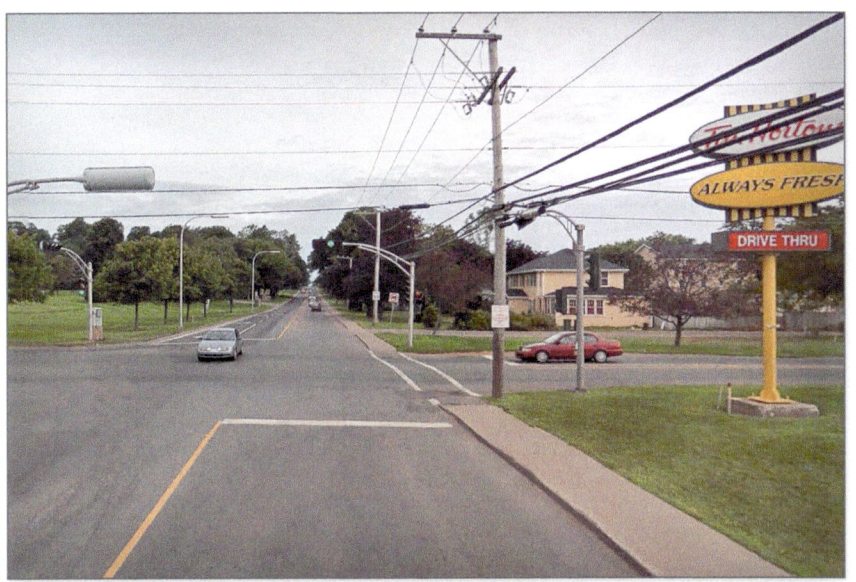

Love them or hate them, roundabouts are all the rage. When the first one opened, do you remember the demo roundabout in the Royalty Mall parking lot to show us how to use it?

The first one was at Travellers Rest between Summerside and Kensington. There are now over 30 throughout the Island.

This one shows the intersection of Allen Street and Mt. Edward Road.

The "Action Corner" once had traffic lights. Now the roundabout keeps the traffic moving. ▪

Do You Remember

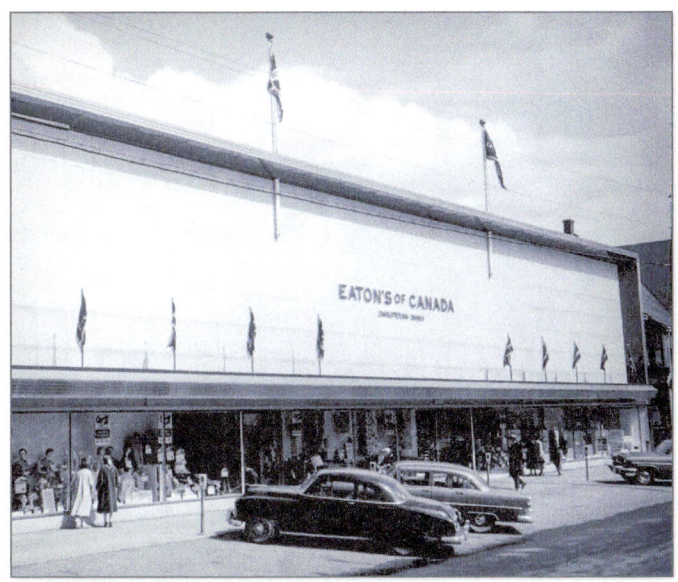

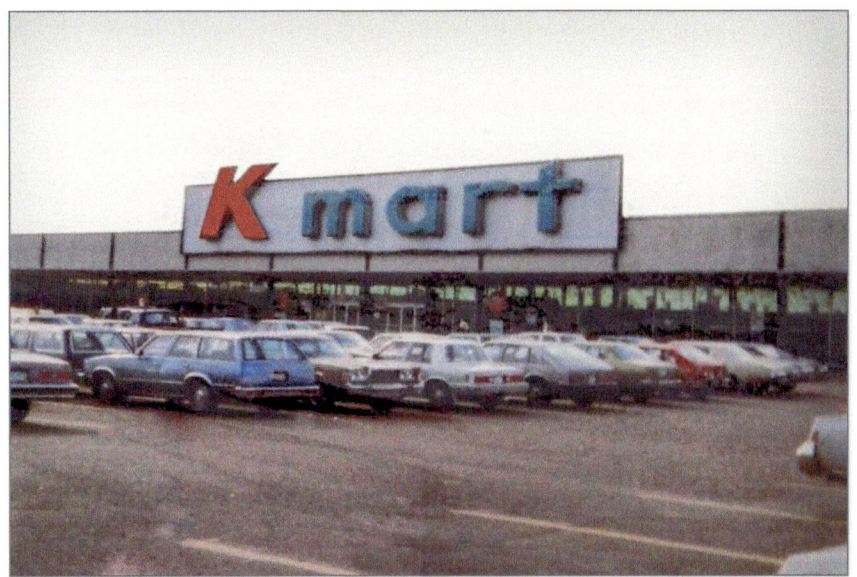

▲ In these pictures from the mid 1960's, shopping at national department stores meant going down town. We had F. W. Woolworth and the Metropolitan on Queen Street, Eaton's and Zellers on Kent Street. ▪

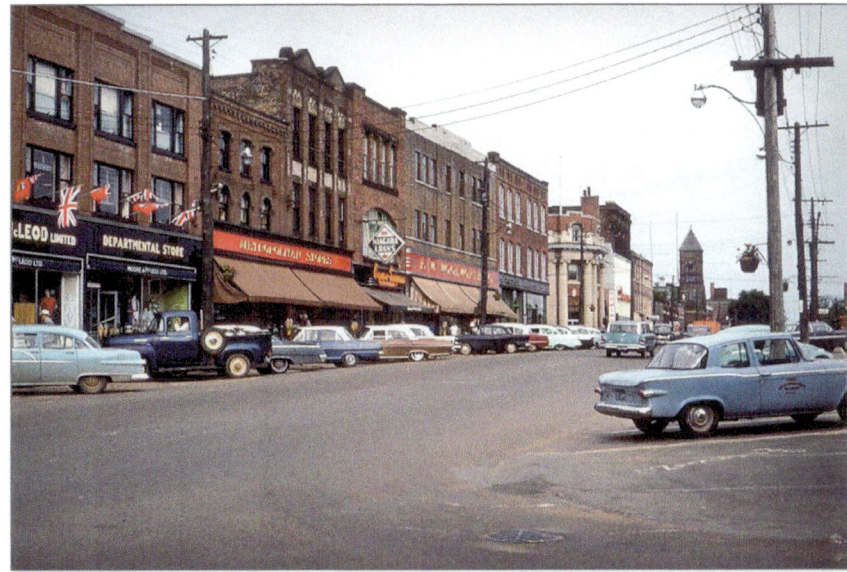

Later, with the malls opening, it spelled the demise of downtown shopping. We had the Kmart Mall where the Atlantic Superstore is on University at Belvedere. The Atlantic Superstore opened on this site in 1999. To accommodate the Kmart Mall, the Kirkwood Motel was demolished. ▶

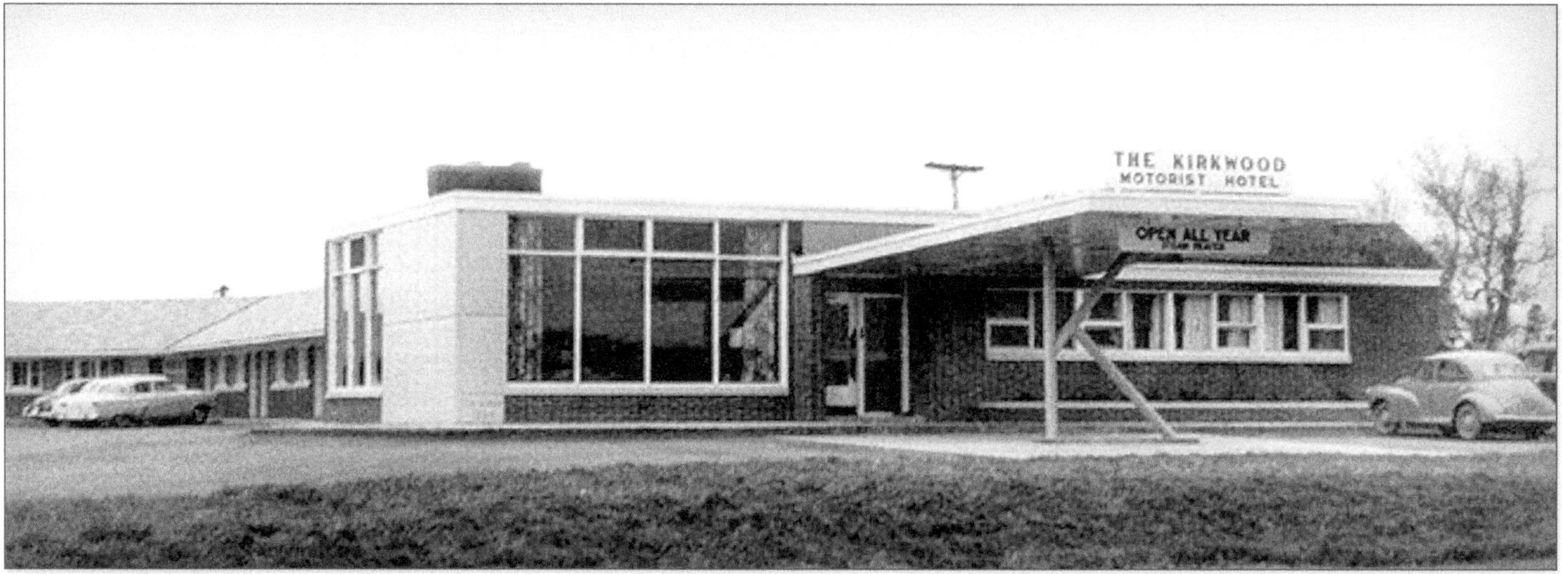

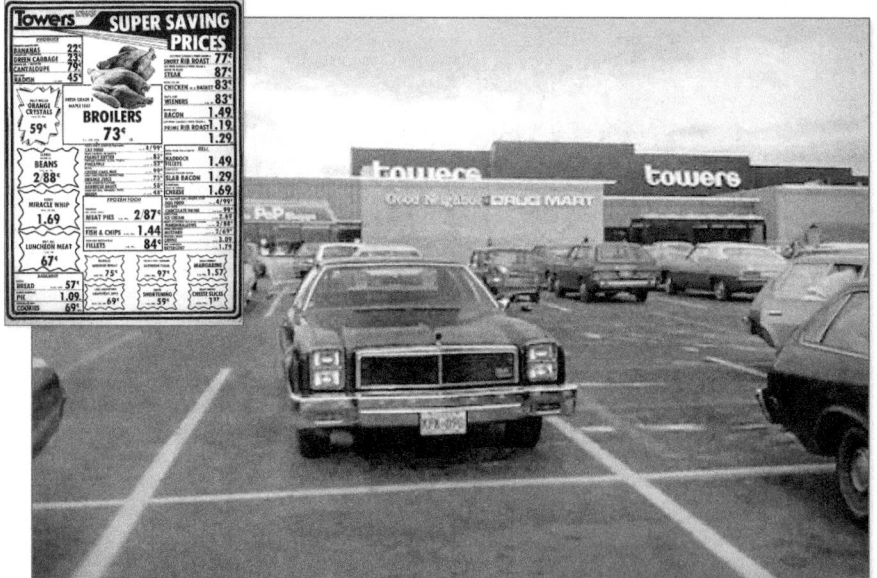

The Kirkwood Motel at 455 University Avenue was built in 1954 by Carl Burke. This property included a swimming pool. ■

The Royalty Mall opened for business on December 1, 1965. At the time it was the only mall on Prince Edward Island and one of only three in the Maritime provinces. The first thee tenants were the Royal Bank of Canada, Co-op and the Liquor store. With the addition of Towers Department Store it was commonly named Towers Mall. The mall has recently been renamed Royalty Crossing, although many still say "I will meet you at Towers Mall". The anchor store was later Zellers and then short-lived by Target. Towers Department Stores, opened in 1974, was bought out by Hudson's Bay Company/Zellers nationally in 1990. In 2013 Zellers closed, with most leases in malls bought out Canada wide by Target. This location of Target opened November 2013 and closed April 8, 2015. This picture of Towers is from 1977. ■

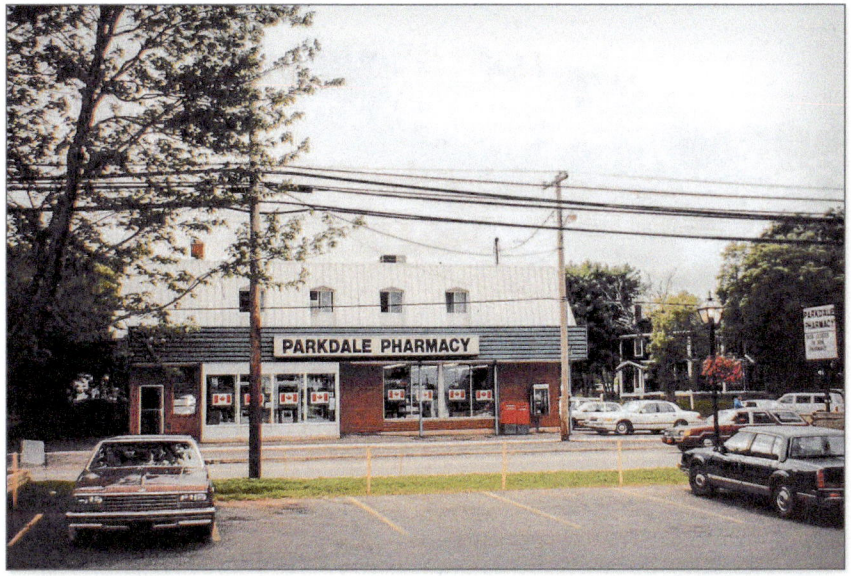

Ray Murphy operated his first pharmacy at 41 St. Peters Road, shown here in 1992. The second picture also from 1992, shows the new Pharmacy and doctors office under construction across the street on St. Peters Road.

In business over 40 years, Murphy's Pharmacy now has thirteen location across the Island. ▪

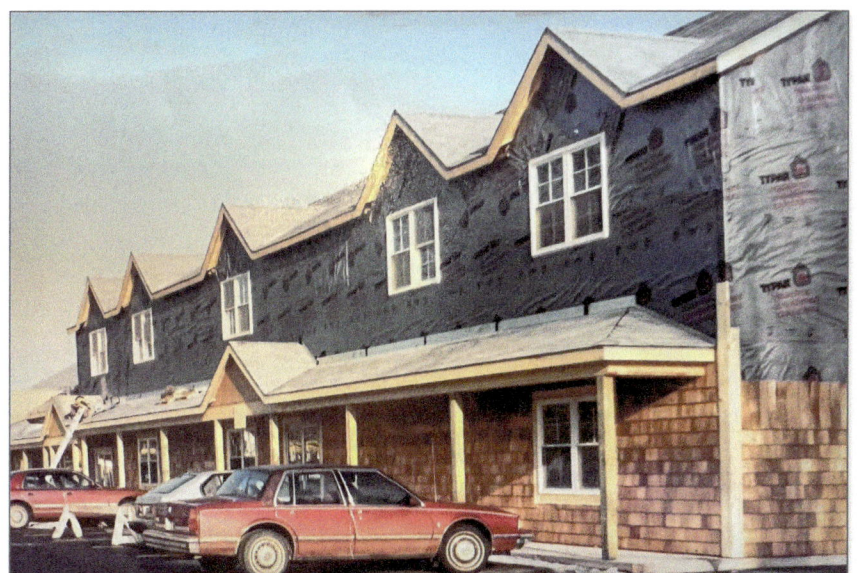

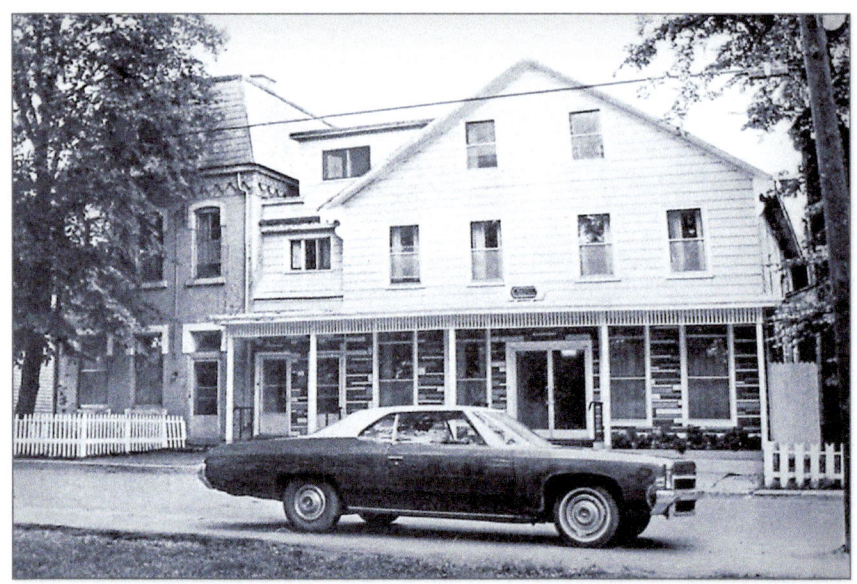

This picture of MacLean Funeral home, King Square c.1970. This site was a grocery store in the 1890's. G. Dudley Wright (mayor of Charlottetown 1918-1920) operated a funeral home here. In 1923 N. D. MacLean took over the funeral home, later run by Jim Allan until 1979. Allison Swan joined the business in 1969 and has been funeral director and later owner since 1979. This building was gutted by fire on January 7, 1974. ▪

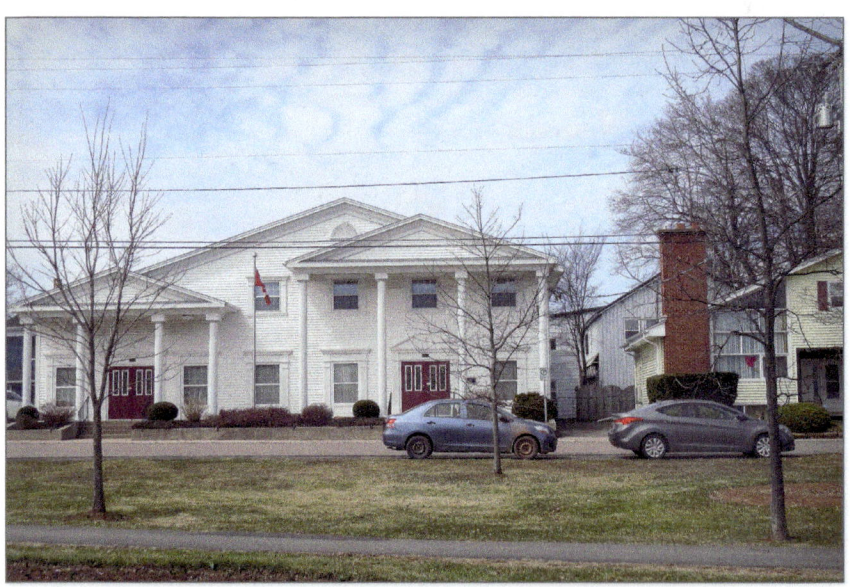

A new building was built on the site. The brick building at the left in the former picture was removed to provide parking. ▪

The Charlottetown Curling Club, incorporated 1915 sold shares, this one from 75 years ago. The first mention of an organized curling club on the Island was January 26, 1876 when the railway started one. On February 3, 1887, the Charlottetown Curling Club was organized and ice time was available at the Citizen's Skating Rink. The first interprovincial match, against Pictou, Nova Scotia was held on February 12, 1889, when the local inexperienced team was soundly trounced by the visitors.

(From the Ronnie Diamond collection)

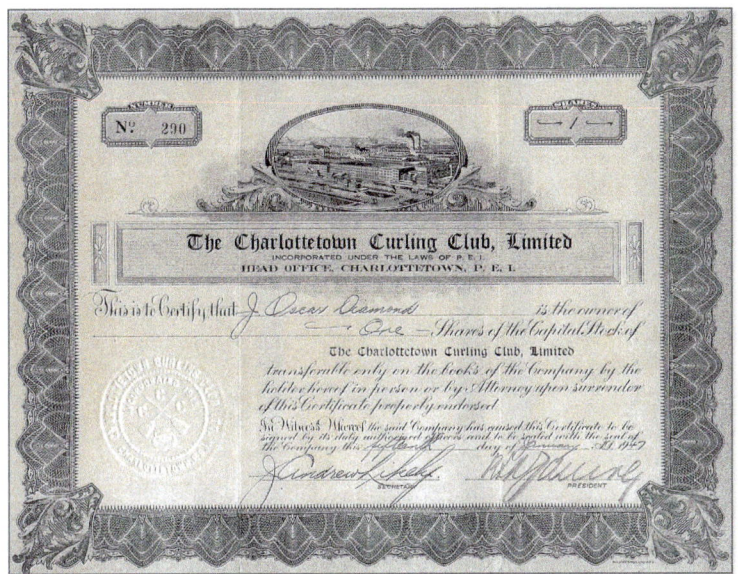

The Charlottetown Forum was incorporated in 1930. Tenders were called on June 17th for construction of the forum to be located on the north side of Fitzroy Street between Weymouth and Cumberland Streets. This rink served well until the construction of the new Civic Centre on Kensington Road.

(From the Ronnie Diamond collection)

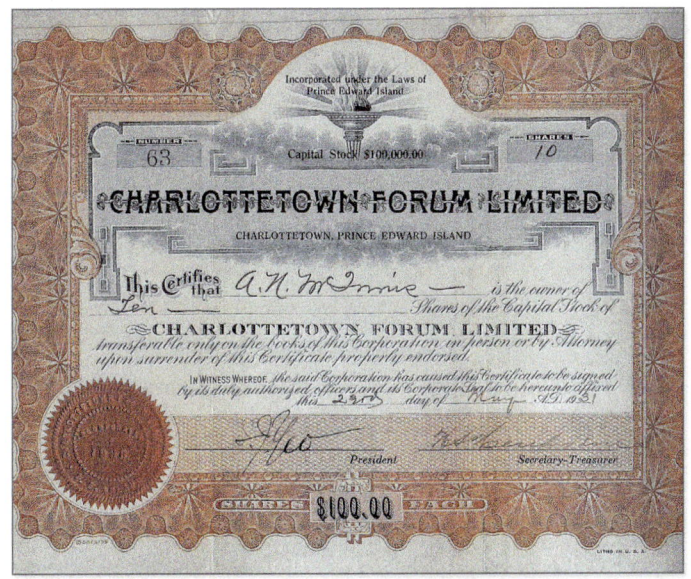

Cornerstones

Cornerstones or markers were placed on building to show date of construction.
Sometimes they listed the owner. It is not a practice that is used as much today.

To the reader: See how many of these markers you can find.
This would make a great scavenger hunt.

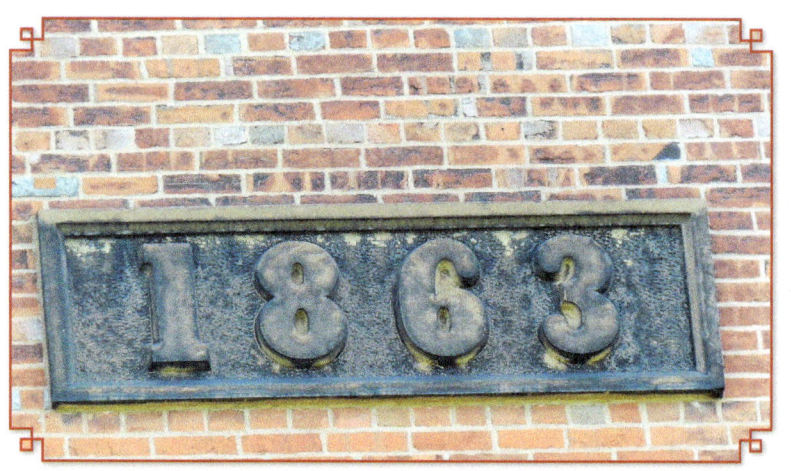

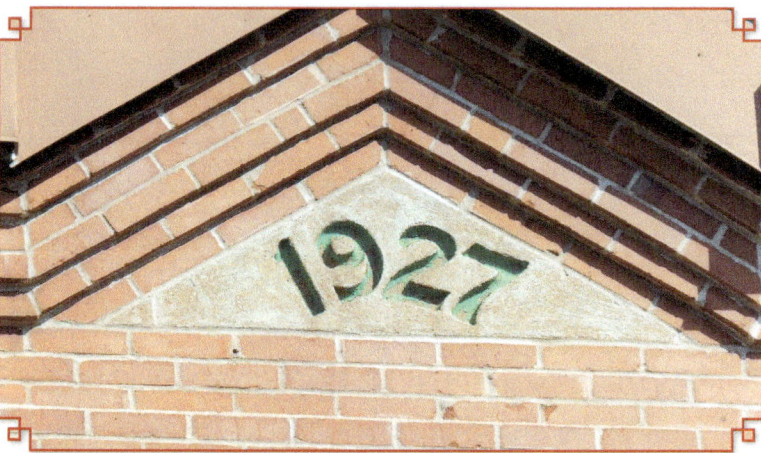

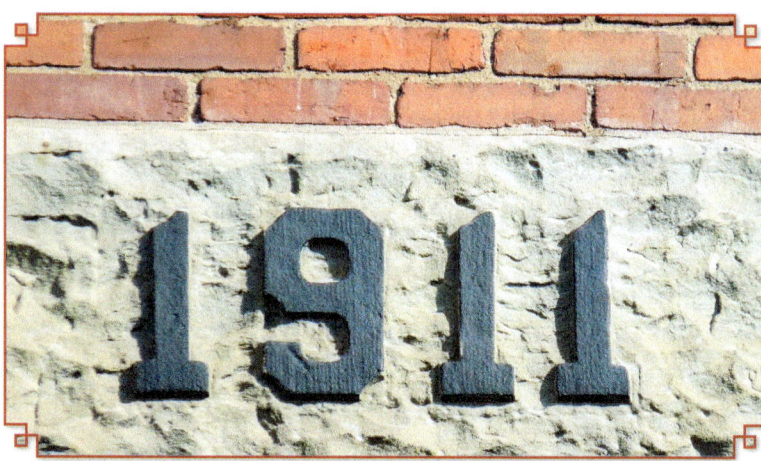

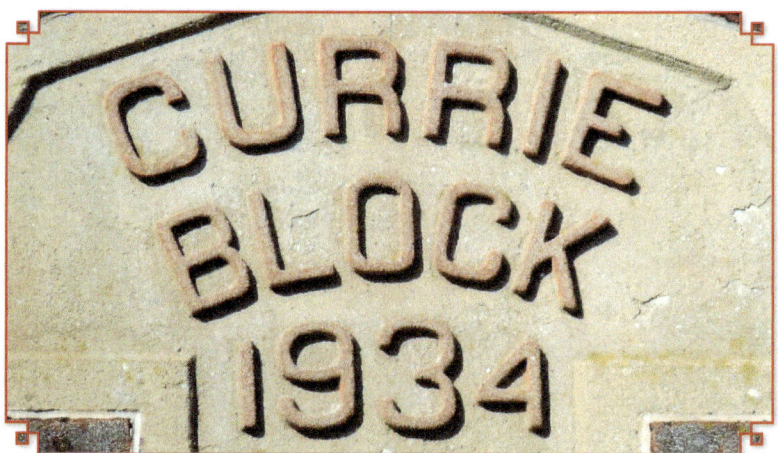

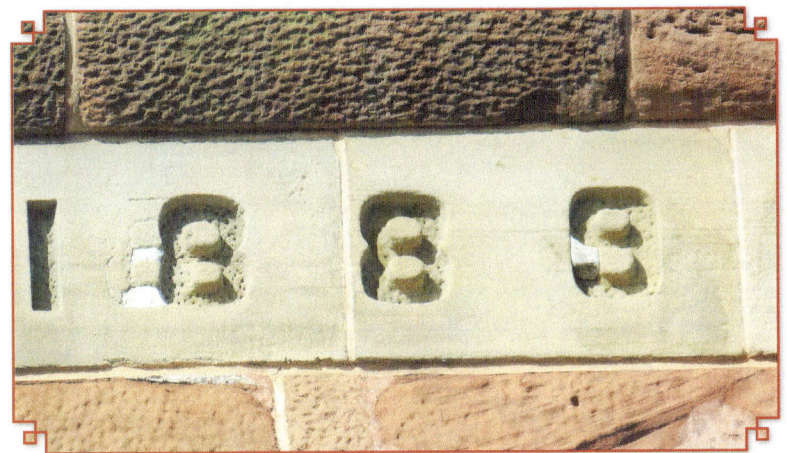

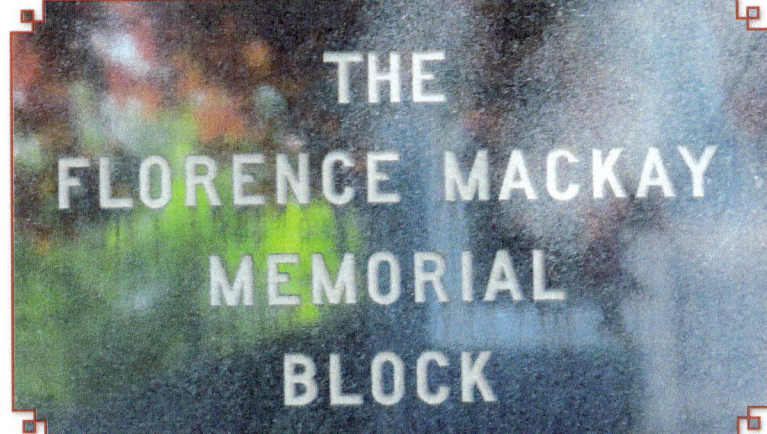

THE
FLORENCE MACKAY
MEMORIAL
BLOCK

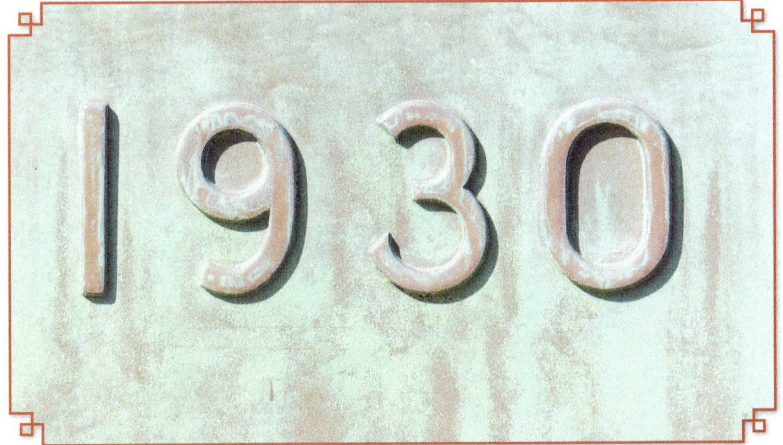

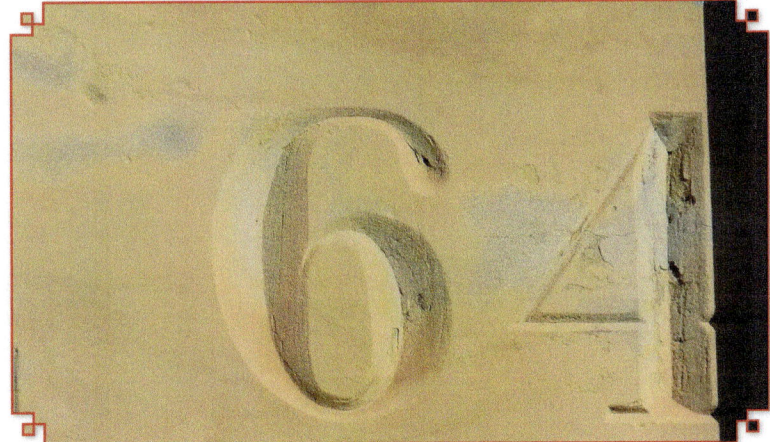

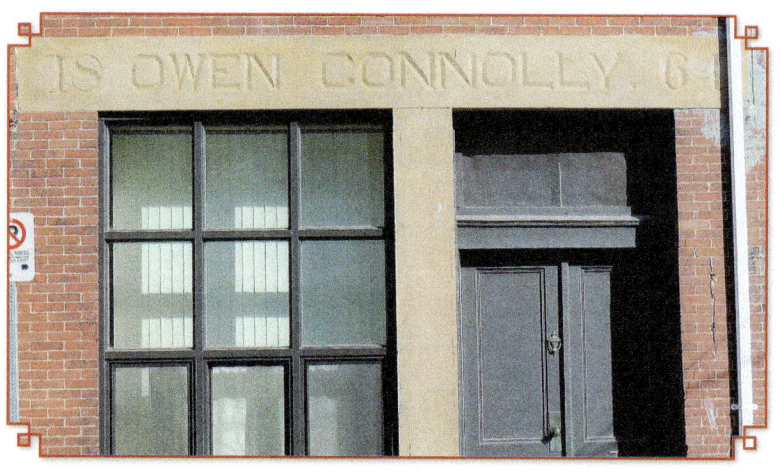

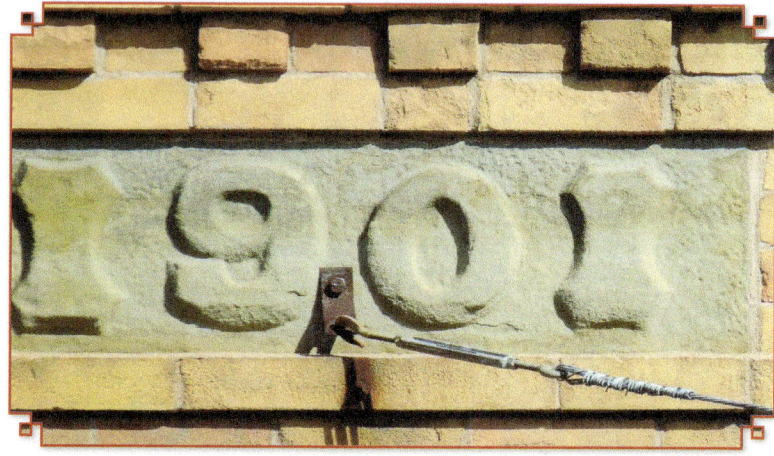

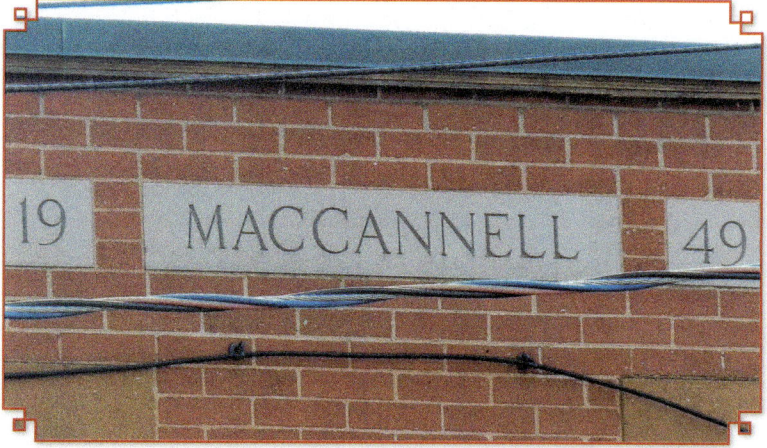

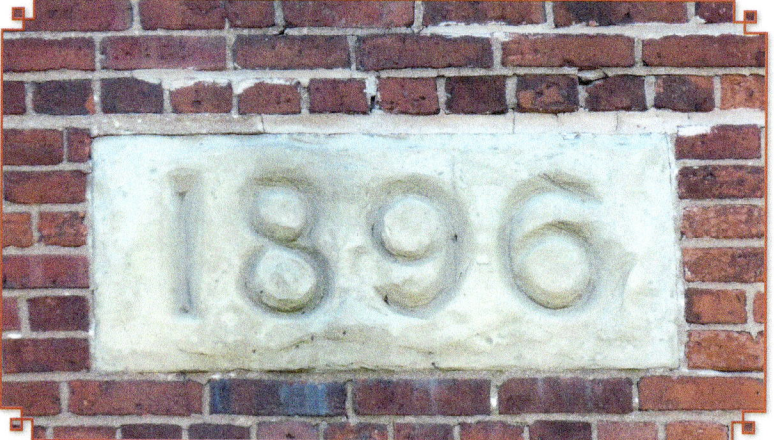

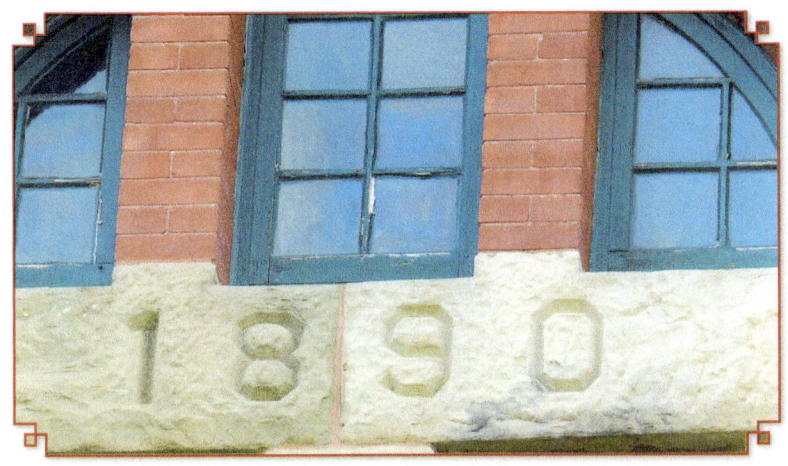

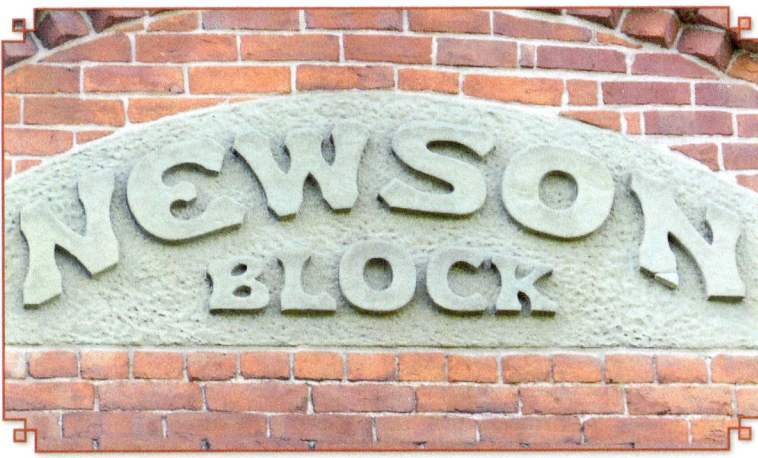

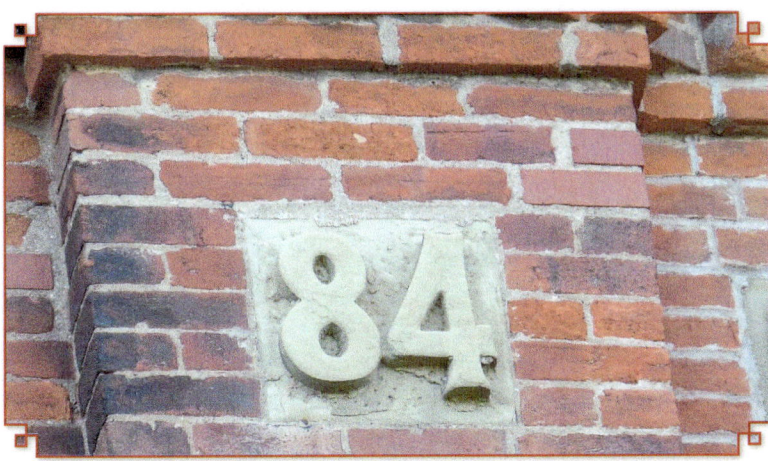

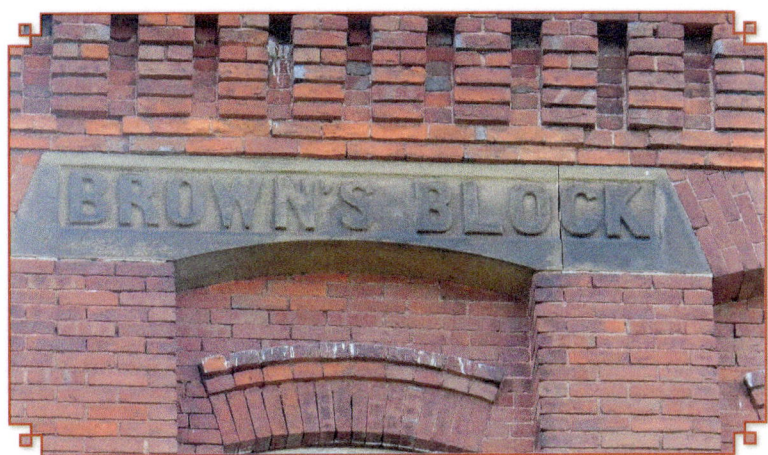

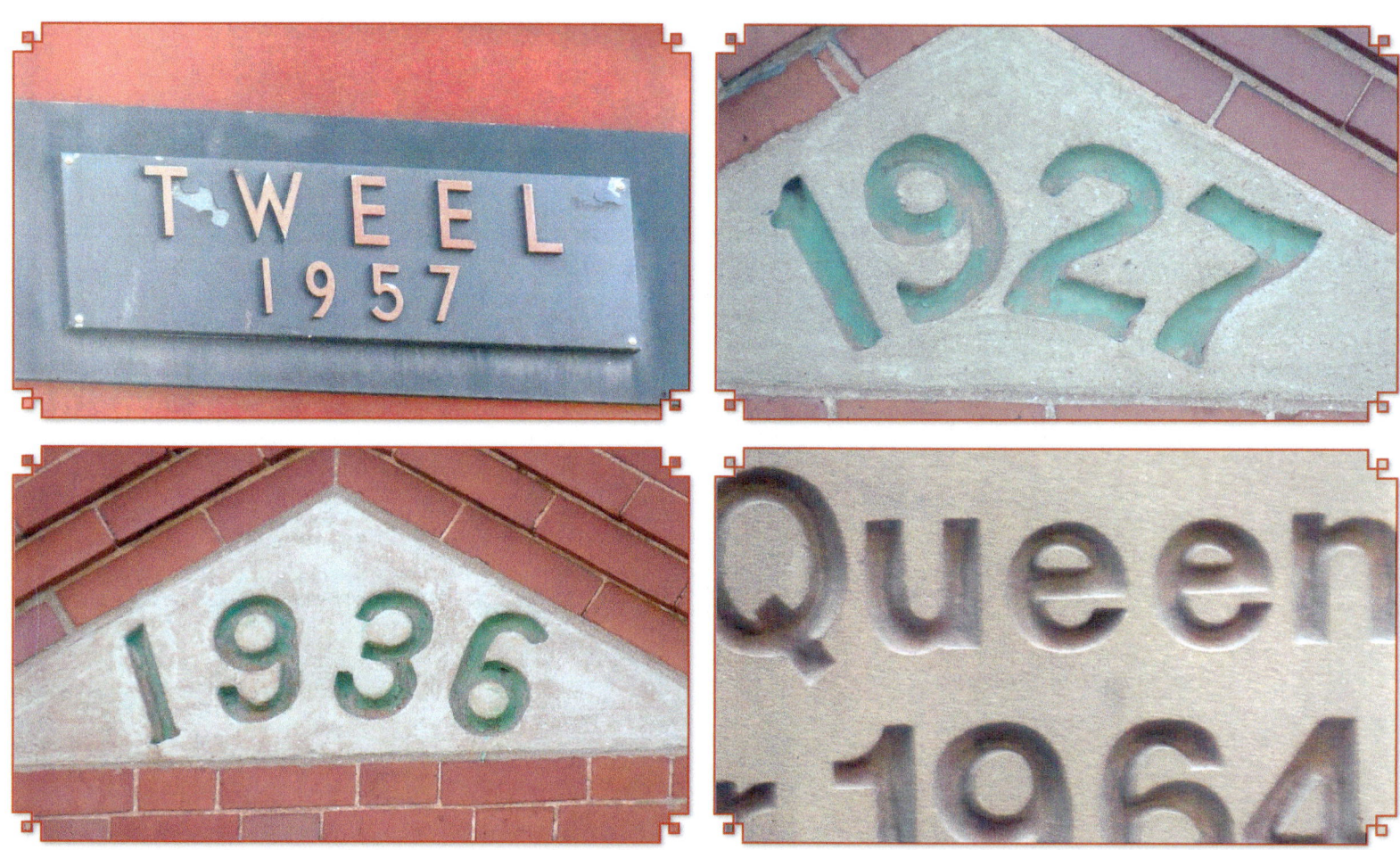

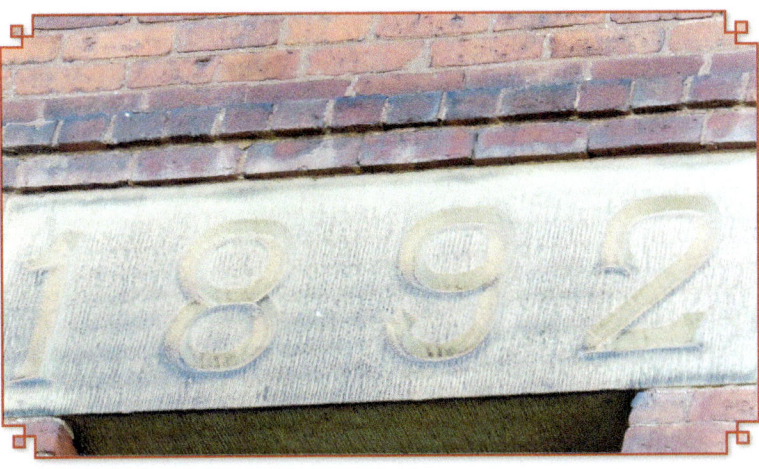

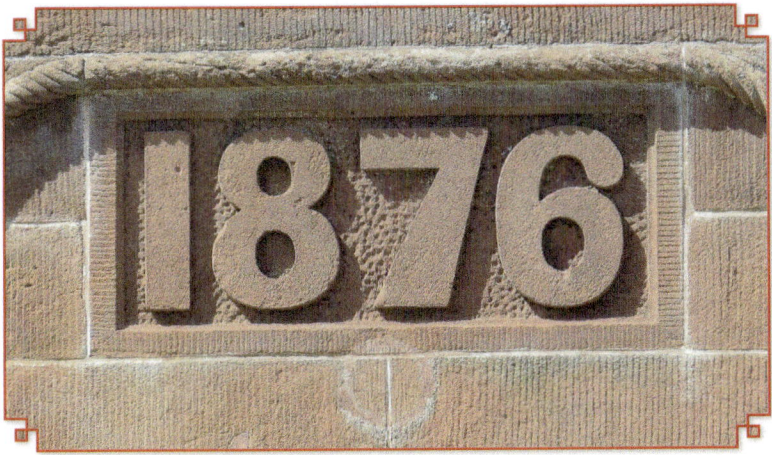

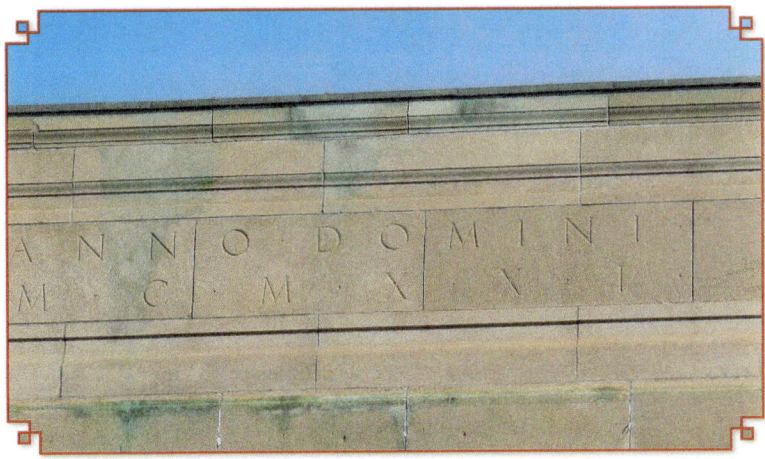

Acknowledgements

My wife Cathy took time to edit, lighten, darken, straighten and size all these photos to make a better presentation in this book. Thank you very much.

A special thank you for encouragement from Natalie Munn of the City of Charlottetown, Catherine Hennessey and Rev. Art O'Shea.

I want to give full credit to the Public Archives and Records Office of the Provincial Government for their collecting, cataloguing and making available to the public, so many pictures and artifacts that enhance our knowledge of our past. I encourage you to find the pleasure and enjoyment one has being a researcher at this fine facility.

Bibliography

Charlottetown Guardian

City Directory 1937, Irwin Printing

Earle's Pictures Restoration

McAlpine's Charlottetown Directory, 1887-88, UPEI

McAlpine's Charlottetown Directory, 1900, UPEI

McAlpine's Charlottetown Directory, 1924-25, UPEI

Meachum & Co, J. H. Illustrated Historical Atlas of PEI 1880

Prince Edward Island phone Book, 1959

Prince Edward Island phone Book, 1972

Public Archives and Records Office of Prince Edward Island (PARO)

Most of the black and white photos in this book are from their vast resources.

Robertson Library of UPEI

Rogers, Irene L.: Charlottetown The Life in its Buildings 1983

Wikipedia